MW00984434

Beads and Prayers
The Rosary in History and Devotion

The Evolution of the Marian Rosary

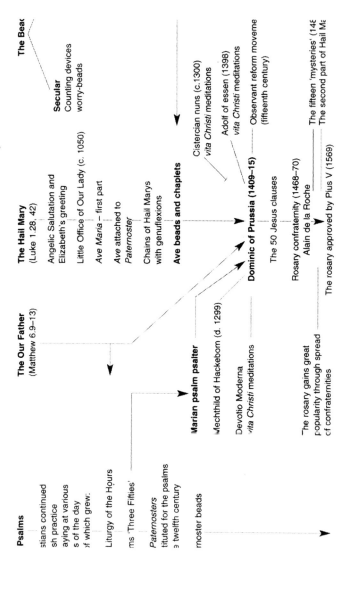

JOHN D. MILLER

Beads and Prayers

THE ROSARY IN HISTORY AND DEVOTION

BURNS & OATES
A Continuum imprint
LONDON • NEW YORK

First published in Great Britain in 2002 by
BURNS & OATES
A Continuum imprint
The Tower Building, 11 York Road
London SE1 7NX
www.continuumbooks.com

British Library Cataloguing-in-Publication Data
A catalogue record for this book is available from the British Library.

ISBN 0 86012 320 0

Typeset by YHT Ltd, London
Printed and bound in Great Britain by MPG, Bodmin

Contents

v

CONTENTS

To the Woman of the Gospel,
Our Mother and Advocate

Chronology of the Development of the Rosary[1]

1750 BC   Various devices for counting prayers found in most cultures from the earliest times.

1700–1450 BC   Beads found in the Aegean culture of Crete, probably for decorative usage rather than prayer.

AD 300–400   The earliest recorded prayer to the Blessed Virgin (c. 300): 'We fly to thy patronage, O Holy Mother of God [*Theotokos*], despise not our petitions in our necessities, but deliver us from all danger, O ever glorious and blessed Virgin.'

Anthony the Great (251–356) supposedly invented the Byzantine rosary: a circular string of knotted wool used in conjunction with the Jesus Prayer. Abbot Paul, a hermit of Thebes in Egypt (d. 347), used a pile of 300 pebbles.

431   Council of Ephesus declares Mary as *Theotokos* (God-bearer) Devotion to Mary increases as a result.

500–600   Akathistos Hymn, written sometime before 560.

The two greetings, that of the Angel and that of Elizabeth, found in the Liturgies of St James of Antioch and St Mark of Alexandria, may go back to the fifth, or even fourth, century. Also found in the Liturgy of the Abyssinian Jacobites, and in the ritual of St Severus (538).

c. 600 Egyptian Coptic ostracon bears in Greek the following inscription: 'Hail Mary, full of grace, the Lord is with thee, blessed art thou amongst women, and blessed is the fruit of thy womb, because you have conceived Christ, the Son of God, redeemer of our souls.'

659 Grave of Abbess Gertrude in Nivelles (Belgium) contained beads.

c. 782 Monks of St Apollinaris would say 300 *Kyrie eleisons* and *Christe eleisons* twice a day in gratitude for the Pope's benefactors.

c. 1050 The Angelic Salutation and the greeting of Elizabeth as a prayer formula became popular through the recitation of the Little Office of Our Lady, consisting of psalms, Marian hymns and antiphons, in which the *Ave Maria* is frequently used as a versicle and responsory.

c. 1080 Lady Godiva, on her death, leaves a string of beads to be hung on the image of Our Lady in the Abbey: 'The circlet of gems on a string she fingered them one by one so as not to fall short of the right number of prayers.'

1096 The *Ancient Customs of Cluny*, collected by Udalrio, record that on the death of 'any brother at a distance', every priest is to offer Mass and the non-priest monks either to say 50 psalms or repeat 50 times the *Paternoster*.

c. 1100 and after Illiterate lay brothers recited Little Psalter: 150 *Paternosters*, or 'Three Fifties', replacing the 150 psalms.
Paternoster cords often carried.
Paternoster knots and beads integrated into a structural framework: 150 *Aves* spaced into decades or groups of ten. Wooden and clay beads replace knotted cords among the people.

1128 Templars, if unable to attend choir, are to repeat the Lord's Prayer 57 times. On death of a brother, each knight to recite the *Paternoster* a hundred times a day for seven days.

c. 1130   Marian psalters (150 rhymed four-line stanzas, each beginning with the word *Ave*, each addressed to the Blessed Virgin, but paraphrasing at the same time some thought from the psalm to which it corresponds).

1140   St Aybert (d. 1140) bent his knees in prayer a hundred times a day while repeating the *Ave*.

1160   Saint Rosalia (relative of Emperor Charlemagne) buried with a string of little beads that end in a cross.

In England and the Netherlands, the full scriptural half of the *Ave* is becoming a formula of prayer: 'Hail Mary, full of grace, blessed art thou amongst women and blessed is the fruit of thy womb.'

1200-1300   The Ancrene Riwle (rule for anchoresses, c. 1200) includes directions for 50 *Aves* divided into sets of ten, with prostrations and other marks of reverence.

The Legend of St Dominic tells how in 1214 Dominic was given the rosary by the Blessed Virgin in order to convert the Cathars.

Guilds of bead-makers had been established (e.g. Guild of Paternosterers). Paternoster Row and Ave Maria Lane near St Paul's in London.

The name '*Jesus*' added to the Angelic Salutation. Development attributed to the initiative of Pope Urban IV (1261) (confirmed by the granting of an indulgence by Pope John XXII (1316–34)). Formula becomes '*Jesus Christus. Amen.*'

c. 1300   Manuscript containing a collection of 98 *vita Christi* meditation prayers recited by the Cistercian nuns at the cloister of Saint Thomas on the Kyll.

German vernacular Marian psalter gives for the first time scenes of the life of Christ inserted within a traditional litany of praise to the Virgin.

1347   Earliest surviving representation of prayer beads in England is on the effigy of Blanche Grandisson at Much Marcle, Herefordshire.

1347   Approx. date of a Viking colony excavated in North America, where a clear round bead is believed to be part of prayer beads worn by a Viking woman.

1350s   Beads now being worn in Germany for adornment rather than devotion. Augustinian canon of Osnabruck outlaws the wearing of coral rosaries around the neck.

1380   The French royal inventories list rosaries of enamelled gold encrusted with jewels.

1390s   Chaucer says of his Prioresse:

> Of small coral about her arm she bare
> A pair of bedes, gauded all with green,
> And thereon hung a broch of gold full shene.

c. 1400   Prayer beads more universally called 'rosaries'. Rose gardens and garlands associated with the Virgin Mary.

1408   Death of Carthusian Heinrich Eghar. In a vision Mary had taught him to say a 'psalter' in her honour and first to say a *Paternoster* and then the ten *Aves* repeated fifteen times. This he communicated to a Carthusian prior in England. This psalter became common in England.

1409–15   Dominic of Prussia (1384–1460), composed a series of 50 Jesus clauses to accompany the *Ave* prayer.

1441   Statutes of Eton College (founded by Henry VI) required the scholars to say daily the complete psalter of the Blessed Virgin, containing a *Credo*, fifteen *Paters* and 150 *Ave Marias*.

1468–70   Alain de la Roche (Alanus de Rupe) (c. 1428–75), a Dominican, founds his first confraternity: 'the Confraternity of the Psalter of the Glorious Virgin Mary' at Douai.

1475   Confraternity founded by Jakob Sprenger in Cologne on 8 September 1475 gains support of Frederick III and approval of Papal

Legate, Alexander of Forli, in 1476. The brotherhood spreads quickly throughout Europe.

1476   The Papal Legate grants to the Cologne confraternity indulgence of one quarantine for reciting the rosary.

1478   Pope Sixtus IV grants indulgence of seven years and seven quarantines and extended indulgences to apply to souls in purgatory '*per modum suffragii*'.

1483   Dominican rosary book, *Our Dear Lady's Psalter*, reduced the 50 meditation points to 15, all of which, except the last two, correspond to the present mysteries: the Coronation was combined with the Assumption and the Last Judgement was the fifteenth mystery. (The word 'mystery' is first used by Alberto da Castello, in 1521.)

1493   Second part of the Hail Mary found in *Compost et Kalendrier des Bergiers*, published in Paris (later translated into English and printed by Richard Pynson (1506) as *The Kalender of Shepardys*): 'Hayle Mary fulle of grace God is with the, thou arte blessyd amonge women and blessyd be the fruite of thy wombe Jesus. Holy Mary moder of God praye for us synners. Amen.'

1517   Luther challenges the interpretation of indulgences as preached by Tetzel; nails 95 theses to the door of the church in Wittenberg on 31 October.

1519   Luther denies the primacy of the Pope and the infallibility of General Councils, in the Leipzig Disputation with Johann Eck. (Luther excommunicated 1521.)

1520   Pope Leo X gives rosary official approbation.

1531   Tenochtitlan (Mexico): Our Lady of Guadelupe visits Juan Diego, and her exquisite image is set on the fragile cloth of his garment. (Recent studies suggest a rosary is draped across her praying hands. Most of the rosary is worn under her garment, only 21 beads show.)

1543–63 The Council of Trent inaugurates the Counter-Reformation.

1559 Pius V gives the Dominican Master-General exclusive control over the rosary confraternities. The blessing of rosaries was reserved for Dominicans or priests having special faculties (continued until 1984).

1569 Pius V, in Bull *Consueverunt Romani Pontifices*, officially approves the rosary.

1572 Pius V establishes Feast of Our Lady of Victory on 7 October, following defeat of the Turks at Lepanto (1571). Victory attributed to the Blessed Virgin through the public recitation of the rosary.

1573 Name of the feast is changed by Gregory XIII to 'Feast of Our Lady of the Rosary' and feast transferred to the first Sunday of October. (Since 1969 it has reverted to 7 October.)

1575 Bull of Gregory XIII makes special arrangements for persecuted Catholics of England for the Jubilee year of 1575. (They are required to say either the rosary or the Corona of Our Lady.)

1600–1700 The *Gloria Patri* (by 1613) and the Apostles' Creed are added to the rosary. Overall configuration and prayer sequence of rosary become more uniform.

1627 Louis XIII orders public recitation of the rosary during Huguenot rebellion at La Rochelle. (Fifteen thousand rosaries distributed to the troops with set hours of prayer.) Rebellion crushed.

1673 St Louis de Montfort born in Brittany. He preaches the rosary and writes *True Devotion to Mary*, *The Secret of Mary* and the *Secret of the Rosary*, still popular today.

1683 Jan Sobieski, King of Poland, invokes Our Lady of the Rosary and defeats Saracens as they storm the gates of Vienna and threaten Western Europe.

1716   Charles VI appeals to Our Lady of the Rosary and conquers the Moors at Peterwardein.

1717   Following victory on Corfu, Pope Clement XI extends the Feast of the Holy Rosary to the whole Church.

1830   Catherine Labouré (Rue de Bac) is instructed to produce Miraculous Medal.

1854   Definition of the Immaculate Conception of the Blessed Virgin Mary (8 December). Pius IX promulgates Apostolic Constitution *Ineffabilis Deus*.

1858   In Lourdes (11 February) Bernadette Soubirous has first vision of a 'beautiful Lady'. (25 March) The Lady identifies herself: '*Que soy era Immaculada Councepciou.*'

1879   Apparition of Mary with St Joseph, St John and an altar on which stands a young lamb appears in Knock, Ireland. During her visit, the people recite the rosary – the 'Irish Catechism'.

1883–98   Pope Leo XIII promotes the rosary as the 'most glorious and effective prayer' for those who want to reach Jesus through Mary. He encourages family rosary and advocates the beads as an antidote to rationalism and liberalism in twelve different Encyclicals and five Apostolic Letters.

1917   (13 May) A Lady with a rosary in her hand appears to three young children in Fatima, Portugal. She exhorts them to 'Say the rosary every day, to obtain peace for the world and an end to the war'. On 13 October the apparition says: 'I am the Lady of the Rosary.' Fatima prayer is added to each decade of the rosary.

1937   Pope Pius XI Encyclical Letter *Ingravescentibus malis* exhorts use of rosary in the struggle against communism.

1942   Patrick Peyton, the rosary priest, begins programme of family prayer and rosary devotion that leads to formal rosary crusades in the late 1940s.

1950   Pius XII Definition of the Assumption: *Munificentissimus Deus.*

c. 1960   *Mysteries of the Rosary* meditations on the rosary composed by Pope John XXIII.

1962–65   Second Vatican Council.

1974   Pope Paul VI, in *Marialis cultus,* recommends rosary, but says 'the faithful should feel serenely free in its regard'.

1981   Medjugorje (Yugoslavia) apparitions. The Blessed Virgin makes most insistent call to 'Pray, pray, pray.'

1987   John Paul II renews devotion to the Blessed Virgin Mary. In his Encyclical Letter *Redemptoris Mater,* the Pope gives an extensive teaching on Mary in anticipation of the Marian year 1988.

2001   Following the terrorist attack on the World Trade Center and the Pentagon on 11 September of this year, Pope John Paul II asks that during the month of October everyone say the rosary daily for peace.

Note

1. This chronology is based on the web page, 'Journaling the Beads', see *www.rosaryworkshop.com/HISTORYjournalingBead.htm*

Introduction

A 'rosary' means but one thing to a Roman Catholic today. It is
a circular string or chain of beads composed of five decades of
small beads separated by five larger beads with a pendant
attached, consisting of a cross or crucifix, and a chain of two
large and three smaller beads. This device is used to count the
prayers recited in honour of the Blessed Virgin Mary while
meditating on scenes from the life of Christ and His Mother. A
complete 'rosary' requires three repetitions of this chaplet,
covering the full fifteen 'mysteries of salvation'. Pope Pius XII
called it 'the compendium of the entire Gospel'.

The Eucharist remains the summit and source of Catholic
worship with the Liturgy of the Hours as the Church's official
prayer. Pope Paul VI tells us that after the Liturgy 'the Rosary
should be considered as one of the best and most efficacious
prayers'.[1] Indeed, the rosary is the most popular and universal
pious devotion in use today. Since Pius V gave it official
approval in 1569, many Popes have promoted the rosary prayer,
especially at times when the Church has been under threat.

The aim of this book is to examine the origins, development
and background of the rosary with particular reference to the
Marian rosary in common use today. It will sometimes be
designated the Dominican rosary to acknowledge that it was the
Dominicans who promoted it and to distinguish it from variants

associated with other orders. It evolved into its present form
during the fifteenth and sixteenth centuries, but it is a flexible
spiritual tool which can be adapted to current needs.

In the English literature one may find accounts of the origins
of the rosary, but none are complete. Indeed, the definitive
history of the rosary is yet to be written. Fr Herbert Thurston
SJ, writing in *The Month* between 1900 and 1916, is the most
important source in English. He had available to him the work
of the Bollandist Fr Thomas Esser, published in German
between 1884 and 1906, the earlier studies of Daniel Rock in
his book *The Church of Our Fathers* and Edmund Waterton's
comprehensive history of devotion to the Blessed Virgin, *Pietas
Mariana Britannica*. Franz M. Willam claims to have produced
'the first complete history of the origin and development of the
Rosary' in *The Rosary: Its History and Meaning* (1948; available
in English translation 1953). This is an important work, but
disappointing in that it is not well referenced. *The Rose-Garden
Game* (1969), by Eithne Wilkins, is an important contribution,
focusing on the symbolism associated with the rosary. More
recently, Anne Winston-Allen studied the German vernacular
literature of the late Middle Ages, throwing more light on the
origins of the rosary at that period. Her book, *Stories of the Rose*,
published in 1997, is informative and lavishly illustrated. A
future scholarly examination of the history of the rosary would
include a review of the German, French, Italian and Spanish
sources. Though one may find in various works of reference,
such as the original version of *The Catholic Encyclopedia* and the
more recent *Theotokos* by Michael O'Carroll, the essential
details, there is no one comprehensive account of the overall
history of the rosary and its associated prayers. This work aims
to draw together the information and insights of these re-
searchers and others to whom I refer in the text, and present
a scheme to show how the four main streams of origin and

other influences came together in the fifteenth century.

Before proceeding to our main study it will be convenient to consider the meaning of the various words used in connection with the rosary:

The word **chaplet** comes from the French *chape* (*un petit chapeau*): a covering or cap, a form of headgear, and hence, a crown, wreath or garland. By the middle of the twelfth century, 'chaplet' can be found referring to prayer beads or to the spiritual exercise of reciting chains of *Aves*.

The word **rosary** may have come into use from the German *Rosenkranz*, meaning a rose garland or wreath, or *Rosenkrenzelin* – a small garland or wreath. The term was certainly in use before the beginning of the fifteenth century. The Latin form *rosarium* meant 'a rose garden' or 'an anthology of prayer or verse'. Today **a rosary** is used to denote a set of rosary beads of five or fifteen decades. However, the term may be used for any sort of prayer beads.

From Italy we have a **corona** – a crown, and less commonly, **sertum** – a wreath.

Bead or **bede** is, according to Waterton, an Anglo-Saxon word, but the dictionary[2] suggests that it is derived from the Old English *gebed*, from the German *gebet*, related to the Dutch *bede*, meaning 'prayer'. The words 'bead' and 'prayer' are connected by association with the rosary, as each bead represents a prayer.

To **bid**, as in the 'bidding prayers' of the Mass, from the Old English *biddan* and German *bitten*, is 'to ask'. To **bid the beads** (*bedes byddying*) is to say one's prayers.

> All night she spent in bidding of her bedes
> And all the day in doing good and godly deeds
> (Edmund Spenser, *The Faerie Queene*)

3

Ich bidde my bedis.

(William Langland, *Piers Plowman*)

Beads-folk, **bedesmen** or **bedeswomen** are those who pray for others, especially for their benefactors. A **bead-house** may be a chapel or an almshouse, from the practice of giving alms to the residents who would in return offer their prayers in gratitude. For a consideration in one's will, a **bedesman** would regularly pray for the repose of one's soul. A **bead-roll** is a list of persons to be prayed for. In the sixteenth century it was common practice to sign one's correspondence 'Your obedient bedesman', or 'Your poor bedeswoman'.[3] We have examples in the letters of Sir Thomas More, writing from prison, and the Franciscan John Forrest, Confessor to Queen Catherine of Aragon and one of the English martyrs. Although in our old English documents 'the bidding of beads' does not necessarily imply the use of the rosary, nor indeed any devotion whatever to the Blessed Virgin, yet from the thirteenth century this was commonly the sense.

We **tell** our beads as we go, that is, we keep a 'tally', count our beads (Old English *tellan*; German *zahlen*). Otherwise we 'say' or 'recite' a rosary.

A **pair** of beads is a set of beads. A circle of beads hanging from one's belt looks like a pair of parallel strings of beads.

Because of his name, some have attributed the rosary to the Venerable Bede, but this is groundless. A more plausible explanation is that he received his name from his assiduity in prayer.

To those readers who have reservations about Catholic devotion to Mary and her role in the history of salvation may draw I their attention to what Cardinal Newman had to say:

4

Mary is exalted for the sake of Jesus. It was fitting that she, as being a creature, though the first of creatures, should have an office of ministration. She, as others, came into the world to do a work, she had a mission to fulfil; her grace and glory are not for her own sake, but for her Maker's; and to her is committed the custody of the Incarnation, this is her appointed office – 'Behold a virgin shall conceive and bear a Son: and His name shall be called Emmanuel.' As she was once on earth, and was personally the guardian of her Divine Child, as she carried Him in her womb, folded Him in her embrace, and suckled Him at her breast, so now, and to the latest hour of the Church, do her glories and the devotion paid to her proclaim and define the right faith concerning Him as God and man. Every church which is dedicated to her, every altar which is raised under her invocation, every image which represents her, every litany in her praise, every Hail Mary for her continual memory, does but remind us that there was One who, though He was all-blessed from all eternity, yet for the sake of sinners, 'did not shrink from the Virgin's womb'.[4]

Mary is honoured by the Church because it was she who was chosen by God and agreed to be the Mother of the Incarnate Word: 'Behold, I am the handmaid of the Lord; let it be to me according to your word' (Luke 1.38). By her wholehearted response to the Holy Spirit she became the medium by which the one Mediator and Saviour, Jesus Christ, came into the world. The Church presents Mary to us a model disciple and a 'type' of the Church. In promoting the rosary devotion, the Church invites us to meditate with Mary on the life of Christ, because she 'kept all these things, pondering them in her heart' (Luke 2.19).

The rosary has been part of my prayer life since childhood. My interest in the history and development of the rosary was aroused initially by Gabriel Harty's excellent short book

Rediscovering the Rosary, and more recently by a lecture given at Aylesford by Dr Sarah Boss in July 1999. This work began as a 30-minute talk on the history of the rosary given to a group of 'over-sixties' in September 1999. In preparation I began to read around the subject, in particular the series of articles by Fr Thurston, 'Our Popular Devotions', published in *The Month*. One article led to another, and so on. It was a happening rather than a planned exercise. I hope the reader will find the subject as interesting as I do.

Notes

1. Paul VI, *Marialis cultus* (1974), n. 54.
2. *The Shorter Oxford English Dictionary*.
3. Edmund Waterton, *Pietas Mariana Britannica: A History of Devotion to the Most Blessed Virgin Marye, Mother of God* (London: St Joseph's Catholic Library, 1879).
4. J. H. Newman, *Sermons and Discourses* (New York: Longmans, Green, 1893), Vol. II, p. 252, in F. M. Willam, *The Rosary: Its History and Meaning*, trans. E. Kaiser (New York: Benzinger Bros, 1953), p. 165.

2

Origins of the Rosary

The Legend of St Dominic

For 400 years or more it was generally accepted that the rosary as a Marian prayer was given by the Blessed Virgin to St Dominic in a dream to assist him in his effort to convert the Cathars. This story was to be found in the lesson for the Feast of the Holy Rosary in the Roman Breviary and was attested by various Popes down to the rosary Encyclicals of Leo XIII (1878–1903).

St Dominic (c. 1172–1221; canonized 1234), born in Calaruega in Old Castile, joined the Augustinian Canons of Osma and became sub-prior. In 1203 he went on an embassy with Bishop Diego on behalf of Alfonso VIII, King of Castile, to ask for the hand of a noble lady of the 'Marches', most probably the Marches of Denmark, for the king's son Fernando. In this they were successful, and were sent again the following year to arrange the marriage. However, on their arrival they found that the lady had since died.[1]

In the course of his journey Dominic had encountered the Albigenses in southern France. (The Albigenses followed the heretical teachings of the Cathari, denying the humanity of Jesus.) On his return from northern Europe (1203–5), Dominic became involved in a mission to the Albigenses in the region of

Figure 2.1   Mary giving the rosary to St Dominic
Source: Photograph by author

Toulouse. He adopted a new style of evangelization as an itinerant mendicant preacher and founded a community which was formally established in 1220. The Order of Preachers maintained elements of monastic observance, but dropped manual labour in favour of study and preaching.

Dominic's mission to the Cathars was not a success and, according to the legend, in the year 1214 he retired to a cave in the woods near Toulouse. After he had spent three days in fasting and prayer, the Blessed Virgin appeared to him, accompanied by three queens and 50 maidens – the number clearly corresponding to the pattern of the psalter. She raised him up and kissed him, and, in the style of medieval mystical eroticism, quenched his thirst with milk from her chaste breast. She then told him that not intellectual thundering against heresy but rather a gentle remedy against sickness was required: 'Therefore if you will preach successfully, preach my psalter.' The Blessed Virgin then vanished together with her entourage. Restored and armed with the rosary, Dominic went forth and reconverted the Cathars to Catholicism. The Cathari, who did not believe that Christ was a real man, born of a real woman (such as he, Dominic, had now experienced her to be), were to be persuaded by the statement proclaiming: 'And blessed is the fruit of thy womb'.

An alternative version of the Virgin's words is given by Augusta Drane:

Wonder not that until now you have obtained so little fruit by your labours; you have spent them on barren soil not yet watered with the dew of divine grace. When God willed to renew the face of the earth, He began by sending down on it the fertilising rain of the Angelic Salutation. Therefore preach my Psalter of 150 Angelic Salutations and 15 Our Fathers and you will obtain an abundant harvest.[2]

She continues:

> For that it was through his hand that the Blessed Virgin Mary
> delivered to us, her children, the devotion of the holy rosary, is the
> firm and constant tradition of the Church supported by a weight of
> authority which can hardly be called into question without
> temerity. Nevertheless it cannot be presented with those precise
> details of times and circumstances which are demanded in a
> narration of historic fact.[3]

Quoting Danzas, Augusta Drane goes on to be more frank:
'The rosary has no history, and will probably never have one.'[4]

The Bollandist Fr Thomas Esser, writing in the 1890s,
examined the origins of this Dominican legend, and Fr Herbert
Thurston reviewed the evidence very fully.[5] He came to the
conclusion that there is a complete absence of St Dominic's
name in connection with this devotion until 250 years after his
death; there is no mention in biography, recorded sermons, in
the documents for the process of canonization, nor in paintings
or sculpture. None of the many early Dominican saints used the
rosary as such, though many of them did recite a multitude of
Aves counting on a knotted cord or circlet of beads. For
instance, Blessed Benventuro Bojani said a thousand *Aves* a day
and two thousand on Saturdays, and in addition 700 *Paters* and
700 *Aves* – each hundred for a different intention.

In 1908 Fr Thurston examined further data on the possible
connection of the rosary with St Dominic.[6] He drew attention
to a document which was reputed to be a contemporary poem
written immediately after the battle of Muret (1213). The
original document no longer exists, but a book published in
1693 by a certain Fr Benoist professes to be a copy of the
original. According to the version of this poem published by Fr
Thomas Esser in his *Rosary Book* (published about 1900), the

unknown author of the poem pays a tribute of gratitude to St Dominic, on the grounds that the victory was due to his prayers and his rosary, as follows:

Verse 4

Dominicus rosas afferre	So soon as Dominic
Dum incipit tam humilis,	begins to bring roses,
Dominicus coronas confrerre	For Dominic quickly hastens
Stastim apparet agilis.	to twine wreaths.

Fr Thurston surmised that perhaps Benoist had made an error when copying the poem. On consulting the original text of Fr Benoist, he found that the first word of the third line of the stanza was in fact '*Dominus*', 'Lord'. Dominic brings the roses and the Lord weaves them into a wreath to crown the victors. It was the copyist of Fr Benoist who had been in error. There is no warrant for supposing that St Dominic was familiar with the practice of saying 50 Hail Marys, and describing the prayers as 'roses' or the whole exercise as a 'rosarium'.

The linkage between the rosary and St Dominic would seem to have been proposed by Alain de la Roche, a Dominican friar and founder of the first rosary confraternity in 1468–70. What is certain is that from that time onwards the Dominican Order of Preachers were the main promoters of the Marian rosary.

The Origins of the Rosary

If it was not St Dominic who gave us the rosary, where then did it originate? A full review of the story of the rosary will show that there was no one point of origin, rather it evolved over a long period and from a variety of sources. The multiplicity of streams of development and other influences are depicted in the Frontispiece to this book (p.ii). If we were to compare it to a river system, there are four main rivers or lines of development. Three have their source in scripture and one in the use of prayer beads. The psalms and Jewish liturgical tradition flow into the Liturgy of the Hours of monastic practice out of which come the Marian psalm psalters and the *Paternoster* beads. The Our Father was always a central prayer in Christian devotion, being incorporated in the celebration of the Eucharist and the Divine Office. In the twelfth century, with the growth of monasticism and the many lay brothers, the recitation of 150 *Paternosters*, counted on a knotted cord or string of beads, was substituted for the psalms.

The Angelic Salutation and Elizabeth's greeting of Mary are found in the Eastern Liturgy from perhaps the fifth century. They are again found in the Little Office of Our Lady, which grew in popularity at the beginning of the second millennium. From about 1050 the Angelic Salutation, with or without Elizabeth's greeting, begins to be used as a popular prayer form, initially perhaps being added to the end of the Our Father. Then the *Ave* develops separately as a greeting to the Blessed Virgin, as popular devotion to Mary grows in the twelfth century. One suggestion is that, being essentially a salutation, the *Ave* was said as an accompaniment to a series of genuflexions repeated 150 times. Alternatively, the *Ave* came to be said as a chaplet of 150 salutations counted on a circlet of beads. The name of Jesus is added in about 1261, so that the prayer commonly ends with 'Jesus Christ. Amen.' The second part of the Hail Mary dates from the end of the fifteenth century and its current form was fixed in the sixteenth.

The use of beads as a counting device is probably universal. It is known that prayer beads were used in Hindu practice from about 1750 BC. We can date the Christian use of beads to the fourth century and the Jesus Prayer has survived to the present day being counted on a knotted woollen rope.

Two streams of Marian devotion continue to flow and develop: the Marian psalm psalter and the *Ave* chaplet.[7] Furthermore, during the fourteenth century the practice of meditation on the life of Christ is an important spiritual development and is taken up by the Devotio Moderna movement and the Observant reform movement. There is a confluence of these three streams when another Dominic, a Carthusian monk, joined meditation on the life of Christ with the repetition of the *Ave Maria* in sets of 50 prayers sometime between 1409 and 1415. This is the essence of the modern rosary. Further experiment and development continued until the rosary was formally approved by Pius V in 1569.

We will now begin a more detailed examination of the origins of the rosary, following it from this confluence of practice and influence through to its general acceptance by the Church. We will then study the elements that constitute the rosary.

Life of Christ Meditations

Exactly when the life of Christ (*vita Christi*) meditations, the essence of the modern rosary, became part of the rosary is a matter for debate. Anne Winston has contributed to the understanding of this problem by her study of the German vernacular texts of the Middle Ages.

> Marian legends of the twelfth century tell of pious individuals being rewarded by the Blessed Virgin for the practice of reciting strings of *Aves*. It was believed that hearing these words brought Mary delight by recalling to her the joy of the Incarnation. The 'Marien Rosenkranz' legend in the German Passional (1280–1300) describes, for example, the reciting of chains of *Aves* as the act of creating a symbolic wreath for the Virgin. In this tale, 50 *Aves*

chanted by a monk miraculously turn into roses and form a chaplet, which is called a '*rosen crantz*'. Originally, the term *rosarium* had been used to designate a garden, an anthology of texts, or a rose wreath. Ultimately, it came to refer to 50 salutations to the Virgin.

For keeping track of these prayers, chains of beads came into use. The beads are called a '*zapel*' (chaplet) in 1220–35. The beads were also known as *Ave* or *Paternoster* beads because they were used for counting repetitions of *Aves* or *Paternosters*. The Beguines of Ghent in 1242 were required by their regulations to pray three chaplets of *Aves* daily. Other religious devoted themselves to marathon repetitions of these prayers. Esser reports that certain Dominican nuns at the cloister of Unterlinden in Colmar prayed a thousand Hail Marys each day, and on special days two thousand.[8]

A parallel development arose from the recitation of the Psalter in private devotions, as a replacement for the traditional canonical hours. In the 'Marian psalm psalters', which originated around 1130, the antiphons that preceded each psalm and announced its theme were replaced by verses that interpreted each of the 150 psalms as a reference to Christ or Mary. Gradually the devotion was shortened to a recitation of the antiphons and, in place of the psalm proper, either a *Paternoster* or an *Ave Maria*. Without the psalm, the connection that the antiphon had to a specific theme was lost. As a result, the antiphons themselves came to be replaced by 150 verses in praise of the Virgin. Partly for ease of recitation, the Marian psalters were subdivided into three sets of 50 stanzas, each set of which was also designated as a 'rosary'.

By the end of the fourteenth century there existed these two forms of the psalter: 'psalters' composed of 150 *Ave Marias* or *Paternosters* and the rhymed Marian psalm psalters composed of 150 stanzas each representing a psalm. The Marian psalm psalters dating from before 1300 do not contain connected narratives but lists of attributes of Christ or Mary related to the themes of the psalms. Thus these alone cannot constitute the source for the narrative meditations linked to the *Ave* prayer that characterize later rosaries.

Dominic of Prussia and the Jesus Clause

We turn now to the Carthusians of the Charterhouse of St Alban at Trier (Trèves) on the River Mosel in southwest Germany, near the Luxembourg border. Adolf of Essen, shortly after his entry to the Charterhouse in 1398, wrote two short treatises in Latin, one of which recommended the rosary and the other, meditations on the life of our Saviour Jesus Christ and his Blessed Mother. It is possible that Adolf may have been influenced by the Devotio Moderna, a revival movement current at that time which promoted meditation on the life and Passion of Christ. Inspired by these meditations, his brother monk Dominic of Prussia,[9] sometime between 1409 and 1415, composed 50 meditation points summarizing the principal mysteries of the life of Christ to be attached to the *Ave* after the words 'Jesus Christ'; for example: 'Jesus Christ, from whose sacred side, opened by the soldier's lance, there escaped water and blood for the remission of our sins'. In his *Liber experientiarum* (1458), Dominic of Prussia explicitly claimed to be the first to have composed the 50 *clausulae*.[10] There is some suggestion that he wrote a set of 150 meditation points at a later date.

The two books written by Adolf were translated into German and presented to Margaret of Bavaria, Duchess of Lorraine (d. 1434), who lived nearby at Sierck. She profited greatly from these and became a benefactress of the Carthusians. In 1415 she established a new Carthusian foundation in an old

Cistercian monastery, Marienfloss, and Dom Adolf of Essen was appointed as the superior, where he remained until 1421 when he returned to Trier as prior. In 1429 Adolf had a vision of the Virgin Mary accompanied by her heavenly court. When they sang the rosary to Mary, each *Ave* was accompanied by one of the *clausulae* which Dominic had first composed. At the name of Mary, all bowed their head and at the name of Jesus all genuflected. Each clause finished with an *Alleluia*. He understood that those who pray the rosary fervently in this fashion will obtain the grace of spiritual advancement, final perseverance and a heavenly reward. Knowledge of this vision came to light from writings found in his cell after his death. Adolf had been instrumental in spreading this form of the rosary until his death in 1439.

Johannes Rode (d. 1439) entered Trier in 1416 and became prior in 1419, but was appointed abbot of the Benedictine monastery of St Mathias in 1421 to carry out a reform. Later he was to be the Visitor-General to all the monasteries in the Electorates of Spire, Worms and Strasburg. In this work he was often accompanied by Adolf of Essen, and together they introduced the rosary with the *clausulae* of Dominic of Prussia.

Dominic himself spent two years as Master of Novices in Cologne, so he too had the opportunity to pass on his form of the rosary. But by far the greatest means of propagating this devotion was by correspondence. It is claimed that Dominic and his brother monks distributed more than a thousand copies of this prayer exercise.[11]

The earliest printed rosary book appeared in 1475: *[Dis ist] unser lieben frowen Rozenkranz* (*This is Our Lady's Rosary*), and included Dominic's 50 *clausulae*. (See Chapter 17 for a full version.) The following are three examples quoted by Fr Thurston:

5th   Jesus Christ whom thou didst wrap in swaddling cloths and
        laid in a manger. Amen.

19th   Jesus Christ whose feet Mary Magdalen washed with her
        tears, and wiped with her hair, kissed and anointed. Amen.

32nd   Jesus Christ who prayed for his executioners, saying 'Father
        forgive them for they know not what they do.' Amen.

Dominic made it clear in a supplementary note that this scheme
was to be taken only as a suggestion. In practice there was much
experimentation and many variations were in use.

The addition of life of Christ meditations changed the nature
of the devotion. Emphasis on the person of Jesus and the events
of his life, in effect, transformed the *Ave Maria* prayer into a
Jesus prayer – a shift that reflects the popular impulse toward
imitatio Christi piety. Instead of simple *Aves*, repeated
ritualistically because the Virgin liked to hear them, or psalms
recited round the clock in order literally to pray without
ceasing, *imitatio* exercises had as their goal the conforming of
the individual worshipper to the model of Christ. This shift
from an outward to an inward focus was directed towards
transforming the person.[12]

Though Dominic was the first to link exactly 50 biographical
meditations on the life of Christ to the *Ave* prayer that marked
the beginning of a new form of the religious exercise, the idea
was not new. In 1977 Andreas Heinz discovered a manuscript
containing a *vita Christi* rosary dated around 1300. This text is
contained in a manuscript collection of prayers that were
recited by the Cistercian nuns at the cloister of Saint Thomas
on the Kyll, located 40 kilometres from Trier. The Cistercian
text contains 98 (originally a hundred, presumably) *vita Christi*
meditations. Despite the relative proximity of Saint Thomas's
to Trier, there appears to be no connection between this
obscure early rosary and Dominic's later, widely disseminated

one. Dominic himself makes no mention of the Cistercian prayer; instead he attributes his inspiration to a passage in Mechthild of Hackeborn's (1241–99) *Liber spiritualis gratiae* (Book of Spiritual Grace), where Mechthild records a vision of a beautiful tree upon whose leaves were written in golden letters the entire life of Christ. 'Jesus Christ, born of a virgin; Jesus Christ, circumcised on the eighth day; Jesus Christ whom the three kings worshipped; Jesus Christ, who was presented in the temple; Jesus Christ, whom John baptised; etc.'[13]

We should also note a German vernacular Marian psalter of the early fourteenth century where we find for the first time scenes of the life of Christ inserted within a traditional litany of praise to the Virgin. The third set of stanzas contain a chronological sequence of 38 events from the life of the Saviour, from conception and birth through to Passion, death and resurrection, ending with the Last Judgement. The story is integrated within the rhymed four-line verse form characteristic of Marian psalters. For example:

> Help us, Lady, on account of the agony
> that Christ suffered on death's journey,
> when Pilate washed his hands,
> that we may find a just end.[14]

In 1483 a rosary book written by a Dominican, *Our Dear Lady's Psalter*, reduced the 50 meditation points to fifteen, all of which, except the last two, correspond to the present mysteries: the Coronation was combined with the Assumption and the Last Judgement was the fifteenth mystery. The Dominican Alberto da Castello, in his book *The Rosary of the Glorious Virgin* (1521), tried to unite the old and the new forms of the mysteries. He was the first to use the term 'mystery' in this context. A mystery was attached to each *Pater*, and the 50 meditation points or *clausulae* were attached to the *Aves*. It was during the sixteenth century that the rosary of fifteen mysteries became the accepted form.[15]

The Rosary Confraternities

It was a Dominican, Alain de la Roche (Alanus de Rupe) (c. 1428–75), influenced by the Carthusians of Trier, who did so much to promote the rosary in the late fifteenth century. Alain was a Breton, a learned and eloquent man, a teacher of theology, a Dominican friar of the monastery of Dinan. In about 1460 he believed that he had been commissioned by the Virgin Mary in a vision to preach the rosary devotion and to found rosary confraternities. He was prone to visions and ecstasies, and was considered by some to be a 'really frantic and crazy man'. He is sometimes given the title 'Blessed' though he was never formally beatified.

Fraternities of many kinds were founded in the Church in the Middle Ages to meet the religious and social needs of clergy and laity. Their primary purpose was to secure for their members mutual support in death through Masses, prayers and alms, as well as intercessions in sickness and other religious benefits. They often catered for various forms of lay piety and many were associated with the orders of mendicant friars.[16]

Alain de la Roche founded his first confraternity, 'the Confraternity of the Psalter of the Glorious Virgin Mary', at Douai in 1468–70. His aim was that the organization should be easy to join, without vows or constraints, and it was free. There were no penalties for failing to say the prayers, no prescribed times for saying them and no prescribed manner – the rosary could be said standing or walking. It was such flexibility that was partly responsible for the success of the confraternities.[17]

Alain died at Zunolle in Flanders on 8 September 1475, the

Figure 2.2   Mary appearing to Alain de la Roche (copy of a woodcut in
the *Rosario* of Alberto da Castello, 1521)
Source: Thurston, H., The Rosary, *The Month*, 97 (1901): 290

very day another and more influential confraternity was
founded by Jakob Sprenger in Cologne. This had the support
of Frederick III, whose name appeared among the earliest
members on the Cologne register. The emperor leant
credibility and prestige to the organization, leading to approval
by the Papal Legate, Alexander of Forli, in 1476.

The brotherhood spread quickly to other cities, not only in
Germany (Rostock 1475, Augsburg 1476), but also in Lille,
Ghent 1475, Lisbon 1478, Venice 1480, Florence 1481 and
Barcelona 1488. Each chapter of the brotherhood was
independent, any location could start one. The only requirement was that members should sign a membership roll with
their name, marital status and whether they were religious or
lay persons. Membership was predominantly, but not exclu-
sively, female.

As a social phenomenon, the brotherhood was attractive because of its lack of discrimination. Sprenger declared membership open to everyone so that the poor and the needy and the languishing 'of this knavish world' could become the equals of the rich. Extra-liturgical religious practice and private devotion flourished in the late Middle Ages because the laity felt they were but spectators at the Eucharist. We can see how easy it was for the practice of reciting the rosary during Mass to develop.

Alain favoured the traditional Marian psalter of 150 *Aves: he thought the term 'rosary' with its worldly connotations and the Carthusian short version with only 50 Aves* were a threat to the traditional psalter. He claimed that the prayer and the confraternity dated back to the days of the Virgin herself. Alain claimed that the Virgin had personally commissioned him to revive her prayer and its languishing confraternity. The Book and Ordinance of the new confraternity recommended dividing the 150 *Aves* into three sections of 50 to be recited morning, noon and evening: (1) the prophecies of Jesus; (2) his childhood; (3) the Passion. They also suggested marking off the *Aves* with fifteen *Paternosters*, thus the number of *Paternosters* recited in the course of a year would equal the number of wounds Christ suffered as reckoned by St Bernard, viz. 5475.[18]

Alain recommended the recitation of the prayers before a picture as an aid to meditation. A picture of Mary and her child, greeting in Mary the eyes that saw Jesus, the ears that listened to his voice, the lips that kissed him, or a beautiful picture of Christ, reciting an *Ave* to the hair that was torn, to the crown of thorns, to the wounded brow, to the weeping eyes, etc., finally to salute the perfection of God and the saints in heaven.

Michael Francisci, a professor at Cologne University, presented a series of lectures in December 1475 defending the devotion of the confraternities against their detractors. The lectures were published first in 1476 and later in his *Quodlibet* in 1480. Michael had been in Douai 1465–8 and active in Cologne 1469–81. He interpreted Alain's ideas to a wider public in a form that was attractive and practical. It was a composite work that suggested three meditations: (1) Mary's earthly joys; (2) her Passion sorrows; and (3) her heavenly joys. He also suggested marking off each ten *Aves* with a *Paternoster.*[19]

Jakob Sprenger recommended in his statutes (1477) that the members of the brotherhood say three rosaries a week, each consisting of 50 *Aves* with five *Paternosters.* He spoke of ten white roses and the insertion of a red rose with which there should be meditation on the rose-red blood of Christ, but does not specify any meditation on the white roses. The statutes of the Colmar confraternity, founded in 1485, called for five Joys – ten *Aves* each – and five Sorrows – one *Paternoster* each. It was an antiphonal format of ten merged Joys and Sorrows.[20]

Indulgences and their Abuse

Promotional writings for the new confraternity founded by Alain marketed the devotion as a way to reduce time in purgatory and as a talisman to protect users against all manner of evil in this present life. The statutes of the Douai brotherhood advertised very generous but unauthenticated indulgences of up to 30,000 years for saying the prayer.

The first of many rosary indulgences was granted to the Cologne confraternity in 1476 by the Papal Legate, Alexander of Forli, who offered 40 days (one quarantine) for reciting the prayer. Pope Sixtus IV, in a Bull promulgated in 1478, granted an indulgence of seven years and seven quarantines. He also extended indulgences to apply to souls in purgatory, '*per modum suffragii*'.[21]

This ability to apply indulgences to the souls in purgatory

partly accounts for the popularity and rapid spread of the rosary confraternities among a population who were concerned about this matter and as an insurance that they too would benefit after death from the prayers of the brotherhood. By 1520 the amassing of all kinds of indulgences as insurance against purgatory reached monumental proportions. Johann Eck criticized the Holy Ghost Order for having acquired for its members a million years and 42 plenary indulgences. There was also the practice of hiring the rosary said by proxy.

Martin Luther challenged his academic colleagues to debate the subject of indulgences and he challenged the interpretation of indulgences as preached by the Dominican Johann Tetzel. No one took up the challenge. Luther wrote his 95 theses and sent them to the bishop who had licensed Tetzel, but got no response. Only then did he nail them to the door of the church in Wittenberg, on 31 October 1517. It was not until 1567 that Pius V acted to prohibit the abuses. (For an explanation of indulgences, and a record of those applied to the rosary, see Chapter 18.)

The Picture Text

William Caxton learnt the craft of printing in Cologne during 1470–72, and printed the first book in English in 1475, but 'the admirable art of typography was invented by the ingenious Johan Gutenberg at Mainz in 1450'.[22] Nevertheless, this was a time when some 95 per cent of the population was illiterate. The principal means of communication was by word of mouth, by sermons, hymns and popular songs. This was supplemented by the visual image in the form of stained glass windows, altar pieces, devotional panels, woodcuts and engravings.

The *Ave* psalm psalter and the 50 *clausulae* of Dominic necessarily required a written text, and were therefore not accessible to the majority of people. However, everyone could read pictures. A popular manual, *Our Lady's Psalter*, published in Ulm by Conrad Dinckmut in 1483 and reprinted in at least seven editions before 1503, included the first picture rosary, fifteen woodcuts depicting the sequence of events in the life of Christ and Mary. According to Thomas Esser[23] they are the earliest record of the fifteen mysteries and were intended to be used for meditation while reciting the rosary.

Figure 2.3   The five Joyful Mysteries (*Unser Lieben Frowen Psalter*, 1495).
Printed by L. Zeissenmair at Augsburg, 1495
Source: Thurston, H., The Rosary, *The Month*, 96 (1900): 626

Figure 2.4   The five Glorious Mysteries (*Unser Lieben Frowen Psalter*, 1489).
Printed by Conrad Dinckmut at Ulm, 1489
Source: Thurston, H., The Rosary, *The Month*, 96 (1900): 627

The idea of using pictures in religious devotions was not
new. Alain had recommended the recitation of the rosary before
an image of Christ or the Virgin. A rosary manual dated 1484
from the Netherlands carried the advice to readers: 'those who
cannot read should look at the illustrations while repeating the
Ave Maria and think about the life and Passion of Our Lord'.

The picture texts in the Ulm manual consist of three sets of five medallions, each medallion framed by ten roses representing ten *Ave Marias*. The first set of five, the 'white rosary', narrates the chief events in the birth and childhood of Jesus, the second set, the 'red rosary', recounts the events of the Passion, and the third set, the 'golden rosary', depicts the Resurrection and the glorious events that followed it. Except for the final illustration, which shows the Last Judgement, these meditations correspond to those that emerged as standard in the course of the sixteenth and seventeenth centuries.[24] Although the pictorial versions show less variety than written ones, the picture sets too were subject to experimentation. Besides the shift in the final scene from Last Judgement to the Coronation, the most common variation was substitution of the Adoration of the Magi in place of one of the other events of Christ's childhood. The Coronation scene appears first in an engraving in Barcelona by Franciscus Domenech in 1488, and then in Florence in a set of fifteen full-page engravings in 1490 by Francesco Roselli.[25] Similar sequences of illustrations narrating the life of Christ or of Mary can be found in altar pieces and serial devotional panels, which were very popular in fifteenth-century Germany.

The Ulm Picture Rosary and Johannes of Erfurt's Venice Statutes

In the statutes of the Venice confraternity (founded in 1480) there appears for the first time in written form a complete set of fifteen specific narrative meditations resembling those of the Ulm picture text, but, instead of the Last Judgement, for the fifteenth meditation we have 'the glory of paradise'. We do not know who compiled the Venice statutes, but they must have been familiar with Sprenger's German handbook and probably also Francisci's *Quodlibet*. The link between Venice and Ulm was the chaplain and founder of the Venice brotherhood, Johannes of Erfurt, a German Dominican who was an alumnus of the convent in Cologne. Similar narrative meditations are found in the statutes of the Florence confraternity (1481) and in Alberto da Castello's Italian rosary book *Rosario dello Gloriosa Virgine* of 1521.[26] It is in this book that the term 'mystery' is used of the narrative meditations for the first time.

The Observant Reformers

The Observant reform movement of the fifteenth century influenced all the major religious orders. Dominic of Prussia, Johannes Rode, Alain de la Roche, Michael Francisci, Jakob Sprengler and Johannes of Erfurt were all intimately and actively involved in the Observant movement and hoped by promoting their confraternities to engender pious devotion among the populace.

The Observant movement had begun in the 1330s among the Franciscans in Italy. It was promoted by the Augustinians in the 1380s and by the Dominicans in the 1390s. The aim was a return to a strict observance of the rule with asceticism and a renewed spirituality. In a few of the convents it included the practice of daily communion. Among the mendicant orders it led to a wave of revivalist preaching and a recommitment to attend to the sacramental life of the laity. It was in this ambience of spiritual renewal/revival that the new manner of reciting the rosary was promoted and the rosary confraternities established as a reformist outreach to the laity.

The earliest licences to preach the rosary were issued to members of the strictly Observant Holland congregation (1481) and Leipzig congregation (1479). Johannes of Erfurt from the Holland congregation's convent in Greifswald in Poland was the founder of the first Italian confraternity at Venice in 1480.[27]

During the sixteenth century the rosary became firmly established and recognized. Pope Leo X gave the rosary official approbation in 1520. It continued to be propagated by the establishment of rosary confraternities which were increasingly under Dominican control. In 1559 Pius V gave the Dominican Master-General exclusive control over the confraternities. At the Dominican General Chapter of 1574 there was great concern because other orders, such as the Franciscans, were showing paintings of the Blessed Virgin giving rosaries to their founder saints, and steps were taken to counter this trend. Their control was such that until 1984 the blessing of rosaries was reserved to Dominicans or priests having special faculties.

In 1569 Pope Pius V, in the Bull *Consueverunt Romani Pontifices*, officially approved the rosary and promoted its use. He himself was a Dominican and a devotee of Our Lady. He called for the public recitation of the rosary throughout Europe to combat the (at that time) invincible Turks. The Feast of Our Lady of Victory was established by Pius V on 7 October 1572, in commemoration of the battle of Lepanto (1571), when the Turkish navy was decisively defeated by the Venetian and Spanish fleets under the command of Don Juan of Austria, son of Charles V of Spain. It is said that for three hours before the battle the rosary was recited before an image of Our Lady of Guadalupe. This picture had been given to Admiral Doria by Phillip II of Spain, to whom it had been sent, in 1570, by Archbishop Montufor of Mexico.[28] During the time of the battle, Pius V was in conference with his cardinals in Rome. Suddenly he arose and went to the window, and looking towards the east said: 'Enough of business, let us thank God for the great victory He has just given our fleet.' These words were recorded, signed and sealed and kept secret. Two weeks later a courier from Venice brought the news of victory. The

Venetian Senate said: 'It was not our valour, nor arms, nor armies that gave us the victory, but Our Lady of the Rosary.' In *Salvatoris Domini* (5 March 1572), Pius wrote: 'We desire in particular that the remembrance of the great victory obtained from God through the merits and intercession of the glorious Virgin, on 7 October 1571, against the Turks, the enemies of the Catholic Faith, may never be forgotten.' In 1573 the name of the feast was changed by Gregory XIII to the Feast of Our Lady of the Rosary and the feast transferred to the first Sunday of October. Since the 1969 revision of the calendar it has reverted to 7 October. Initially the feast was granted only to churches which had an altar dedicated to the rosary.

During the Jubilee year of 1575 Gregory XIII issued a Bull making special arrangements for the persecuted Catholics of England. To obtain the Jubilee blessing, they were required to say either the rosary or the corona of Our Lady.

The 'Glory be to the Father' and the Apostles' Creed had been added to the rosary prayer by the early seventeenth century. The overall configuration and prayer sequence of the rosary were becoming more and more uniform. It has been said that during the seventeenth century (the baroque era), the rosary became the Marian prayer *par excellence*, recited at births and wakes, in church and at home – virtually omnipresent within Catholicism.

Fr Fernandez OP, in his *Historia de los Insignes Milagres* (1613), Chapter 25, gives an account of the manner in which the rosary was said publicly in choir in the Dominican church of Santa Maria Sopra Minerva in Rome: beginning with *Deus in adjutorium*, followed by a hymn, meditation, antiphon, and then the *Paternoster* followed by ten *Aves* ending with the *Gloria Patri*, said or sung antiphonally by two choirs, and concluding with a versicle, prayer and an anthem to Our Lady, according to the season.[29]

King Louis XIII of France ordered public recitation of the rosary against the rebellious Huguenots in 1627. Fifteen thousand rosaries were distributed to the troops with set hours of prayer. The battle was won and France was saved.

St Louis de Montfort (1673–1716), born in Brittany, had great devotion to the Blessed Virgin and strongly promoted the rosary. He founded two religious orders, and his books *True Devotion to Mary*, *The Secret of Mary* and *The Secret of the Rosary* are still popular. He draws on the early handbooks of the rosary confraternities, and his writing gives an insight into this popular devotion as found at the end of the seventeenth century. In *The Secret of the Rosary* St Louis wrote: 'My *Ave Maria*, my rosary, is my prayer and my most certain touchstone for distinguishing between those who are guided by the Spirit of God and those who work under the illusion of the evil spirit.' The rosary as taught by St Louis was that which we know as the Dominican rosary in common use today. Already the rosary devotion was so widespread as to been seen as a badge of the Roman Catholic.

Jan Sobieski, King of Poland, invoking Our Lady of the Rosary, defeated the Saracens in 1683 as they stormed the gates of Vienna and threatened all Western Europe. In 1716, on the Feast of Our Lady of the Snows, the Emperor Charles VI, appealing to Our Lady of the Rosary, conquered the Moors at Peterwardein. After another victory on Corfu, in 1717, Pope Clement XI extended the Feast of the Holy Rosary to the whole Church.

In the chapters that follow, we shall examine in detail the elements that constitute the rosary: the Hail Mary, the Our Father and other associated prayers.

Notes

1. Augusta T. Drane, *A History of St Dominic* (London: Longmans Green, 1891), pp. 12–22.
2. Ibid., p. 22.
3. Ibid., p. 21.
4. A. Danzas, Etude sur les temps primitif de l'Order de St Dominique, quoted ibid., p. 121.
5. The Rosary: Was the Rosary Instituted by St Dominic?, *The Month*, 97 (1901): 67–79.
6. Fr Herbert Thurston, The Name of the Rosary (I), *The Month*, 111 (1908): 518–29.
7. Waterton refers to them as the 'Ave-Psalm-Psalter' and the 'Ave-Psalter', see *Pietas Mariana Britannica*, p. 150.
8. Anne Winston, Tracing the Origins of the Rosary, *Speculum*, 68 (1993): 619–36.
9. Also known as: Dominicus Prutenus (Latin), Dominikus von Preussen (German) and Dominique Hélion (or de Prusse) (French).
10. For further consideration of the origins of the narrative meditation see Anne Winston-Allen, *Stories of the Rose* (Pennsylvania: Pennsylvania State University Press, 1997), p. 17 and notes 24 and 25.
11. Ibid., p. 26. See Herbert du Manoir (ed.), *Maria: Etudes sur la Sainte Virge* (Paris: Beauchesne, 1949–71), Vol. II, pp. 661–75, for a detailed examination of the early history of 'Les "clausules" ou "formules" de Dominique'.
12. Anne Winston, Tracing the Origins of the Rosary, *Speculum*, 68 (1993): 620–1.
13. Anne Winston-Allen, *Stories of the Rose*, p. 17, see note 25.
14. Ibid., p. 20.
15. Michael O'Carroll, The Rosary, *Theotokos: A Theological Encyclopedia of the Blessed Virgin Mary* (Wilmington, DE: M. Glazier, 1982), pp. 313–14.
16. See Fraternities, in *The Oxford Dictionary of the Christian Church*, 3rd edn, F. L. Cross and E. A. Livingstone (New York: Oxford University Press, 1997).
17. Anne Winston-Allen, *Stories of the Rose*, see rosary confraternities, pp. 24–5; 28–9; 116–22; 127–8.

18. Ibid., p. 66.
19. Ibid., p. 67.
20. Ibid., p. 68.
21. Ibid., p. 122.
22. *Encyclopaedia Britannica CD 2000* (Chicago: Encyclopaedia Britannica Inc.), 'The invention of typography – Gutenberg (1450?)'.
23. Anne Winston-Allen, *Stories of the Rose*, p. 65, note 1.
24. Ibid., p. 34.
25. Ibid., p. 54.
26. Ibid., p. 69.
27. Ibid., p. 73.
28. Francis Johnston, *The Wonder of Guadalupe* (Chulmleigh, Devon: Augustine Publishing, 1981), p. 75: 'After remaining in the Doria family for several centuries, [this picture] was donated in 1811 by Cardinal Doria to the growing shrine of Our Lady of Guadalupe at San Stefano d'Aveto, Italy, where it remains an object of veneration to this day.'
29. Herbert Thurston, The Rosary: The Fifteen Mysteries, *The Month*, 96 (1900): 637.

3

The Hail Mary

Hail Mary, full of grace, the Lord is with you,

Blessed are you among women, and blessed is the fruit of your
womb, Jesus.

Holy Mary, Mother of God, pray for us sinners, now and at the
hour of our death. Amen.

Scriptural Origin[1]

We find the origin of the first part of the Hail Mary in the
Gospel of St Luke. It is a combination of the first words of
Gabriel to the virgin identified as Mary (Luke 1.28) and the
greeting of Elizabeth to her cousin Mary (Luke 1.42).

These words of the Angel to Mary are a form of greeting:

Chaire, kecharitōmenē, ho kyrios meta sou (1.28)

(Nestle)

Hail, O favoured one, the Lord is with you

(RSV)

Greetings, favored one! The Lord is with you

(NRSV)

Hail, full of grace, the Lord is with thee: blessed art thou among women

(Douay, from the Vulgate)

'*Chaire*' was a normal form of greeting in secular Greek. Hence its translation as '*Ave*' in the Latin or 'Hail' in English. 'Hail' is an archaic form and perhaps today we would say 'Hello', though that might sound too familiar. The contemporary Jewish greeting would have been '*Shalom*', meaning 'peace', but the use of '*Chaire*' alerts us to the scriptural context of the composition. Thus '*chairein*' may be translated as 'to rejoice'. When used in this sense in the Greek Septuagint it often refers to a joy that greets a divine saving act (Exodus 4.31; 1 Kings 5.21; Isaiah 66.7). For example the specific form '*chaire*' is used in the Greek Septuagint (LXX) when addressing the Daughter of Zion:

> Rejoice greatly, O daughter of Zion!
> Shout aloud, O daughter of Jerusalem!
> Lo, your king comes to you ...
> (Zechariah 9.9; RSV from the Hebrew)
>
> Rejoice, O Daughter of Zion ...
> The King of Israel is in your midst...
> (Zephaniah, 3.14 17; from the LXX)

The Daughter of Zion is the female personification of the people of God, Israel, and later of the Church. Although this is an interesting symbolism, and Luke hints at other Old Testament characters in his infancy narrative, we have no proof that Luke had this in mind when he wrote his gospel.

'*Kecharitōmenē*' means to bestow favour on, highly favour, or bless. Occasionally it has the sense of plenitude, hence the translation 'graciously favoured', or 'highly favoured'. This is reflected in the Vulgate as *'gratia plena'* – 'full of grace', and hence its use in our prayer, the Hail Mary. In this context it is more than a simple statement of fact. One might consider it to be a title of honour or even a new name. The name 'Hannah' is very similar, coming from the Hebrew *hannāh*, possibly an abbreviation of *Hananiah*, meaning 'Yah[weh] is gracious'.[2]

'The Lord is with you': this affirmation of the Angel gives divine assurance and comfort. It is not to be taken literally in the sense of a conception that has already occurred.

'Blessed are you among women' is found in some Greek scriptural texts, the Vulgate and the King James Version. Biblical scholars suggest that this was added later in anticipation of the words of Elizabeth to Mary in Luke 1.42, 'and she exclaimed with a loud cry, *"Blessed are you among women, and blessed is the fruit of your womb!"* ' This is the second phrase of the Hail Mary.

'Blessed': in the Greek this is written as *'eulogēmenē'* and *'eulogēmenos'*; *'eulogeo'* is 'to praise, to celebrate with praises'. Literally, it is to speak well of someone: a eulogy, a benediction. This form of address was used in the Old Testament of women who had helped to deliver God's people from peril. For example:

Most blessed of women be Jael.

(Judges 5.24)

O daughter, you are blessed by the Most High God above all women on earth.

(Judith 13.18)

Blessed shall be the fruit of your body.

(Deuteronomy 28.4)

In the Old Testament the Hebrew word translated as 'blessed' is
'*berak*', meaning 'to bless' or 'to praise'. It is the basic form of
Jewish prayer. It recalls God's mighty deeds and gives him
praise and thanks.[3]

'*Jesus*' comes from the Greek form of the Hebrew 'Joshua',
meaning 'Yahweh saves'.

The Angel tells Mary: 'you will conceive in your womb and
bear a son, and you shall call his name Jesus' (Luke 1.31). Later
'*Christ*' is added as further identification. Jesus is the 'Anointed
One', the 'Messiah', expressed in Greek as *Christos*.

The second part of the Hail Mary is not biblical. It is a
supplication by the Church to the Holy Mother of God, that by
her advocacy she will obtain for us sinners the necessary grace
for our salvation now and at the hour of our death, thus
recognizing her universal mediation.

'*And the virgin's name was Mary*' (Luke 1.27). The name
'Mary' is derived from the Hebrew *Miryam*, rendered *Maria* or
Mariam in Greek. The meaning of the name is uncertain.
Surprisingly Strong's Lexicon gives it as 'their rebellion', a
reference to the rebellion of Aaron and his sister Miriam against
Moses. Other dictionaries suggest a possible derivation from the
Egyptian *Maryë* (*mrjt*), meaning 'beloved',[4] which seems more
appropriate for the Mother of the Lord. John Damascene, who
was born in Damascus, interprets the name 'Mary' as 'Lady'
according to Syriac etymology.[5] '*Holy Mary*' reminds us that
Mary is the Immaculate One, filled with the Holy Spirit from
the first instant of her conception. The perfect fruit of the
perfect redemption by the perfect Redeemer.

'*Mother of God*', or more accurately, '*Theotokos*', the birth-
giver of God, the one who gave birth to the one Person who
was man and God, recalls Mary's Divine Motherhood and her
cooperation with God in the redemptive Incarnation, and the
redemptive sacrifice of her Son at Calvary.

The only belief of the Roman Catholic Church about Mary not specifically mentioned is her perpetual virginity.

Early Devotion to Mary

Although Thurston says 'It was antecedently probable that the striking words of the Angel's salutation would be adopted by the faithful as soon as personal devotion to the Mother of God manifested itself in the Church',[6] the earliest recorded prayer to the Blessed Virgin is that of the *Sub tuum praesidium* found on a fragment of papyrus dating from approximately AD 300, (now in the John Rylands Library in Manchester). It reads:

> Under your mercy, we take refuge, Mother of God [*Theotokos*], do not reject our supplications in necessity. But deliver us from danger, [You] alone chaste, alone blessed.[7]

Or:

> Mother of God, [hear] my supplications: suffer us not [to be] in adversity, but deliver us from danger. Thou alone ...[8]

Or, as we pray it today:

> We fly to thy patronage, O Holy Mother of God, despise not our petitions in our necessities, but deliver us from all danger, O ever glorious and blessed Virgin.

It is important to note that this is the first written record of the title *Theotokos* (though it may have been used earlier by Origen) and was to be officially approved by the Council of Ephesus in 431.

There was a great development of Marian devotion in the Eastern Church following the Council of Ephesus. In the East, the Marian cult was manifest particularly in the liturgy in homiletics, poems and hymns. The Akathistos Hymn is undoubtedly the finest of all Greek poems in honour of the Blessed Virgin Mary. In the Greek practice it is sung on the first five Fridays of the Fast, i.e. in Lent, at the service of Small Compline. It was probably written in the first half of the sixth century and is attributed to St Romanos the Melodist, who died in about 560. It contains 24 stanzas, alternately long and short.

The long stanzas are a series of acclamations each beginning with the Angel's greeting at the Annunciation, '*Chaire*', 'Hail' or 'Rejoice' (cf. Luke 1.28).

Ikos One

A prince of the angels was sent from heaven, to say to the Mother of God, Hail! Hail! Hail!

And seeing thee, O Lord, take bodily form at the sound of his bodiless voice,

filled with amazement he stood still and cried aloud to her:

Hail, for through thee joy shall shine forth:

Hail, for through thee the curse shall cease.

Hail, recalling of fallen Adam:

Hail, deliverance from the tears of Eve.

Hail, height hard to climb for the thoughts of men.

Hail, depth hard to scan even for the eyes of angels.

Hail, for thou art the throne of the King;

Hail, for thou holdest him who upholds all.

Hail, star causing the Sun to shine:

Hail, womb of the divine Incarnation.

Hail, for through thee the creation is made new:

Hail, for through thee the Creator becomes a new born child.

Hail, Bride without bridegroom!

Choir   Hail, Bride without bridegroom! [In Greek, *Chaire, Nymphi anympheute*]

Kontakion One

The Holy Maiden, seeing herself in all her purity, said boldly unto
Gabriel:
'Strange seem thy words and hard for my soul to accept.
From a conception without seed how dost thou speak of
childbirth, crying: Alleluia!'
Choir Alleluia.[9]

The Evolution of the Hail Mary as a Prayer

The Hail Mary, as we know it, may be considered in four parts:

- Hail [Mary], full of grace, the Lord is with thee

    (Luke 1.28)
- Blessed art thou amongst women, blessed is the fruit of thy
  womb

    (Luke 1.42)
- Jesus
- Holy Mary, Mother of God, pray for us sinners now and at the
  hour of our death. Amen.

The union of the two greetings, that of the Angel and that of
Elizabeth, in one formula is found in the Liturgies of St James of
Antioch and St Mark of Alexandria, which may go back to the
fifth, or even fourth, century – likewise, in the Liturgy of the
Abyssinian Jacobites, and in the ritual of St Severus (538).
Confirmation of its early use in the Eastern Church is found on
an Egyptian Coptic ostracon dated about AD 600, which bears
in Greek the following inscription:

> Hail Mary, full of grace, the Lord is with thee, blessed art thou
> amongst women, and blessed is the fruit of thy womb, because you
> have conceived Christ, the Son of God, redeemer of our souls.[10]

In the Western liturgy, this prayer formula is assigned from the seventh century as an offertory antiphon for the Feast of the Annunciation, the Ember Wednesday of Advent, and the fourth Sunday in Advent in the Antiphonary traditionally attributed to St Gregory the Great.[11]

Mary Clayton, in a study of the Blessed Virgin Mary in Anglo-Saxon England, found the cult of the Virgin to be an unexpectedly important aspect of Anglo-Saxon spirituality. It flourished in two different periods: firstly in the late seventh to the early ninth century in Northumbria and Mercia, and secondly in southern England as a product of monastic reform in the tenth and eleventh centuries. The prayer books of the Anglo-Saxon period contain significant numbers of prayers to the Virgin, thus acknowledging her power of intercession. However, there is no mention of the Angelic Salutation as being among those three *florilegia* of private prayers found in manuscripts from the end of the eighth century to the beginning of the ninth century in Northumbria. In southern England prayers to Mary are found in manuscripts associated with Winchester and Canterbury. The Winchester manuscripts were particularly important.

Titus D. xxvi is a small prayerbook written between 1023 and 1035 for Aelfwine, dean of the New Minster at Winchester. It has this prayer which anticipates the late Middle Ages in that it makes a request that Mary deflect the anger of God by her prayers and is specifically concerned with the day of death:

> Holy Mary, pray.
> Holy Mary, intercede for me, a wretched sinner.
> Holy Mary, help me on the day of my departure from this present life.
> Holy Mary, help me in the day of my distress.
> Holy Mother of God, pray.
> Holy Virgin of virgins, pray.[12]

There is little or no trace of the Hail Mary as an accepted devotional formula before about 1050. All the evidence suggests that the Angelic Salutation and the greeting of Elizabeth as a prayer formula became popular through the recitation of the Little Office of Our Lady, consisting of psalms, Marian hymns and antiphons, in which the *Ave Maria* is frequently used as a versicle and responsory:

Ave Maria, gratia plena, Dominus tecum.
Benedicta tu in mulieribus.

This rite appears first as a private devotion in the tenth century and is attested in the Life of Bishop Ulrich of Augsburg (d. 973). The Little Office was an addition to the Divine Office, becoming popular among the monastic orders in the eleventh century. Its use on Saturday was ordered by Pope Urban II at the Synod of Clermont in 1095 for both the regular and secular clergy in order to obtain Mary's help for the First Crusade. By the twelfth century the daily recital of the Little Office of Our Lady was a devotion firmly established in popular favour. Two Anglo-Saxon manuscripts at the British Museum, one of which may be as old as 1030, show that the words '*Ave Maria*', etc. and '*benedicta tu in mulieribus et benedictus fructus ventris tui*' occurred in almost every part of the Cursus, and though we cannot be sure when these clauses were first joined together so as to make one prayer, there is conclusive evidence that this had come to pass only a very little later.[13] St Peter Damian (1007–72) was an enthusiastic advocate of the Little Office of Our Lady. He leaves us the story of a clerk who came before Our Lady's altar every day to chant 'this versicle of the Angel which the Gospel records: Hail Mary, full of grace, the Lord is with thee, blessed art thou amongst women.'[14]

It was Thurston's opinion that the words of the Angel Gabriel, having become familiar through the Little Office, came, in the course of the eleventh century, to be used by pious persons as an independent formula of salutation to the Blessed Virgin, and that this custom spread widely among all classes in the following century. He quotes Franco, Abbot of Afflinghem, who wrote sometime before 1125: 'Of good right [he says] does every condition, every age, every degree honour Mary with the angelic salutation; of good right does every voice, every tongue, every conscious being cry aloud to Mary with the angel: *Ave Maria, gratia plena, Dominus tecum; benedicta tu in mulieribus.*'[15]

The great collections of 'Mary legends' which began to be formed in the early years of the twelfth century show us that this salutation of Our Lady was fast becoming widely prevalent as a form of private devotion, though it is not quite certain how far it was customary to include the clause: 'and blessed is the fruit of thy womb'. But Abbot Baldwin, a Cistercian who was made Archbishop of Canterbury in 1184, wrote before this date a sort of paraphrase of the *Ave Maria* in which he says:

> To this salutation of the Angel ... we are accustomed to add the words, '*and blessed is the fruit of thy womb*', by which clause Elizabeth at a later time, on hearing the Virgin's salutation to her, caught up and completed, as it were, the Angel's words, saying: '*Blessed art thou amongst women and blessed is the fruit of thy womb.*'[16]

The oldest prescription relative to the recitation of the Hail Mary occurs in the statutes of Odo of Silliac, Bishop of Paris, dated 1198: 'Let priests ceaselessly exhort the people to say the Lord's prayer, the "I believe in God" and the salutation of the Blessed Virgin.'[17] After this date similar enactments become frequent in every part of the world, beginning in England with the Synod of Durham in 1217.[18]

The Hail Mary as a Salutation

To understand the early developments of this devotion it is important to grasp the fact that those who first used this formula recognized that the *Ave Maria* was essentially a form of greeting. It was therefore customary to accompany the words with some external gesture of homage, a genuflexion, or at least an inclination of the head.[19]

Fr Thurston, writing in 1916,[20] made a strong case for this hypothesis. He presented evidence that from the fourth century onwards, the practice of multiple genuflexions existed in the East and continues to the present day. As a form of asceticism it was adopted with special ardour in Ireland. From these two geographical extremities, the practice had spread throughout the greater part of Europe by the year 1200. These genuflexions were performed in fifties, hundreds or multiples of a hundred, deriving from the practice of reciting the psalms fifty at a time – the 'Three Fifties'. Furthermore, they were frequently accompanied by the repetition of a short prayer. This was a particular feature when prescribed in the penitential codes.

St Athanasius, in *De Virginitate* (in the mid fourth century), instructed consecrated virgins to recite the psalms standing, and at the end to genuflect. John Cassian, writing at the beginning of the fifth century, advised a prostration, with a prayer, at the end of each psalm. St Columbanus (d. 615), abbot and missionary, who was noted for his encouragement of private penance and his strict adherence to the practices of the Irish Church, advocated kneeling after each psalm. This idea of punctuating the recitation of the psalms with a genuflexion and a prayer seems to have spread very widely in both the East and the West.

In the Orthodox tradition the practice of repeated genuflexions, together with the recitation of a prayer such as

'O God make haste to help me', was used as an ascetical discipline. The number of prayers were counted in multiples of a hundred using a knotted cord, the *komvoschinion*.

The same practice might be given as a penance. For example, it was the custom in some monasteries that if a monk should doze off in choir, a brother monk would silently light a taper and place it by his side so that when he awoke he would be convicted of his misdemeanour. He would then arise and complete a series of genuflexions accompanied by a short prayer of repentance: 'Lord Jesus Christ, Son of God, have mercy on me a sinner.' Thus he does his penance and wakes himself up.

Irish hagiography provides many examples of the practice. Of St Patrick himself, Tirechan (see the *Book of Armagh*) tells us that during three days and three nights he besought the King of Kings with a hundred prayers and assiduous kneelings.

The most striking evidence of this form of austerity is found in the penitential books where the *arreum*, that is, the price or the tariff for commutation of canonical penance, might be, for example, 700 genuflexions, and seven blows, and a crossfigil (holding the arms extended) at the end of every hundred until the arms are tired, in place of a week of strict penance, on bread and water. To compensate for one day's penance on bread and water, for those who could read, a man should recite 50 psalms in church with genuflexions, or for a month of fasting – 1200 psalms with genuflexions.

When we speak of a 'genuflexion' today we think of going down on one knee, but in the present context we should understand the act of 'genuflexion' or 'prostration' as going down on both knees, bowing so as to touch the ground with the forehead. This is known in the Orthodox Church as a great metany (*metanœa*), referred to in Latin as a *veniae* (a pardon), and to the Irish monks as the *slectain*. The Muslims have a similar practice at Friday prayers. Those who practised this form of asceticism on a regular basis developed hard callouses on the knees and bumps on the forehead.

From the close of the eleventh century, and during the two centuries that followed, there was a great wave of Marian devotion in Europe, marked, especially in religious houses, by the adoption of the Little Office of Our Lady. In this office the versicle *Ave Maria*, etc. occurs frequently, and as it is of its nature a salutation, the more devoted would genuflect. The same greeting accompanied by a genuflexion was used to honour images and statues of Our Blessed Lady. Gradually this practice evolved into a separate formula consisting, as it did in the beginning, of only six words, *Ave Maria, gratia plena, Dominus tecum*: it was found suitable for the purpose, a penitential exercise combined with devotion to the Mother of God. The addition of the words of St Elizabeth may have made it yet more penitential and more meritorious but less suitable as an accompaniment to the genuflexions, and so ultimately the genuflexions were omitted. In the East the practice remains unchanged but in the West, the *Ave* has been extended and adopted in place of the series of genuflexions. The original importance of the genuflexions accounts for the numbers of *Aves*, namely 100, 200, or even 1000 *Aves* corresponding with the numbers of prostrations. The adoption of the number 150 reflects the importance of the psalter.

Records of the use of genuflexions and *Aves* are numerous. A few examples will suffice. Of St Aybert (pre-1140) it is recorded that he recited 150 *Aves* daily: a hundred with genuflexions and 50 with prostrations. (It is particularly noted that his *Ave* included the clause 'and blessed is the fruit of your womb'.) Of Blessed Mary of Oignies (1177–1213) it is said:

> first of all without pause ... she bent the knee 600 times; secondly reading the entire psalter upright, she offered to the Blessed Virgin

the angelic salutation, kneeling, at the conclusion of each psalm; thirdly, when the spirit of devotion moved her yet more strongly, striking herself 300 times with the rod of discipline, she made a genuflexion at each blow, offering herself as a victim to God and our Blessed Lady in this long-drawn martyrdom and with the three last blows, to give honour to the others, she drew blood freely. Finally she consummated the sacrifice with 50 more simple genuflexions.[21]

Thierry tells us of St Louis of France (1214–70) that 'without counting his other prayers the holy King knelt down each evening fifty times and each time he stood upright repeated slowly an *Ave Maria*'. A Dominican nun, St Margaret (d. 1292), daughter of the King of Hungary, on the vigil and during the octaves of the feasts of Our Lady would '[offer] up to her the Angelic salutation a thousand times with a thousand prostrations, sweetly bedewing each with the spiritual savour of her tears'. Just how they kept count of such large numbers of prayers we do not know, but some device such as a string or circlet of beads would have been helpful.

Fr Thurston's thesis is that during the twelfth century the *Ave* (i.e. the Angelic Salutation alone) was rather the adjunct of the genuflexion, than the genuflexion the adjunct of the *Ave*. In nearly all the early examples which are commonly appealed to as foreshadowing the multiple recitation of the *Aves*, the element of austerity was especially prominent.

This form of prayer is akin to that of the 'Holy, Holy, Holy' which we are taught to think goes up continually before the throne of the Most High. It fulfils the injunction to pray constantly. To bow the head at the sacred name of Jesus was commanded by Gregory X on 12 October 1274. Today we are still encouraged to bow our heads at the name of Jesus, and to genuflect during the Nicene Creed at the words 'and was made man' (at Christmas and on the Feast of the Annunciation). We also genuflect during the recitation of the Angelus at 'The Word was made flesh.' In the Liturgy of Good Friday the priest prostrates himself in reverence before the altar at the start of the celebration. During the intercessions of Good Friday, and after each scripture reading of the Easter Vigil, we are bidden by the Deacon: '*Oremus* ... *Flectamus genua* ... *Levate*' (Let us pray ... Let us kneel ... Arise). Reflecting courtly etiquette, we genuflect to the Tabernacle when we enter the church and make a double genuflexion when the Blessed Sacrament is exposed. 'As I live, says the Lord, every knee shall bow to me, and every tongue shall give praise to God' (Romans 14.11).

The Marian Psalters

The so-called '*Ave* psalm psalters'[22] are made up of 150 rhymed four-line stanzas, each beginning with the word *Ave* and each addressed to the Blessed Virgin but paraphrasing at the same time some thought from the psalm to which it corresponds.

The following example, attributed to St Anselm, is the 109th stanza, corresponding to Psalm 110, verse 1:

The Lord says to my lord: 'Sit at my right hand, till I make your enemies your footstool.'

Ave David tu filia	Hail! thou David's daughter
Ex qua nostra substantia	From whom our nature,
Sedet in patris dextera	Sits at the Father's right hand,
Jesus Christus in gloria	Jesus Christ in glory.

Compare with the line of the psalm which reads: 'sit at my right hand'. If this sample is genuinely the work of Anselm then it must have been written prior to 1109.[23]

47

Many of these *Ave* psalm psalters are known, and some of them belong to the twelfth century. A further example is taken from the *Analecta Hymnica*, edited by Fr Dreves.[24] It is the sixth stanza, recalling the opening words of Psalm 91, verse 1:

He who dwells in the shelter of the Most High, who abides in the shadow of the Almighty

Ave, quam inhabitat Verbum	Hail! thou in whom the Word
caro factum,	made flesh dwells
Qui collapsos vetiti ligni per	He who, grieved that, ruined
contactum	by touching the forbidden
Nos fecisse condolens cum inferno	tree,
pactum	We have made a pact with
Ligno vitae reparat figuli vas	hell,
fractum	Repairs the potter's broken
	vessel with the tree of life

This *Ave* psalm is thought to have been written by Stephen Langton (d. 1228), Archbishop of Canterbury from 1207 and one of the great scholars of his time. He is credited with the division of the books of the Bible into chapters which, with small modifications, is still in use. It is probable that he was the author of the sequence *Veni Sancte Spiritus*.

This format demonstrates the practice of addressing the Blessed Virgin 150 times instead of reciting the 150 Davidic psalms. The *Ave* psalm psalter is a devotion for the literate. Those who could not read may well have substituted 150 simple *Aves* of whatever length.[25]

In her book *Stories of the Rose* Anne Winston-Allen quotes examples of German vernacular Marian psalters dating from the thirteenth century. They too are four-lined rhymed stanzas, each beginning with the salutation *Ave Maria* in place of, or indicating, the entire salutation. The 50 verbal 'roses' consist of Marian iconographic symbols and titles of honour, each followed by a supplication, as in the example:

> *Ave Maria*, rose without thorns,
> you were born to comfort me.
> A queen of high birth,
> help me that I shall not be lost.

A second work dates from the late thirteenth century and is a fragment of a longer one that consisted of 50 or 150 stanzas.

> Hail Mary, branch of Jesse,
> from you came the noble one,
> Jesus your child, whose sweet name
> took away from us all our sins.

Together the verses make up a typical list of unconnected accolades.

A third work, from the early fourteenth century, refers to itself as a 'rôzenkranze' or rosary. Instead of beginning with the Latin '*Ave Maria*' it begins with the German equivalent – 'I greet you' or 'Hail to you'. It praises the Virgin for her purity, piety and beauty.

> I greet you, rose garden of heaven,
> the chosen, the pure, the tender one.
> You noble sweet rose blossom,
> entreat God for me through your goodness.

In a fourth vernacular Marian psalter, dating from the early fourteenth century, there is for the first time a series of scenes from the life of Christ inserted into a traditional litany of praise to the Virgin. The first two sets of 50 stanzas list the attributes of the Virgin. The third set of 50 recount events in the life of Christ.

> Help us, because of the glances
> that he often cast toward you
> as a child toward its mother.
> Whatever you wish, he does for your sake.
>
> Help us, Lady, on account of the agony
> that Christ suffered on death's journey,
> when Pilate washed his hands,
> that we may find a just end.

Thus Anne Winston-Allen shows how the life of Christ narrative first grew out of the Marian psalm psalter and later became attached to the rosary.[26]

The Name of Jesus

As regards the addition of the word '*Jesus*', or as it usually ran in the fifteenth century '*Jesus Christus. Amen*', it is commonly said that this was due to the initiative of Pope Urban IV (1261) and confirmed by the granting of an indulgence by Pope John XXII (1316–34). The evidence does not seem sufficiently clear to warrant a positive statement on the point.[27]

The Invocation to Mary

The final part of the prayer, prompted by the need to join petition to praise, may have been influenced by the litanies of the Saints, introduced towards the end of the seventh century, with the invocation to Mary, '*Sancta Maria, ora pro nobis.*' Such a petition is found in a hymn recorded in the *Analecta Hymnica* (edited by Fr G. M. Dreves), which dates from the twelfth century and is to be found in a gradual, now in Stuttgart. This has been accurately dated 1151, and the first and last verses read:

Ave Maria,	Hail Mary,
gratia plena,	full of grace,
Dominus tecum,	the Lord is with you,
benedicta tu in mulieribus.	blessed are you among women.

Hic nobis et mortis in	Come to our help now
hora succurre	And at the hour of our death
ac in orbis examine	and at the world's judgement
nos tuos recognosce.	acknowledge us as thine own.

The hymn is attributed to Gottschalk, a monk of Limburg and a contemporary of Peter Damian. Each of the stanzas except the first ends with a prayer, an appeal. The whole hymn finds its climax in the supplication that the Blessed Mother would lend her aid to her clients 'here (i.e. now) and at the hour of death'.[28]

Another early suggestion of a second part is found in a poetic paraphrase of the *Ave Maria* which was assigned (wrongly) to Dante (d. 1321):

O Blessed Virgin, do thou continually pray to God for us
that He may pardon us and give us grace so to live here below,
that paradise may be bestowed on us at our end.[29]

By the end of the fifteenth century, two endings to the *Ave Maria* are found:

Sancta Maria, Mater Dei, ora pro nobis peccatoribus.

Holy Mary, Mother of God, pray for us sinners.

(used by St Bernardino of Siena, the Carthusians, and in the Synodal Constitutions of Augsburg and Constance), and:

> *Sancta Maria, Mater Dei, ora pro nobis nunc et in hora mortis nostrae. Amen.*
>
> Holy Mary, Mother of God, pray for us now and at the hour of our death. Amen.

(used by the Servites, in a Roman breviary, and, with variations, in some German dioceses).

St Bernadino of Siena (d. 1444) when reciting the *Ave* in public said on one occasion, after the words '*et benedictus fructus ventris tui*', 'nor can I refrain from adding *Sancta Maria, ora pro nobis peccatoribus*'.[30]

It is thought probable that the current form of the Hail Mary came from Italy. Fr Thomas Esser asserts that it is to be found in a manuscript of St Antonius of Florence, who died in 1459, but this has not been confirmed. We can be sure that the current form of the Hail Mary was fixed during the sixteenth century. At the very end of the fifteenth century, an *Ave Maria* identical with our own, except for the omission of the single word '*nostrae*', is to be found in Savonarola's commentary on the *Ave Maria* printed about 1495, of which there is a copy in the British Museum. Two years earlier than this in a French edition of the *Compost et Kalendrier des Bergiers*, which appeared in 1493, the invocation is added to the Hail Mary, which is repeated in Pynson's English translation *Kalender of Shepardys* in 1506 in the form:

> Holy Mary moder of God praye for us synners. Amen.

A form of the Hail Mary as we know it now, but with the word *Christus* inserted after Jesus and the omission of *nostrae* before the *Amen*, is found in the Sarum Breviary of 1531. The official recognition of the *Ave Maria* in its complete form, though the prayer in that form is found in the Catechism of the Council of Trent, was finally given by inclusion in the Roman Breviary authorized by Pius V in 1568.

Cardinal Wiseman, writing of Dr Challoner's translation of *Dominus tecum* in the revised Rheims version of the New Testament as 'our Lord is with thee', makes the point that 'In the *Ave Maria* Catholics have always, till lately, been accustomed to say, "*Our* Lord is with thee"; as it is in that version, and as it has always been used in England, even before that translation was made.'[31]

Thurston observes that in some places, and notably in Ireland, the feeling survived during the nineteenth century that the Hail Mary is complete with the word 'Jesus'. Indeed, it was said that it was not uncommon for Irish peasants, when bidden to say Hail Marys for a penance, to ask whether they were required to say the 'Holy Marys' too.[32]

Conclusion

Thus we may say that two phrases of the Hail Mary are scriptural, and that the devotion arose from the versicles and responsories of the Little Office of Our Lady. The early twelfth-century Marian legends show that this salutation of Our Lady had become prevalent as a form of private devotion, though it is not certain whether it included the clause: 'and blessed is the fruit of thy womb'. The addition of the word '*Jesus*' or '*Jesus Christus. Amen*', dates from the thirteenth century, and the final invocation to Mary was added towards the end of the fifteenth century. The current form was fixed in the sixteenth century. It is found in the Catechism of the Council of Trent and was included in the reformed Breviary (1568) by Pius V.

Notes

1. R. E. Brown, K. P. Donfried, J. A. Fitzmyer and J. Reumann (eds), *Mary in the New Testament* (Philadelphia: Fortress Press, 1974), p. 136.
2. John L. McKenzie, Hannah, *Dictionary of the Bible* (London: Geoffrey Chapman, 1968), p. 337.
3. R. E. Brown *et al.* (eds), *Mary in the New Testament*, p. 136.
4. John L. McKenzie, Miriam, *Dictionary of the Bible*.
5. Luigi Gambero, *Mary and the Fathers of the Church* (San Francisco, CA: Ignatius Press, 1991), p. 401.
6. Herbert Thurston, Hail Mary, *Catholic Encyclopedia*, Vol. VII (1910), online edition.
7. Michael O'Carroll, The Hail Mary, *Theotokos*, pp. 165–6.
8. Hilda Graef, *Mary: A History of Doctrine and Devotion*, 2 vols (London: Sheed & Ward, 1985), Vol. 1, p. 48.
9. Mother Mary and Bishop Kallistos of Diokleia (trans.), *The Akathistos Hymn to the Most Holy Mother of God: With the Office of Small Compline* (Wallington, Surrey: The Ecumenical Society of the Blessed Virgin Mary, 1986).
10. Herbert Thurston, The Origins of the Hail Mary, *The Month*, 121 (1913): 163, quoting Dr Crum, *Coptic Ostraca*, p. 3.
11. Michael O'Carroll, The Hail Mary, *Theotokos*, pp. 165–6.
12. Mary Clayton, *The Cult of the Blessed Virgin Mary in Anglo-Saxon England* (Cambridge: Cambridge University Press, 1990), pp. 110–11, note 71, quoting H. Barré, *Prières ancienne de l'Occident à la mère de Sauveur*, Paris, 1963.
13. Herbert Thurston, Hail Mary, *Catholic Encyclopedia*, Vol. VII, and *The Month*, 98 (1901): 486–8.
14. Herbert Thurston, The Origins of the Hail Mary, *The Month*, 121 (1913): 169.
15. Herbert Thurston, *Familiar Prayers: Their Origin and History*, arranged and selected by P. Grosjean (London: Burns & Oates, 1953), p. 101.
16. Herbert Thurston, Hail Mary, *Catholic Encyclopedia*, Vol. VII.
17. Michael O'Carroll, The Hail Mary, *Theotokos*, p. 165, note 6: 'Statuta Odonis', in Mansi, 22, 681.
18. Herbert Thurston, Hail Mary, *Catholic Encyclopedia*, Vol. VII.
19. Ibid.
20. Herbert Thurston, Genuflections and Aves (I) and (II), *The Month*,

127 (1916): 441–51 and pp. 546–59.

21. Ibid., p. 551.

22. Herbert Thurston, *Familiar Prayers*, p. 107; Edmund Waterton, *Pietas Mariana Britannica*, p. 147.

23. Herbert Thurston, The Origins of the Hail Mary, *The Month*, 121 (1913): 176.

24. Herbert Thurston, *Familiar Prayers*, p. 70.

25. Herbert Thurston, The Origins of the Hail Mary, p. 176.

26. Anne Winston-Allen, *Stories of the Rose*, pp. 18–21.

27. Herbert Thurston, Hail Mary, *Catholic Encyclopedia*, Vol. VII.

28. Herbert Thurston, The Second Part of the Hail Mary, *The Month*, 121 (1913): p. 379, see note: *Analecta Hymnica*, Vol. XI, p. 115 and Vol. I, p. 363.

29. Ibid., p. 382.

30. Ibid., p. 383.

31. Cardinal Wiseman, *Essays on Various Subjects*, Vol. I, pp. 76–7, in E. Waterton, *Pietas Mariana Britannica*.

32. Herbert Thurston, Hail Mary, *The Catholic Encyclopedia*, Vol. VII.

4

The Our Father

The rosary as a spiritual exercise is comprehensive, Marian in its approach but fundamentally Christocentric. The 'Our Father' is integral to the devotion. The Father is the first principle and final end of all prayer. Our prayer is directed to the Father through Jesus in the power of the Holy Spirit. Our faith is in a Trinitarian God and we remind ourselves of this by making the sign of the cross as we commence our prayers. The end of each decade is marked by the 'Glory be', giving glory to the Blessed Trinity. We also recite the Creed, affirming our faith in the Triune God, the Paschal Mystery, the Holy Spirit and the Church.

From the earliest times the sign of the cross began all prayer, and so it would with the rosary. It was common practice to end each psalm of the Divine Office with the *Gloria Patri* and so it would be natural to add this to each decade of the rosary. This practice was adopted possibly in the sixteenth, and certainly by the early seventeenth, century. The Apostles' Creed came to be said in conjunction with the rosary during the seventeenth century.

Having dealt in detail with the development of the Hail Mary and the natural progression of devotion to Mary towards the practice of the rosary we will now consider briefly the historical development of these other prayers.

The Lord's Prayer

To quote the Catechism of the Catholic Church:

> The Lord's Prayer is the quintessential prayer of the Church. It is an integral part of the major hours of the Divine Office and of the sacraments of Christian initiation: Baptism, Confirmation and Eucharist. Integrated into the Eucharist it reveals the eschatological character of its petitions, hoping for the Lord, 'until he comes'[1]

And, we may add, an integral part of the Dominican rosary and many other chaplets and devotions. It is called 'the Lord's Prayer' because it comes to us from the Lord Jesus in response to his disciples' request 'Lord, teach us to pray' (Luke 11.1). 'The Lord's Prayer is truly the summary of the whole gospel', the 'most perfect of prayers'.[2]

The scriptures give us two versions of the prayer. It may well be that Jesus taught the prayer on more than one occasion.

> Pray then like this:
> Our Father who art in heaven, hallowed be thy name. Thy kingdom come, thy will be done, on earth as it is in heaven. Give us this day our daily bread; and forgive us our debts, as we also have forgiven our debtors; and lead us not into temptation, but deliver us from evil.
>
> (Matthew 6.9–13)

> When you pray, say:
> Father, hallowed be thy name. Thy kingdom come. Give us each day our daily bread; and forgive us our sins, for we ourselves forgive every one who is indebted to us; and lead us not into temptation.
>
> (Luke 11.2–4)

It seems probable, from the form in which the Our Father appears in the *Didache*,[3] that the version in St Matthew was that which the Church adopted from the beginning for liturgical purposes. A concluding doxology was probably added in early times. It is based on 1 Chronicles 29.11:

> Thine, O Lord, is the greatness, and the power, and the glory, and the victory, and the majesty; for all that is in the heavens and in the earth is thine; thine is the kingdom, O Lord, and thou art exalted as head above all.

It is found in the *Didache* and some later Greek gospel manuscripts.

The Our Father is essentially a simple, natural and spontaneous prayer, pre-eminently adapted for popular use. A great deal has been written by way of interpretation, but it is sufficient here to indicate that the prayer is divided into an address and seven petitions. The first three ask for the grace that God be glorified, his reign be established and his will be done. The remaining four make request for our basic physical and spiritual needs – our daily bread, forgiveness, protection and deliverance from the evil one. Our petitions are an acknowledgement of our total dependence on God's gratuitous love. As a prayer given to the Church by the Lord himself, it has always been regarded by Christians as uniquely sacred. Tertullian called it 'the epitome of the whole Gospel', and St Cyprian, 'the public and common prayer'. From early times it was taught to the catechumens before baptism, and it was included in the Eucharist. The author of the *Didache* gives the prayer in full and suggests it be recited three times a day. The prayer has always had a prominent place in the Divine Office. The Breviary of 1568 laid down that it be recited before each office except Compline.

We turn again to Thurston for an account of the Our Father in its familiar English form.[4] He tells us that although the Latin term *oratio dominica* is of early date, the phrase 'Lord's Prayer' does not seem to have been generally familiar in England before the Reformation. Prior to the time of Henry VIII, the 'Our Father' was usually said in Latin, even by the uneducated. Hence it was known as the *Paternoster*.

After his break with the Holy See, Henry VIII in his capacity of Supreme Head of the Church began to enforce his ideas of a suitable liturgy for popular use. In 1545 Henry, noting that the youth were taught the *Paternoster*, the *Ave Maria*, Creed and Ten Commandments in Latin, and hence were not brought up in knowledge of their faith, duty and obedience, because they had no understanding of the Latin tongue, decreed that: 'every schoolmaster and bringer up of young beginners in learning, next after their ABC now by us also set forth, do teach this Primer or book of ordinary prayers unto them in English'.

The new authoritative versions of the Our Father and Creed were found first in *The Manuall of Prayers or the Prymer in Englyshe* (1539), which was prepared by Bishop Hilsey at the instance of Thomas Cromwell, the king's vicegerent in ecclesiastical affairs. The same text is also found in a primer of 1541, in which the following is printed:[5]

The King's Commandment

The King's Highness greatly tendering the weal of his realm hath suffered heretofore the *Pater noster*, *Ave*, Creed and the X Commandments of God to be had in the English tongue. But His Grace perceiving now the great diversity of the translations, hath willed them all to be taken up and in stead of them hath caused an uniform translation of the said *Pater noster*, *Ave*, Creed and X Commandments to be set forth, as hereafter followeth, willing all his loving subjects to learn and use the same. And he straightly commandeth every parson, vicar and curate to read and teach the same to their parishioners, and that no man imprint or set forth any other translation upon pain of His Highness' displeasure.

The text of this official version of the Our Father follows, and in reproducing it here the spelling of the 1541 edition is retained:

> Our father whiche arte in heven, halowed be thy name. Thy kingdom come. Thy wil be done in earth as it is in heven. Gyve us this day our dayly bread and forgyve us our trespasses as we forgyve them that trespass against us. And let us not be led into temptacyon. But delyver us from evyll. Amen.

During the rest of Henry's reign this was accepted as the authoritative and official text.

The English text now in use among Catholics is derived from the above text authorized by Henry VIII in 1541 and employed in the 1549 and 1552 editions of the Book of Common Prayer.

During the reign of the Catholic Queen Mary, the Latin liturgy was restored, but no serious attempt was made to induce the laity to say the Lord's Prayer or Creed in Latin. As the English text had become familiar to the majority during the reign of Edward VI no alterations were made.

Our present Catholic text differs only in two very slight particulars: 'which art' has been modernized into 'who art', and 'in earth' into 'on earth'. These changes were adopted towards the end of the seventeenth century. The Anglicans added the doxology: 'For thine is the kingdom, the power and the glory' during the reign of Charles II (1660–85).

During recent years the Anglican Church has experimented with various modern versions of the Our Father, which has caused heated debate. (There has always been great resistance to any change in the wording of familiar prayers.)

The *Paternoster* and the Beads

The repetition of the *Paternoster* most certainly preceded the repetitive use of the *Ave Maria*. The general understanding is that at some stage 150 *Paternosters* were substituted for the 150 psalms of the Divine Office.

The practice of praying 50 Our Fathers for the deceased is said to have been prescribed for the lay brothers as early as 800 in the monasteries of St Gall and Reichenau.[6] The *Ancient Customs of Cluny*, collected by Udalrio in 1096, record that when the death of 'any brother at a distance' was announced, every priest was to offer Mass and the lay brothers either to say 50 psalms or repeat 50 times the *Paternoster*.[7]

For the recitation of the psalms it was necessary that a book be available, and that the monks could read. The first document of Cistercian history, the *Exordium Parvum*, speaks about the *conversi*, the lay brothers being admitted at Cîteaux at the very beginning of the 'New Monastery', in 1098, 'because without their help they [the monks] were unable to observe the commandments of the Rule in its entirety, day and night'. Candidates for brotherhood would be of humble birth and hence illiterate. They were accepted for a one-year noviciate, during which time they were trained for their future duties and in monastic discipline, memorizing a few prayers, *Pater, Credo, Miserere*, with some short responsories. The brothers' simple life was spent at the monastery in different workshops or domestic duties, but the majority of them were put to work on the granges as farmers and herdsmen. Except for Sundays and holy days they were not present at the Divine Office, but, under the direction of the oldest of the group, recited a certain number of *Paternosters* at the time of the canonical hours wherever they happened to be working.[8] It is probable that they prayed in multiples of fifty or 150. In the Cistercian Order deceased members were remembered annually – a priest would say twenty Masses, a lay brother ten Psalters, or 1500 *Misereres*, or 1500 *Paters*, for which purpose 'beads' or a counting string would surely be a necessity.

There is a record from 1128 which tells of the Templars – the Poor Knights of Christ and of the Temple of Solomon (whose role was to protect pilgrims) – who if unable to attend the choir were to repeat the Lord's Prayer (normally sung) 57 times. When one of the brethren died, each knight was to say the *Paternoster* a hundred times a day for seven days.

The Rule of Albert of Jerusalem (1206–14) directed that the hermits of Mount Carmel who could read should recite the psalms in divisions proportionate to the liturgical hours, while those who could not were to recite an appropriate number of Our Fathers, also divided according to the Office hours.[9]

When the Angelic Salutation, the *Ave*, first became a popular prayer separate from the Little Office of Our Lady, one form of usage was to insert it before the words '*et ne nos inducas in tentationem*' when the *Paternoster* was said privately. Subsequently the recitation of strings of *Aves* overtook the popularity of the *Paternoster*.

The use of a counting device to keep tally of the repetition of prayers will be dealt with in a later chapter. The earliest specific association of a counting string for use with the Our Father cannot be determined. Willam gives a reference to the existence of a counting string in the family of John Svenson dating back to c. 900.[10] What we do know is that by the twelfth century it became common practice for lay people to carry a 'Paternoster cord' of 50 knots or beads.

Notes

1. *Catechism of the Catholic Church* (English edn; London: Geoffrey Chapman, 1994), n. 2776.
2. Ibid., n. 2774.
3. See *Didache*: a short early Christian manual on morals and Church practice; author, date and origin unknown; written between AD 60 and late second century, *The Oxford Dictionary of the Christian Church* (Oxford: Oxford University Press, 1997).
4. Herbert Thurston, *Familiar Prayers*, Chapter 2.
5. Ibid., p. 33.
6. Franz M. Willam, *The Rosary: Its History and Meaning*, p. 96.
7. Herbert Thurston, The Rosary, *Catholic Encyclopedia*, Vol. XIII (1912).
8. Louis J. Lokai, *The White Monks: A History of the Cistercian Order* (Okauchee: Cistercian Fathers, Our Lady of Spring Bank, 1953), p. 231.
9. James Boyce, *Praising God in Liturgy: Studies in Carmelite Liturgy* (Washington, DC: The Carmelite Institute, 1999), p. 232.
10. Franz M. Willam, *The Rosary: Its History and Meaning*, p. 192.

5

The Sign of the Cross, the *Gloria Patri* and the Creed

The Sign of the Cross

Among the early Christians, the sign of the cross was probably the most universal expression of faith. In most places, the custom was simply to trace the cross upon the forehead. Some writers (such as St Jerome and St Augustine) describe Christians tracing the cross on the forehead, then the lips, and then the heart, as modern Western Catholics do before the reading of the Gospel. To mark the forehead in this fashion is to apply the seal of God's ownership and protection.

The Hebrew homes in Egypt were marked by the seal of the blood of the lamb (cf. Exodus 12.13). In the days of Ezekiel the Lord said to him:

> Go through the city, through Jerusalem, and put a mark upon the foreheads of the men who sigh and groan over all the abominations that are committed in it ... Pass through the city after him, and smite ... but touch no one upon whom is the mark.
>
> (Ezekiel 9.4–6)

In the Book of Revelation:

> Then I saw another angel ascend from the rising of the sun, with the seal of the living God ... 'Do not harm the earth or the sea or

4

the trees, till we have sealed the servants of our God upon their foreheads.'

Then I looked, and lo, on Mount Zion stood the Lamb, and with him a hundred and forty-four thousand who had his name and his Father's name written on their foreheads.

(Revelation 7.2–3, 14.1)

During the third and fourth centuries there are frequent references in the writings of the Fathers to the use of the sign of the cross. Tertullian writes in c. 202: 'At every step and movement, whether we come in or go out, in dressing or putting on our shoes, at the bath, at table, at the lighting of the lamps, in going to rest, in sitting down, whatever employment occupies us we mark our foreheads with the sign of the cross.'[1] St Cyril of Jerusalem (d. 387) says:

Let us, then, not be ashamed to confess the Crucified. Be the cross our seal made with boldness by our fingers on our brow, and on everything; over the bread we eat and the cups we drink, in our comings in and goings out; before our sleep, when we lie down and when we awake, when we are on the road and when we are still.[2]

It was the invariable practice of the early Christians to make the sign of the cross on the forehead. Towards the end of the fourth century there develops the custom of signing the lips and the heart, in addition to the forehead. Gaudentius of Brescia (early fifth century) urges us: 'Let the word of God and the sign of Christ be on thy heart, on thy mouth, on thy forehead, whether thou sittest at meals, whether thou goest to the baths, whether thou retirest to rest, in going out and coming in, in time of joy and in time of sorrow.'[3]

The practice was to make the sign with the thumb or one finger. Sozomen, the ecclesiastical historian (writing c. 420–40), describes how Bishop Donatus in a rather surprising emergency 'made the sign of the cross with his finger in the air and spat upon the dragon'. The Hieronymian Martyrology has the story of St Saturus, in Achaia, who on passing a certain idol hissed at it, signing his forehead, and the idol at once fell down, for which cause he was beheaded. (So beware, it is a powerful symbol.) St Gregory the Great tells how Martyrius made the sign of the cross with his finger over some bread which was being baked and the loaves in consequence came out marked with the emblem of the cross which the baker had forgotten to do. (The origin of hot cross buns perhaps?)

The large sign of the cross made over the body, as we make it today, originated in the East between the fifth and eighth centuries, but there is no satisfactory evidence of its use in the West until the thirteenth century. The Ancrene Riwle, written in the early thirteenth century, gives directions for the beginning of the Little Office of Our Lady:

> Immediately thereafter . . . Say the *Paternoster* and the *Credo*, both in a low voice, and then stand up and say *Domine labia mea aperies* and make the sign of the cross on your mouth with your thumb, and at the *Deus in adjutorium* [make] a large cross with the three fingers from above the forehead down to the breast.

Pope Innocent III (1198–1216) discussed whether in making the sign of the cross one should trace the bar of the cross from left to right, or from right to left. It is probable, although not certain, that he was talking about the large cross, but it is unclear whether he was concerned with blessing others or oneself:

The sign of the cross is to be made with three fingers because it is traced under the invocation of the Trinity, of whom the prophet says 'Who hath poised with three fingers the bulk of the earth', so that it descends from above to below and crosses over from the right hand to the left, because Christ came down from heaven to earth and crossed over from Jews to the Gentiles. Some, however, make the sign of the cross from left to right because we ought to go from misery to glory, like as Christ also passed from death unto life and from the place of darkness to paradise, the more so, that they sign both themselves and others in one and the selfsame manner. But it is agreed that when we make the sign of the cross over others we sign them from left to right. But if you notice carefully, the fact is that we trace the cross over others also from [their] right to [their] left, for we do not sign them as they turn their backs to us but as they face us.[4]

Lucas Tudensis, a Spanish bishop writing a few years later, is more explicit:

A question occurs regarding the sign of the cross, whether when the faithful make the sign of the cross over themselves or others the hand ought to pass from the left to the right or from the right to the left. To which we answer, as we honestly believe and hold, that both methods are good, both holy, both able to overthrow the might of the enemy, providing only the Christian religion uses them in Catholic simplicity. Seeing, however, that many people presumptuously endeavour to put an end to one of these methods, maintaining that the hand ought not to pass from left to right, as has been handed down to us from our fathers, let us in the interests of charity say a few words on this subject.

For when our Lord Jesus Christ for the redemption of the human race, mercifully blest the world, He proceeded from the Father, He came into the world, He descended, on the left hand as it were, into hell, and ascending to Heaven He sitteth on the right hand of God. Now it is this which every faithful Christian seems to portray, when, on guarding his face with the sign of the cross, he raises three extended fingers on high, in front of his forehead saying 'In nomine Patris', then lowers them towards his beard with the words 'et Filii', then to the left saying 'et Spiritus Sancti', and finally to the right as he utters 'Amen'.[5]

One might point out that a long beard reaches to the chest. It would appear that there was a diversity of practice even as late as 1550 with some people crossing themselves from right to left, as do the Greeks.

In a Portuguese catechism of the sixteenth century we are instructed that in making the sign of the cross the hand should be placed lower than the breast, this practice being justified by its symbolism: that by the Incarnation Christ our Lord came down for heaven into the womb of Our Blessed Lady; that after, he descended into hell – represented by the left shoulder – to rescue sinners; and then ascended into heaven to restore them to himself at the right hand of the Father – for which reason it is on the right shoulder that the sign of the cross finds its term.

Another practice current in England before the Reformation was to 'kiss the thumb', as it appeared, but in reality what was kissed was the thumb placed over the index finger so as to make a cross.

The sign of the cross is a most profound gesture. It is the Christian faith: Trinity, Incarnation, Redemption, summarized in a single gesture. When we cross ourselves, we renew the covenant that began with our baptism. With our words, we proclaim the Trinitarian faith into which we were baptized: 'In the name of the Father, and of the Son, and of the Holy Spirit'. With our hand, we proclaim our redemption by the cross of Jesus Christ by which we become partakers in the divine nature (2 Peter 1.4).

The *Gloria Patri*[6]

Glory be to the Father, and to the Son, and to the Holy Spirit, as it was in the beginning, is now and ever shall be, world without end. Amen.

After the Our Father the *Gloria Patri* is the earliest example of an ancient Christian prayer still in use today. It is known as the 'lesser doxology' to distinguish it from the *Gloria in excelsis Deo*, the 'greater doxology'. ('*Doxa*' means 'glory', hence a doxology is a formula of praise.)

The practice of ending a prayer with a doxology goes back at least to the psalms. Psalm 41 ends with the verse, 'Blessed be the Lord, the God of Israel, from everlasting to everlasting! Amen and Amen.' And Psalm 106 with: 'Blessed be the Lord, the God of Israel, from everlasting to everlasting! And let all the people say, "Amen!" Praise the Lord!'

Two examples from the New Testament give glory to the Father and the Son. Ephesians 3.21, 'to him be glory in the church and in Christ Jesus to all generations, for ever and ever. Amen' and Jude 25, 'to the only God, our Saviour through Jesus Christ our Lord, be glory, majesty, dominion, and authority, before all time and now and for ever. Amen'.

An early Trinitarian formula is given in 2 Corinthians 13.14: 'The grace of the Lord Jesus Christ and the love of God and the fellowship of the Holy Spirit be with you all.' The prayer of St Polycarp before his martyrdom in AD 155 is a Trinitarian doxology:

For this cause, yea and for all things, I praise Thee, I bless Thee, I glorify Thee through the eternal and heavenly High Priest, Jesus Christ, Thy beloved Son, through whom with Him and the Holy Spirit be glory both now [and ever] and for ages to come. Amen.

(*Letter to the Smyrneans*, Chapter 14)

Origen, in his *Treatise Concerning Prayer*, written before 231, says that 'we ought to end every prayer with a doxology of God through Christ in the Holy Spirit'. And St Hippolytus (d. c. 235) gives the following direction: 'But in every blessing let the words be used: "To Thee be glory, Father and Son with the Holy Spirit, in holy Church, both now and always and world without end. Amen."' The earliest clear example of the form: 'Glory be to the Father and the Son and to the Holy Spirit' is found in the treatise *De Virginitate* of St Athanasius (d. 373).

The lesser doxology was connected to the antiphonal singing of the psalms in the Mesopotamian Church from an early date, and a second part was added, resembling that in use in the Greek Church today:

> Glory be to the Father and the Son and to the Holy Spirit, both now and for always and unto ages of ages. Amen.

What differentiated the Western form from that of the East was the insertion of the clause: 'as it was in the beginning'. It is probable that in Rome during the fourth century the psalms ended with:

> *Gloria Patri et Filio et Spiritui Sancto, sicut erat in principio et nunc et semper et in saecula saeculorum. Amen.*

However, it is in 529 that the Council of Vaison, in France, decreed:

> seeing that not only in the Apostolic See, but all through the East and in all Africa and Italy, on account of the subtlety of the heretics who blasphemously affirm that the Son of God was not from eternity with the Father but had a beginning in time, the words *sicut erat in principio* are recited in every conclusion, we have also decreed that the same form should be used in all our churches.[7]

This form of the lesser doxology remains in use throughout the West to the present day.

It was the custom in monasteries to make a prostration at the end of every psalm, while singing the *Gloria Patri*. Generally this would be a greater or lesser metany (*metanœa*), either kneeling and making a profound bow or simply a deep bow from the hips. The practice of bowing during the singing of the *Gloria Patri* is retained today.

As with the Our Father, the English version of the *Gloria Patri* is identical with that of the Book of Common Prayer. Roman Catholics have been using a translation prepared by the Reformers since the sixteenth century. Dr Lingard, writing to the *Catholic Magazine* in 1833, pointed out that 'That the English form is erroneous and should be corrected, there cannot, I think, be a doubt.' He considered that *sicut erat in principio* can only be a parenthesis. An alternative rendering was suggested in 1901:

> Glory be to the Father and to the Son and to the Holy Ghost, as it was in the beginning, so be it now, and for ever, world without end. Amen.

The *Gloria Patri* and the Beads

The lesser doxology begins to be associated with the rosary during the sixteenth century. In a manuscript prayer book, dated about 1500, of the Danish widow Jesperdatter there is a directive that the prayer to the Holy Trinity be added to every Our Father of the Psalter.[8] Louis Blosius (d. 1566) suggested in his prayer book that the following prayer of the Most Holy Trinity be added after each decade: 'Praise be to the glorious Trinity, to the Father, and the Son and the Comforter: praise be to the Virgin Mother of God, now and throughout eternity. Amen.'[9] By the year 1613 we have an account of the manner in which the rosary was said in the Dominican church of Santa Maria Sopra Minerva in Rome, when the *Gloria Patri* is sung after each decade of *Aves*.

Richard Gribble points out that the *Gloria Patri* has never been formally designated as an essential part of the rosary. The current *Enchiridion indulgentiarum* (4th edn, 1999) states: 'The Rosary is a form of prayer in which fifteen decades of Hail Marys are divided up by the Our Father whilst the mysteries of our redemption are recalled.' However, today it is common usage to say the 'Glory be' at the conclusion of each decade of Hail Marys, and it seems most appropriate that this should be so.

The Apostles' Creed[10]

The Apostles' Creed is one of many expressions of the Christian faith which legendary tradition maintained was composed by the Apostles themselves. It was first called the Apostles' Creed by Rufinus and St Ambrose in the latter part of the fourth century because it legitimately represented the apostolic faith. It states the Christian belief in Jesus Christ and the Triune God, and is derived from the profession of faith required of all at baptism.

> I believe in God the Father Almighty, creator of heaven and earth.
> I believe in Jesus Christ, his only Son, our Lord.
> He was conceived by the power of the Holy Spirit and born of the
>   Virgin Mary.
> He suffered under Pontius Pilate, was crucified, died, and was buried.
> He descended to the dead. On the third day he rose again.
> He ascended into heaven and is seated at the right hand of the
>   Father.
> He will come again to judge the living and the dead.
> I believe in the Holy Spirit, the holy catholic Church, the
>   communion of saints,

the forgiveness of sins, the resurrection of the body, and the life
everlasting. Amen.[11]

The Catechism of the Catholic Church[12] teaches that:

From the beginning, the apostolic Church expressed and handed
on her faith in brief formulae normative for all. But already very
early on, the Church also wanted to gather the essential elements of
her faith into organic and articulated summaries, intended
especially for candidates for Baptism . . .

Such syntheses are called 'professions of faith' since they
summarize the faith that Christians profess. They are called 'creeds'
on account of what is usually their first word in Latin: *credo* ('I
believe'). They are also called 'symbols of faith'.

The Greek word *symbolon* meant half of a broken object, for
example, a seal presented as a token of recognition. The broken
parts were placed together to verify the bearer's identity. The
symbol of faith, then, is a sign of recognition and communion
between believers. *Symbolon* also means a gathering, collection or
summary. A symbol of faith is a summary of the principal truths of
the faith and therefore serves as the first and fundamental point of
reference for catechesis.

The first 'profession of faith' is made during Baptism. The
symbol of faith is first and foremost the *baptismal* creed. Since
Baptism is given 'in the name of the Father and of the Son and of
the Holy Spirit', the truths of faith professed during Baptism are
articulated in terms of their reference to the three persons of the
Holy Trinity.

The earliest professions of faith, found in the New Testament,
focus on Christ, as in the brief statement: 'Jesus is Lord'
(Romans 10.9). St Paul gives a brief summary of Christian belief
in 1 Corinthians 15.3–8:

For I delivered to you as of first importance what I also received, that Christ died for our sins in accordance with the scriptures, that he was buried, that he was raised on the third day in accordance with the scriptures, and that he appeared to Cephas,⁕ then to the twelve. Then he appeared to more than five hundred brethren at one time, most of whom are still alive, though some have fallen asleep. Then he appeared to James, then to all the apostles. Last of all, as to one untimely born, he appeared also to me.

By the beginning of the third century the rite of baptism had been formalized and the catechumen was required to acknowledge his faith in answer to questions about the Holy Trinity, the life, death and resurrection of Christ, and his Church. An example is that given by Hippolytus (c. 215–17):

Do you believe in God, the Father Almighty?

Do you believe in Jesus Christ, the Son of God who was born of the Virgin Mary of the Holy Spirit, has been crucified under Pontius Pilate, died [and was buried], who on the third day rose again, alive, from the dead, ascended into heaven and took his seat at the right hand of the Father, and shall come to judge the living and the dead?

Do you believe in the Holy Church and the resurrection of the body in the Holy Spirit?[13]

This format is familiar to us in the renewal of baptismal vows during the Easter Vigil.

Many professions or symbols of faith were drawn up by local churches and synods. The Apostles' Creed, the Symbol of the Apostles, was first mentioned by St Ambrose in c. 390. By this time the legend that it was written by the twelve Apostles was already current. The title is justified in that it faithfully represents the teaching of the Apostles, but it was not written by them. It relies rather on the ancient Roman baptismal creed, that of the See of Peter. Its present form was first quoted by St Pirminius (Priminius), the Benedictine Abbot of Reichenau, in his missionary manual of c. 724. It became widely accepted as authoritative in the West by the twelfth century.

The Nicene Creed is familiar to us from its use in the Sunday Mass. It has great authority from the fact that it stems from the first two Ecumenical Councils (in 325 and 381). It remains common to all the great Churches of both East and West.

Notes

1. Herbert Thurston, *Familiar Prayers* (1953), p. 22, see n. 4: Tertulian, *De Corona Mil.*, c.iii.
2. Ibid., p. 3, see n. 2, Cyril of Jerusalem, *Catech*, xiii, 36.
3. Ibid., p. 5, see n. 2, Guadentius, *De Lect. Evang.* (Migne, P.L., 20, 890).
4. Ibid., p. 11, see n. 3, Innocent III, *De Sacro Alturis Mysterio*, bk ii, ch. 45.
5. Ibid., p. 12, see n. 1, Lucas Tudensis, *De Altera Vita, Adversus Albigenses*, bk ii, ch. 15.
6. Ibid., *Gloria Patri*, pp. 178–92.
7. Ibid., p. 188, see n. 1, Maassen, *Concilia Aevi Mero Vingici* (M.G.H.), p. 57.
8. Richard Gribble, *The History and Devotion of the Rosary* (1992), p. 43, see n. 50: Wilhelm Schmitz, SJ, *Das Rozenkranzgebet im 15 und am Angang des 16 Jahrhunderts* (Freiburg: Herder & Herder, 1903), p. 95.
9. Ibid., p. 44, see n. 51, S. Beissel, *Geschichte der Verehrung Maria*, in *Deutschland Warhend des Mittelalters*, Vol. 1 (Freiburg: Herder & Herder, 1909), p. 71.
10. For a full treatment of the Creeds see J.N.D. Kelly, *Early Christian Creeds*, 3rd edn (London: Longmans, 1972).
11. *The Catechism of the Catholic Church*, n. 197.
12. Ibid., nn. 185–9.
13. Kelly, *Early Christian Creeds* (1972), p. 35.

6

The Pre-Christian Origin of Prayer Beads

The use of various devices for counting prayers must have arisen in most cultures from the earliest times, our ten fingers being the obvious and most primitive. Prayer beads as such, on which the sum of prayers is worked out, are not a discovery or invention that can be attributed to a single source. The earliest string of prayer beads we know of were found in India and associated with the cult of Siva, in the pre-Aryan period (i.e. before 1700 BC).

It may be that from India the use of prayer beads spread, northward through Tibet to China and eventually to Japan (as did the spread of Buddhism), and simultaneously westward through Persia to Arabia, and so to Europe. However, the Buddha lived about 500 BC, and the great Persian empire under Cyrus was around 550 BC – both much later. It is much more likely that such a simple device as a knotted string or a string of beads evolved among any group that required a means of counting. The recitation of multiple prayers would also seem to be widespread.

The most sophisticated counting device, the abacus, originated in Babylon. It was originally a board with soft sand for writing, but evolved into a board with lines and counters. It has fifteen rods of five beads divided into two rows – the upper row of single beads representing five units and the lower row of four beads representing a single unit.

The highest development of a system of knots as a means of aiding the memory and for keeping records is seen in South America, where the *quipu* (a Peruvian word meaning 'knot') served as a means of record and communication in a highly organized society. It was a system of knot-writing, each kind of knot having a separate meaning, and different coloured cords each having its own significance. The Chinese in the times of Yung-chingche used a contrivance similar to the *quipu* of the Peruvians – little cords marked by different knots, which, by their numbers and distances, served them instead of writing.

Among the Wagogo of Central Africa the time of a woman's pregnancy is reckoned by knots: at each new moon one knot is untied. Indeed, knot-tying seems to be a fairly universal practice. In this country it is a common practice to tie a knot in a handkerchief as an aid to memory, and the same custom is found in India: the knot usually being tied in the strings of the pyjamas.

Notched sticks are also universally used for record-keeping: witness the tally-sticks which were used in England and Ireland until quite recently. In Ireland these sticks were employed to record the number of prayers uttered, and the suppliant would leave such a stick as a votive offering.

Prayer Beads or Rosaries among Non-Christian Religions[1]

Hindu or Brahman

The oldest reference to prayer beads to be found in the literature of India is in the Jaina canon as a device used by Brahman monks. (Mahavira the founder of Jainism lived from 599–527 BC and the Jaina canon evolved from the oral tradition becoming systematized at the end of the fourth century.)[2] The two names given to these prayer beads are *ganettiya* and *kantchaniya*. References in later literature occur in Brahman works only, the *mata* 'garland' and *sutra* 'string' names referring to the shape of the string. The following passage from the Buddhist *Forty-two Points of Doctrine* alludes to the rosary or chaplet (if we may call it such): 'The man who, in the practice of virtue, applies himself to the extirpation of all his vices is like one who is rolling between his fingers the beads of the chaplet. If he continues taking hold of them one by one, he arrives speedily at the end. By extirpating his bad inclinations one by one, a man arrives at perfection.' It is generally considered that the Hindus were the first to evolve the rosary known in Sanskrit as the *japa-mala*, 'muttering chaplet' or *smarani*, 'remembrancer', because by means of its beads the muttering of a definite number of prayers may be counted. But the pious Hindu not only computes his daily prayers as if they were so many rupees to be added to his capital stock in the bank of heaven, he sets himself to repeat the names of his favourite god, and will continue to do so for hours together.

The rosary differs according to the sect. The number of beads varies. A worshipper of Siva uses a rosary of 32 beads; a votary of Vishnu, on the other hand, uses one with 108 beads. This number is also sometimes found on a Saivite rosary, indeed the beads may run into several hundreds, irrespective of the sect. There are usually one or more terminal beads to each rosary, they are not generally counted in with those on the main string. The Sikhs have a rosary which consists of knots made of many strands of wool, knotted together at intervals – 108 knots in all. The Saktas use rosaries made of dead men's teeth and similar relics.

The materials of which rosaries are made vary greatly and each has a specific purpose. A favourite bead of the Saivites is that called *rudraksa*, 'eye of the god Rudra' (Siva). This is a seed from the *Eleocarpus ganitrus*. In the Punjab, however, the name *rudraksa* is applied to the seeds of the jujube-tree, and importance is here attached to the number of facets on the seeds. The seeds, according to a Siva legend, are said to be the tears of Rudra (or Siva) which he let fall in a rage (some say in grief) and which crystallized into this form. The five facets are also sometimes thought to stand for the five faces or the five distinct aspects of the god. The worshippers of Vishnu, on the other hand, prefer smooth beads, and favour those made of the *tulasi*. The materials vary according to the use to which they are put and the wealth of the owner. The poorer Jains generally use rosaries made of cotton thread and sandalwood; the richer use beads of red coral, crystal, cornelian, emerald, pearl, silver and gold.

There are also small rosaries called *boberkhas*. These are used when the more costly rosaries with the usual number of beads are not obtainable, or when the user cannot afford to buy the more expensive beads. Devotees attach much importance to the size of the beads – the larger they are, the more effective is the rosary, and the greater the merit attained by the user of it.

While counting his daily prayers on the beads a high-caste Brahman is careful to conceal his hand in a bag made for this purpose, so that he may not be seen to pray. The favourite mantra is the *Gayatri* from the *Rigveda*: 'Let us adore that excellent glory of the divine Vivifier: may he enlighten our understandings.' A Brahman may attain beatitude by simple repetition of the *Gayatri*, and having repeated the *Gayatri* 3000 times he is delivered from the greatest guilt.

Lutheran pastor Sam Schmitthenner writes:

Once, travelling on a train in India, I was in a compartment with a Brahmin family. The daughter was a teenage movie star. Before going to bed her mother said, 'Remember to say Siva's names.' So the daughter sat cross-legged, yogi-style, folded her hands and said his 108 names, touching a bead for each one: 'Nata Raj, dancing Siva who shows his grace, peace and creative power, and destroys and treads the evil dwarf ... Blue Throated One, he drank the poison churned up on the cosmic sea, saving the world. Source of the Ganges ... Bairagi, smeared with ashes, he dances in the graveyards,' etc. She knew them all. Her devotion was touching!

Buddhist

The Buddhist rosary is probably of Brahman origin, and here again the number of beads on the string is usually 108. This is said to correspond with the number of sinful inclinations, which are to be overcome by reciting the beads. Moreover, 108 Brahmans were summoned at Buddha's birth to foretell his destiny. In Burma, the footprints of Buddha have 108 subdivisions; in Tibet, the sacred writings (*Kahygur*) run into 108 volumes; in China, the white pagoda at Peking is encircled by 108 columns, and also in China, 108 blows are the customary punishment for malefactors. Again, in Japan, at the festival of the dead, observed from 13–15 July, 108 welcome fires are lighted on the shores of sea, lake or river, and in India 108 rupees are usually given in alms. Besides the full rosaries of 108 beads, smaller ones of 18 beads are also used – the number of beads representing the chief disciples of Buddha.

India

In India, the Buddhist rosaries do not seem to differ very much from many of those used by Hindus. Some are made of more costly materials than others, the more valuable being of turquoise, coral, amber, silver, pearls, or other gems. The poorer people usually have their rosary beads made of wood, pebbles, berries, or bone, and they are often satisfied with only 30 or 40 beads.

Burma

The Burmese rosary has 108 beads. It is used as a means of counting the repetitions of the names of the Buddha trinity, viz. *Phra* (Buddha), *Tara* (*Dharma*) and *Sangha*. On the completion of a round of the rosary the central bead is held and the formula 'All is transitory, painful and unreal' is repeated.

Tibet

The rosary, *phreng-bas* (pronounced *theng-wa*), 'a string of beads', is an essential part of a Lama's dress, and is also worn by most of the laity of both sexes. The act of telling the beads is called *tan-c'e*, which means 'to purr' like a cat. The rosaries have 108 beads on the main string. The reason given for this number is that it ensures the repetition of a sacred spell a hundred times, the eight extra beads being added for fear of omission. There are three terminal beads to the rosaries, which are called collectively 'retaining beads', symbolizing 'the Three Holy Ones' of the Buddhist trinity.

Tibetan rosaries usually have a pair of pendant strings on which are threaded small metal beads or rings, to serve as counters. At the end of one string is a *dorje* (the thunderbolt of Indra), the other terminating in a bell. The strings are usually attached at the eighth and 21st bead on either side of the large central bead, though there is no rule about this and they can be placed anywhere on the string. By means of these counters 10,800 prayers may be counted, but the number uttered depends largely on the leisure and fervour of the devotee. (Old women are especially zealous in this respect.)

The materials of which the beads are made vary according to the sect, the god or goddess addressed, and the wealth of the owner. The abbots of some of the wealthy monasteries have their beads made of valuable gems and precious stones. Importance is often attached to the colour of the beads, which should correspond with the complexion of the god or goddess to be worshipped.

The Lamas use certain mystical formulas which are prescribed for repetition, each formula having its own special rosary. Different formulas are used for different deities, and are supposed to act as powerful spells as well as to contain the essence of a prayer. These mantras are more or less unintelligible to the worshipper, and are indeed usually gibberish. They are probably of Sanskrit origin. The laity, on the other hand, seldom make use of any other formula than the well-known '*Om mani padme Hūm!*' ('Hail thou jewel in the Lotus!')

China

The full Buddhist rosary in China has the usual number of 108 beads, with three dividing beads of a different size or colour. As in other countries, the materials composing them vary. There is also a smaller rosary of 18 beads, corresponding to the 18 *lohans* (chief disciples of Buddha). In some rosaries each of these 18 beads is carved into an image of a *lohan*. Sometimes the laity wear this smaller rosary at the waist, when it is perfumed with musk and bears the name *heang-chu*, 'fragrant beads'.

As a religious instrument the prayer beads seem to be used to count the repetition of set phrases, whereby the devotee stores up merit for himself. If these repetitions are performed at temples, the greater the merit of the votary. The rosary may also be used to count prostrations in which the devotee goes down on his knees, bowing so as to touch the ground with his forehead, while uttering a prayer formula.

Korea

The Buddhist rosaries of Korea have 110 beads, though, according to the classics, the number is 108, the two extra beads being large ones – one at the beginning usually containing a swastika, the other dividing the rosary into two parts. Each of these beads is dedicated to a deity. Every bead on the string has its own special name. The devotee, when using the rosary, repeats the '*Om mani padme Hūm*', holding each bead till he has counted a certain number. On laying the rosary aside he repeats the following sentences:

> Oh! the thousand myriad miles of emptiness, the place which is in the midst of the tens of hundred myriad miles of emptiness, eternal desert where the true Buddha exists, there is eternal existence with Tranquil Peace.

Japan

It is in Japan that the Buddhist rosary reaches its most complicated form, each sect having its own special rosary. There is also the one known as the *sho-zuku-jiu-dzu*, or the rosary used by all sects in common. It consists of 112 beads, divided into two equal parts by two large beads, called the upper parent bead and the lower parent bead. From the upper parent bead hang two strings, on which are threaded 21 beads smaller than those on the main string, with terminal beads of elongated form called 'dewdrop beads'. From the lower parent bead hang three strings, two with five small beads each and the terminal dewdrop beads. These are used as counters. The rosary represents metaphorically the Buddhist pantheon, and the position of the dewdrop beads is thought to symbolize their actual positions of power and authority, as, according to Buddhist philosophy, they preside for good or evil over this and all other worlds.

The *sho-zuku-jiu-dzu* is the rosary usually carried by monks and laity of all sects, on all occasions of religious state, on visits of ceremony, at funerals, etc. It is said that rosaries were carried by all the Japanese soldiers in the Russo-Japanese War (1906–7). The dead may have a rosary slipped on the wrist, whether they are buried or cremated. At some of the larger temples and at all places of popular pilgrimage there are special shops for the sale of rosaries, having as their sign an enormous rosary hung outside. The devout attach especial value to a rosary that has been consecrated over the sacred flame and incense smoke of a venerated temple.

Muslim

The rosary used by followers of Islam generally consists of 99 beads with a terminal bead called the *imam*, 'leader'. Its chief use is for counting the recital of the 99 names, or attributes, of God, the *imams* being sometimes used for the essential name, Allah. This rosary is divided into three parts, 33 beads in each, by beads of another material or shape, or by tassels which are often made of gold thread or of brightly coloured silks. A smaller rosary of 33 beads is very commonly used, and the devotee will go round this three times to get the full repetition of the 99 names. In Persia and India the Muslim rosary is called *tasbih*; in Egypt *subhah*, from an Arabic verb meaning 'to praise', 'to exalt'. On the *tasbih* is prayed: '*Subhana-llah*' (Glory be to Allah) (33 times); '*Alhamdu-li-llah*' (Praise be to Allah) (33 times); and '*Allahu akhbar*' (Allah is great) (33 times).

Muslim tradition points to a very early use of the rosary, dating it back even to the time of the Prophet himself. In support of this belief it is related that Muhammad reproached some women for using pebbles in repeating the *tasbih*, suggesting that they should rather count them on their fingers. Tradition has it that the Prophet attributed great merit to those who recited the names of God and repeated certain formulas. 'Verily', he says, 'there are ninety-nine names of God and whoever recites them shall enter into Paradise', and, 'Whoever recites the *tasbih*, "I extol the holiness of God" and the *tahmid*, "God be praised" a hundred times, morning and evening, will have all his sins forgiven.'

Wooden beads are used by all sects, and beads made of clay from Mecca are highly valued. Date stones are much used, as also are horn and imitation pearls and coral. Beads made of earth from Kerbala, where Husain is buried, are sacred to the Shiahs and are used by members of this sect only.

In Egypt, on the first night after a burial certain ceremonies take place at the house of the deceased, among them being that of the *subhah*, or rosary. After nightfall a number of *faqirs*, sometimes as many as fifty, assemble, one of them bringing a large rosary of a thousand beads, each bead being about the size of a pigeon's egg. Certain passages from the Qur'an are recited, after which the formula 'There is no deity but God' is repeated 3000 times. A count of these repetitions is kept by one of the *faqirs* by means of the rosary. They often rest and refresh themselves with coffee at the end of each round. Certain other sentences are recited after this and then one of the officiants asks his companions, 'Have ye transferred (the merit of) what ye have recited to the soul of the deceased?' They reply, 'We have transferred it', adding, 'and peace be on the Apostles, and praise be to God, the Lord of all creatures.'

Jewish

Among the Jews the rosary has lost all religious importance; having taken it from the Turks and Greeks, it is used merely as a pastime on the Sabbath and holy days. No manual labour being permitted on those days, they occupy themselves with passing the beads through their fingers. In this context they are no more than 'worry-beads'.

Notes

1. Winifred S. Blackman, Rosaries, *Encyclopaedia of Religion and Ethics*, ed. James Hastings (Edinburgh, T. & T. Clark, 1918).
2. Jainism, *Encyclopaedia Britannica CD 2000*.

7

The Use of Beads in the
Christian Tradition

The introduction of the rosary among European Christians has been attributed to various people, among them Peter the Hermit (d. 1115), who preached the First Crusade, thus suggesting that the rosary was an imitation of that used by the Muslims. The strongest tradition, as previously described, was that in a vision St Dominic 'was admonished by the Blessed Virgin to preach the rosary as a special remedy against heresy and sin'. These legends have no historical foundation.

The use of repetitive prayer in the Christian Church seems to have evolved among the desert monks, and for this purpose various means of counting were used. Sozomen, in his *Ecclesiastical History*, relates how Abbot Paul, a hermit of Thebes in Egypt (d. 347), daily recited 300 prayers, keeping count by means of pebbles gathered in his cloak, dropping them one by one at the end of each prayer. This primitive system of counting suggests that the rosary evolved independently and was not borrowed from other traditions. St Anthony of Egypt (251–356), a disciple of Paul of Thebes, began to practise an ascetic life at the age of twenty, and after fifteen years withdrew for absolute solitude to a mountain by the Nile called Pispir (now Dayr al-Maymun), where he lived from about 286 to 305. During the course of this retreat, he began his legendary combat against the devil. He attracted a number of disciples, and is regarded as the founder of organized (in so far as it could be said to be organized) eremitical monasticism. The development of the *komvoschinion*, or Byzantine rosary – a circular string of knotted wool – is attributed to St Anthony. However, we cannot exclude the possibility of an eastern influence. Egypt had trade links with Persia and Persia with India, where the Hindu Brahmans used beads to count their prayers.

In Christian Ethiopia, prayer-sticks were devised and notches made on staffs used as supports for people standing during the long services. Forty-one notches were made since the prayer 'Lord have mercy' is repeated 41 times in honour of the 41 lashes the Coptic tradition believes Christ received during his Passion.

John Cassian (c. 360–430) studied monasticism in Egypt. In about 415 he founded two monasteries near Marseilles, where he wrote his *Conferences*, which take the form of conversations with the leaders of Eastern monasticism. It is from these that we learn of the Eastern method of repetitive meditative prayer. Perhaps he also introduced the Eastern prayer-rope.

During the next 700 years we have only a few hints that suggest the use of repetitive prayer and the beads. There is a remote connection with the Irish Celtic Church. The Irish monks had a practice of singing the 150 psalms in three sets of 50 – which became known as the 'Three Fifties' – recalling the doctrine of the Trinity as emphasized by St Patrick. In the penitential books, a common penance was the recitation of 50 psalms. This practice was carried into Europe by the Irish missionaries, hence the possible connection with the 'three fifties' of the rosary. It is suggested that the Irish Celtic Church had been influenced by Eastern monasticism, probably by way of John Cassian. Did they have any knowledge of prayer beads? St Brigid of Kildare (d. 523) is said to have used strings of wooden beads.[1] Present-day scholars of the early Celtic Church are unable to confirm this – could it be a confusion with St Bridget of Sweden? The grave of a certain Abbess Gertrude, who died in 659 at Nivelles, Belgium, was found to contain a set of beads. No description of the beads is given in this reference so the relevance is uncertain.

The continuing practice of repeating a prayer many times is well documented. During the eighth century (c. 782) it was traditional for the monks of St Apollinaris to say 300 *Kyrie eleisons* and *Christe eleisons* twice a day in gratitude for the Pope's benefactors. As already mentioned, the lay brothers in the monasteries of St Gall and Reichenau in c. 800 had the practice of praying 50 Our Fathers for the deceased, as did the monks of Cluny from 910.

It is in the eleventh century that we have the first firm reference to the use of prayer beads in England. It is stated by William of Malmesbury that the Lady Godiva of Coventry, wife of Count Leofric, bequeathed to the monastery which they had founded 'a circlet of gems which she had threaded on a string, in order that by fingering them one by one as she successively recited her prayers she might not fall short of the exact number'. Which prayers were used is not known. (See Chapter 8, p. 95, for a more detailed discussion on Lady Godiva and the rosary.)

During the twelfth century it became a common practice for lay people to carry a 'Paternoster cord' of 50 knots or beads, a 'fifty', to be repeated three times, instead of the traditional longer strand of 150.

A contemporary of St Aybert (d. 1140) wrote how Aybert bent his knees in prayer a hundred times a day and prostrated himself, 'raising his body by his fingers and toes', 50 times, while repeating the *Ave Maria*.

Aelred of Rievaulx (d. 1167) wrote a treatise *De vita eremetica ad sororem*, which was a source for the Ancrene Riwle. Aelred's rules for anchoresses, so common in the England of his time, are particularly interesting because they contain meditations on the life of Our Lady that are surprisingly modern. For example, when reflecting on the Annunciation, the recluse should in imagination enter Mary's chamber together with the Angel and salute the 'sweetest Lady' with him, frequently repeating the *Ave Maria*. She should enter into Mary's feelings on hearing the greeting, follow her when she visits Elizabeth and when she gives birth to Jesus at Bethlehem; at the Passion she should unite her own to the tears of the sorrowful Mother. In this we have an early indication of the rosary meditations.

Repetition of numbers of *Aves* was recommended by the author of the early-thirteenth-century Ancrene Riwle (Ancrene Wisse), which provided three anchoresses with an elaborate celebration of the Five Joys of Our Lady based on the repetition of five *Aves* with appropriate prayers and antiphons, and recommended saying five decades or more of *Aves*, each decade marked by a different physical posture, standing, kneeling, bowing, etc. The custom of accompanying the saying the Angelic Salutation by some act of reverence, genuflexion or inclination seems to have been widespread among religious at this time. It makes no mention of beads with which to count the *Aves*, nor did it suggest any meditations to accompany them.

Beads are not mentioned even in the devotion of a thousand *Aves* recorded in several early-sixteenth-century manuscripts, where some means of keeping count must surely have been needed. A hundred *Aves* were to be said every day for ten days, whether 'standing, kneeling, going, or riding', while a sum of money was held in one hand. After repeating the *Aves* and saying a prayer, the alms were to be kissed and then given to a poor person in honour of the Angel's joyous greeting to Our Lady. The attraction of the devotion was the promise that all would go well on the day it was used, and that no reasonable prayer would go unanswered.[2]

Paternoster Beads

By the thirteenth century the making of paternosters, as the beads were then called, had become a specialized industry both in Paris and in London. In Paris, the workers were divided into four different guilds or companies, each company being distinguished according to the material in which its members worked. In London, at the same period, certain citizens were known as 'paternosterers'. These craftsmen probably resided in Paternoster Row and Ave Maria Lane, being thus conveniently close to the great devotional centre of London, under the shadow of St Paul's Cathedral. Thurston says that there was also in the fourteenth century another Paternoster Lane located beside the Thames in the Vintry ward, close to the church called Paternoster Church, or St Michael's the Royal. This quarter of London was then inhabited by Gascon vintners who brought their goods by ship up the Thames. They would require their own forms of this devotion, and Thurston suggests that French 'paternotriers' settled in this locality to supply this want.[3] Near the Abbey of Eynsham in the village of Yarnton in Oxfordshire, there is a Paternoster Lane – so named because the distance while walking was measured by the number of *Paternosters* recited.

Prayer-Ropes in the Eastern and Coptic Churches

The knotted cord is a primitive form of rosary. It survives in both Greek and Slavic monasteries as part of the investiture of the Little Habit and the Great Habit when it is bestowed ceremonially upon a monk or nun by the Superior saying:

'Take, Brother N., the sword of the Spirit, which is the word of
God, for the continual prayer to Jesus; for thou must always
have the Name of the Lord Jesus in mind, in heart, and on thy
lips ever saying: "Lord Jesus Christ, Son of God, have mercy on
me a sinner."'

Among the Greeks the knotted cord is known as a
komvoschinion. The Russians give it the old Slavic name of
chotki or *vervitsa* (string); in popular language it bears the name
lestovka because of its resemblance to a ladder (*lestnitsa*). A
komvologion is similar to a *komvoschinion*, but made with beads.
The *komvoschinion* used by the monks on Mount Athos has a
hundred knots, divided by three beads of larger size into four
equal parts with a pendant of three more knots terminating in a
small cross-shaped tassel. This cord may be used for counting
any kind of prayer or devotional exercise, but typically the Jesus
Prayer: 'Lord Jesus Christ, Son of God; have mercy on me, a
sinner.' In the book *The Way of a Pilgrim*[4] it is suggested that a
shorter version, 'Lord Jesus Christ, have mercy on me', be
repeated up to 12,000 times a day.

A similar prayer, 'Lord Jesus Christ, Son and Word of the
Living God, through the intercessions of thine all-pure Mother
and of all thy Saints, have mercy and deliver us', may be
accompanied by a hundred prostrations repeated twelve times
daily with 300 more in the evening.

Prostrations vary in character. A 'great metany' (*metanœa*) is a
prostration in which one kneels, making a profound bow with
the forehead touching the ground, and a 'little metany' a deep
bow, flexing the hips so as to touch the ground with the hand.

Another practice is to make ten great metanies and thirty
little metanies repeating the prayer 'Lord Jesus Christ, Son of
God, have mercy upon me, a sinner' 60 times; this to be done
five times a day, making 300 in all. The significance of the
figure 300 is its correspondence with the number of the psalms

and lesser doxologies said at the canonical hours. This form of *komvoschinion* is used by Hellenic monks in Greece, Turkey and the East generally, as well as on Mount Athos.

Among Russian monks the knotted cord used is the old Slavic *vervitsa*. It has 103 knots or beads, which are separated into unequal groups by larger beads. The groups of beads are as follows: 17+33+40+12, and an additional small bead at the end. In the Slavic *vervitsa* the lower ends are fastened together; they terminate in three flat triangles, inscribed and ornamented.

The use of the *komvoschinion* or *vervitsa* is primarily a monastic or ascetic devotion; it is not so widely used by the Orthodox laity, though the laity of the Russian sect called Old Believers have adopted it. Whenever this devotion is seen in use among the Uniates outside the monasteries, it has been copied from the rosary as used among the laity in the West.

The rosaries used by the Copts in Egypt have 41 beads, or sometimes 81. They are used for counting a similar number of repetitions of the *Kyrie eleison*. This petition is repeated in Arabic or Coptic, with the addition, at the end, of a short prayer in Coptic. Sometimes the Copts resort to what is presumably a more primitive method of keeping record of their prayers, and count on their fingers.

Notes

1. Eithne Wilkins, *The Rose-Garden Game* (London: Victor Gollancz, 1969), p. 53.
2. Jan Rhodes, The Rosary in Sixteenth-Century England (1), *Mount Carmel*, 31/4 (1983): 180–91.
3. Herbert Thurston, in *Journal of the Society of Arts*, 1: 262, as quoted in *Encyclopaedia of Religion and Ethics*, ed. James Hastings (Edinburgh: T. & T. Clark, 1918), p. 853b.
4. *The Way of a Pilgrim*, trans. from the Russian by R. M. Freoch (London: Triangle, SPCK, 1986). A literal translation of the original

Russian title reads: 'A candid narrative of a Pilgrim to his Spiritual Father'. Written between 1853 and 1861 by an unknown author, it came into the possession of a monk of Mount Athos. It was copied and published by the Abbot of St Michael's Monastery at Kazan, 1884.

8

The Use of Prayer Beads in England

We have evidence of the use of prayer beads in England from the eleventh century onwards. They were particularly popular during the fifteenth and early sixteenth centuries until their use was attacked by the Reformers, when they became a badge of Catholicity.

Lady Godiva

During the first half of the eleventh century Leofric, earl of Mercia, chose the site of a ruined convent on which to build a magnificent abbey at Covnentria (Coventry). His wife Godgifu (God's gift), better known to us as Lady Godiva, was a pious woman of whom it was said: 'Lovely as Godgifu was, the beauty of her soul and her virtues far eclipsed her personal charm.' The Countess Godgifu endowed the monastery church with all her treasure. Her final gift was a circlet of gems on a string which she used for her prayers. On her deathbed she desired that this chaplet be hung round the neck of 'Our Ladye of Coventry', whom she had so dearly loved. 'In a word, for the love of God and the service of the Church, she literally denuded herself of all her personal property.'[1]

The memory of this remarkable woman was kept alive by the local populace and evolved into a folk-tale which was first recorded by Roger of Wendover (d. 1236) in the *Chronica*. He recounts that Leofric, in exasperation over his wife's ceaseless imploring that he reduce Coventry's heavy taxes, declared he would do so if she rode naked through the crowded marketplace. This she did, her hair covering all of her body except her legs. Ranulf Higden (d. 1364), in his *Polychronicon*, says that as a result Leofric freed the town from all tolls save those on horses. (An inquiry made in the reign of Edward I shows that at that time no tolls were paid in Coventry except on horses.) A later chronicle asserts that Godiva required the townsmen to remain indoors at the time fixed for her ride. Peeping Tom, a citizen who looked out of his window, apparently became a part of the legend in the seventeenth century. In most accounts he was struck blind or dead. There are no contemporary accounts of this part of the legend. The chronicler Florence of Worcester (d. 1118) mentions Leofric and Godiva with respect, but does not refer to the ride. Nor was it mentioned by William of Malmesbury writing about Leofric and Godiva in 1125.

Representations of the Rosary

According to Jan Rhodes,[2] who gives an account of the use of prayer beads in England during the sixteenth century, the earliest surviving representation of prayer beads in England is on the effigy of Blanche Grandisson (1347) at Much Marcle, Herefordshire. But it was not until the later fifteenth century that they came to be pictured at all frequently. Then they become quite common on funeral monuments and brasses, for instance, they are held by mourners on the tombs of Richard Beauchamp (1439, Warwick); Sir Nicholas Fitzherbert (1493, Norbury, Derbyshire); Sir Robert Harcourt (1490, Stanton Harcourt, Oxfordshire). Beads are also depicted on the brasses

Figure 8.1   Rosaries from late brasses at Meissen
1. Rosary beads from the brass of the Duchess Sidonia, wife of Duke Albert of Saxony, 1510
2. Decade beads from brass of Frederick, Duke of Saxony, 1517
3. Beads from the brass of Barbara, Duchess of Saxony, 1534
4. Beads from brass of Amalie, Duchess of Bavaria, 1502
Source: Thurston, H., The Rosary, *The Month*, 97 (1901): 394

of William Gybhys of Chipping Camden (1484); John Jay of St Mary Redcliff, Bristol (1490); the wife and daughters of T. Pownder of St Mary Quay, Ipswich (1525). In stained glass, kneeling donors quite often carry prayer beads, for example the Borlase window, St Neot's, Cornwall.

Thomas Bridgett[3] tells us that by the end of the fifteenth century it had become almost a matter of fashion to carry the rosary publicly. There was an effigy of Richard Patten, father of Bishop Wainflete, which was in the south aisle of Wainflete church, showing him with three things hanging from his girdle – a purse, a dagger and a rosary – being thus provided for every emergency. Fr Bridgett goes on to say that in the church of All Hallows by the Tower (London) may still be seen the effigy of John Rulche, carrying a rosary on his arm. (This is no longer so as it was destroyed in the bombing of December 1940. However, the memorial brass of Andrewe Evyngar (died 1533) and his wife Ellyn, who has a long rosary with tassel suspended from the girdle, survives.) In St Helen's, Bishopsgate, opposite the NatWest Tower Building there is to be found on the floor of the south transept the brass memorial of Thomas and Margaret Williams. The husband has a short rosary at his waist; the date is 1495. On the north wall is a very fine memorial brass of an 'Unknown civilian and his wife, c. 1465'; looped over his belt the man carries a single string of 21 large beads with a tassel at either end. The absence of inscriptions on the brasses of this church has been attributed to their deliberate removal. The parish accounts for 1644 show that an engraver was paid one pound and two shillings for 'defacing the superstitious inscriptions'. To pray for the dead was considered to be unwarranted, purgatory being a 'fond thing vainly invented'.[4] The church of St Mary at Lambeth, just by the entrance to Lambeth Palace, became the Museum of Garden History in 1979, but it retains a brass dated about 1520 depicting a lady of the Howard family with a rosary suspended from the waist. It is now placed on the left-hand pillar of the chancery arch and is in good condition. The rosary is unusual, being made up of ten sets of nine beads separated by a larger bead plus two sets of five beads, making one hundred in total. Almost certainly it was a fashion accessory.

Jan Rhodes[5] describes how rosaries and the text of the *Ave*

Maria were to be found carved on bench-ends at Kingston and Milverton in Somerset and Trent in Dorset. In some churches beads were provided for general use, as a rhyme recorded by Robert Reyneys of Acle, Norfolk, says:

> Man in the church not idle thou stand
> But take thy beads in thy hand
> And if thou have here none of thine
> I pray thee take these for the time
> And say a psalter with glad cheer
> In worship of Our Lady dear . . .
> And thou shalt have for one Psalter
> Of pardon two thousand four hundred years
> Eleven score of days and fourteen . . .
> And therefore pray with heart and mind
> And make the Queen of Heaven thy friend . . .
> And when thou wilt no longer stand
> Leave the beads where thou them found.

The custom was obviously widespread, for Thomas Becon in his *Relics of Rome* of 1563 recorded that anyone who presumed to remove a set of pardon-beads from a church was liable to be cursed in the general 'sentence' or excommunication read publicly four times a year in all churches.

St Michael and the Scales[6]

In the fourteenth and fifteenth centuries images were painted on the walls of English churches. A typical example might show Michael holding the scales with Mary standing to one side. In the scale pans are a soul balanced against a devil. The Virgin either places her hand on the scale beam to weigh it down or adds a rosary. This type of image, known as a 'psychostasis', indicates 'the soul's status or standing before God'.

The image is better understood when we recall Daniel's interpretation of the writing on the wall at Belshazzar's feast – 'you have been weighed in the scales and found wanting' (Daniel 5.27) – indicating that weighing light is the way to damnation, and Psalm 62.9: 'Men of low estate are but a breath, men of high estate are a delusion; in the balances they go up.' The weighing of the soul is an ancient metaphor for salvation, known to Israel, the Egyptians and Greeks. The psychostasis was a pictorial teaching about redemption and the Last Judgement, the conflict between good and evil, the application of justice and mercy. It shows the judgement of the soul after death, its merits weighed against its misdeeds, a task undertaken by St Michael, prince of the heavenly angelic host. Mary, the Mother of Mercy, comes to the aid of the soul, dispensing the graces obtained by her own intercession. The placing of the rosary on the scales is unique to Britain, whereas the placing of Mary's hand, a roll of *Aves*, or a candle was common everywhere.[7] With the foundation of the rosary confraternities from c. 1470, praying for the deceased members by means of the rosary became a very popular devotional practice. Pope Sixtus IV allowed indulgences to be applied to the souls in purgatory in 1478. So it is an interesting observation that the earliest wall-paintings of the psychostasis in English churches have been dated to about 1350. Is it Mary's rosary prayer or the graces obtained by the devout recitation of the Marian psalter by the faithful that are being made available to the poor soul?

Woodcuts illustrating the folio edition of the *Canterbury Tales* printed by Caxton in the 1390s show a number of the pilgrims wearing or carrying their beads in a variety of ways (see Figure 8.2 for examples). In the prologue, Chaucer writes of Dame Eglentine, the Prioresse:

The Clerke's Tale

The Nonne's Tale

Figure 8.2   Woodcuts illustrating *The Canterbury Tales*
Source: Rock, D., *The Church of Our Fathers* (1903), p. 271

Of small coral about her arm she bare
A pair of bedes, gauded all with green,
And thereon hung a broch of gold full shene.

The Variety of Beads

At the beginning of the sixteenth century there was a wide
diversity of prayer beads available for use in England. Some
were made of costly materials, others of wood or bone; some
were open strings, others closed circles. The number and
arrangement of the beads varied greatly. A rosary of 70 beads,
six decades of small beads plus three small beads divided by
seven large beads, was in use which had the advantage that it
was possible to pray the Corona of Our Lady: 63 *Aves*, seven
Paters and a *Credo*, or the Crown of Our Lord: 33 small beads
on which were recited the *Paternoster*, or the Dominican rosary
of 50 *Aves* and five *Paters*.[8] Only as the sixteenth century
progressed, and particularly in the recusant period during the
last quarter of the century, did the familiar five-decade rosary
come to predominate.

There was an equally wide diversity of devotions associated
with the use of prayer beads at this time. They tended to be
based on the numbers five, fifteen or fifty, but sevens and other
significant numbers were also used. Number played an
important part in many devotions of the period. The most
popular tended to focus on the Passion of Christ, which
dominated late medieval devotion, and Passion prayers and
devotions often used beads.

The famous pardon-beads of Syon, the Bridgettine religious
house at Isleworth, Middlesex, founded by Henry V in 1415,
consisted of an open string of five beads, two black, two white
and one red. A rhymed prayer containing 33 words,
representing the age of Christ, was to be said on them:

Jesu for thy Holy Name
And for thy bitter Passion
Save us from sin and shame
And from endless damnation
And bring us to the bliss
Which never shall miss
Sweet Jesu, Amen.

And for that a pardon of 5475 years was promised – the traditional number of the total of the wounds Jesus was believed to have suffered in his Passion.

These examples show the universality of the devotion of the rosary in England at the beginning of the sixteenth century, when the beads were thus publicly carried not only by priests and nuns but by men and women of all classes.

Rosaries Recorded in Old Documents

Evidence of the existence of valuable sets of beads constructed of a variety of precious materials is found in old documents as recorded by Thomas Bridgett.[9] Edmund Waterton[10] also quotes a most interesting inventory and valuation of stock in a jeweller's shop for a year 1381, found in the early archives of the City of London:

One forcer [i.e., coffer or box], value 6d, with divers jewels in the same contained – namely, 4 sets of *paternostres* of white amber, value 2s; 16 sets of *paternostres* of amber, 20s; 5 sets of *paternostres*, namely coral, and one of geet [jet], 10s; 6 sets of *aves* of geet, and *paternostres* of silver gilt, of one pattern, 8s; 38 sets of *aves* of geet with *gaudees* of silver gilt of another pattern 38s; 14 sets of *aves* blue glass, with *paternostres* silver gilt, 3s 4d; 28 sets of *paternostres* of geet, 3s. 4d; 15 sets of *paternostres* of mazer [probably wood inlaid with metal], and 5 of white bone for children, 5s; 29 necklaces of geet, the tongues of silver, 3s 4d; and two crucifixes of silver gilt, 3s.[11]

By his will, dated 2 August 1400, Richard, Lord Scrope of Bolton, leaves to his dear son and heir a pair of paternosters of coral, 'which formerly belonged to my lord father as well as a cross of gold, which I have used and worn'; Roger was that son and heir, and so the third owner of the paternosters, and he in his turn by his will dated 23 September 1403, using the words of his father, bequeaths the pair of paternosters to his son and heir Richard. This is cited as evidence of the reverence and value in which a pair of beads were held in Catholic England, descending from father to son for four generations.

Precious rosaries are often mentioned in the wills of great people. Humphrey de Bohun, Earl of Hereford (1361), leaves to his nephew 'a nouche [clasp] of gold surrounded with large pearls with a ruby between four pearls, three diamonds, and a pair of gold paternosters of fifty pieces with ornaments, together with a cross of gold, in which is a piece of the true cross of our Lord'. John of Gaunt, Duke of Lancaster (1397), leaves 'a chain of gold of the old manner, with the name of God in each part, which my most honoured lady and mother the queen, whom God pardon, gave me, commanding me to preserve it, with her blessing; and I desire that he [his son Henry, Duke of Hereford, Earl of Derby and afterwards King Henry IV] will keep it, with the blessing of God and mine'. In an account presented by the chamberlain to King Henry VI of the various jewels which had been delivered to His Majesty to make his New Year's gifts in 1437, it is mentioned that 'a handsome set of rosary-beads was considered a fitting present to be offered to a king, and to be given by him again to an honoured subject'.

The rosary was therefore clearly a favourite devotion with the great and noble. It was no less so with the learned and the saintly. William of Wykeham, the famous Bishop of Win-chester, who died in 1404, bequeaths to the Archbishop of Canterbury, Thomas Fitzalan, 'a pair of beads of gold appended from a bracelet of gold, having these words engraved on them: "I.H.S. est amor meus" '.

The rosary was said on beads of gold by kings and nobles, and on beads of coral by bishops and prioresses, but it was said no less devoutly by the poor on beads of wood or bone. We should note that it was not only the very rich who bequeathed their rosaries, and there are very many wills to attest to this.

The Spread of the Marian Psalter in England

The Carthusian Chronicle of Cologne records how the famous Carthusian Heinrich Eghar, who died in 1408 aged eighty, had a vision of Mary in which she taught him to say a 'psalter' in her honour and 'first to say a *Paternoster* and then the ten *Aves*', repeated fifteen times. He communicated this revelation to a Carthusian prior in England, and from that time this psalter became so widely spread throughout almost the whole of England that there was hardly any citizen in that country who did not possess one or who broke his fast until he first recited it.[12] At the close of the fourteenth century and the beginning of the fifteenth, we hear more of the rosary in England than anywhere else, and it is particularly true that that form of Our Lady's psalter in which the *Aves* are divided into decades by *Paters* seems first of all to have become general in England.

Thurston examined many *Horae*, including that which was printed for Wynkyn de Worde in 1495. All find a place for the rosary – invariably the Carthusian rosary with 50 *clausulae*. However, there was greater diversity throughout Europe.

The rosary was a devotion enjoined on the students of colleges. In the statutes of Eton (1441), Henry VI orders that

Figure 8.3 The Langdale gold rosary (c. 1500) and the Chatsworth paternoster. A Crown copyright. Reproduced by permission of the Trustees of the Chatsworth Settlement
Source: Rock, D., *The Church of Our Fathers* (1903), p. 112

before the High Mass, in either the church, the cemetery, or the cloister, they shall say, for the remission of the sins committed by the five senses, five decades of the beads with the Creed – thus making up, with what had been said during Matins and the other Hours, the whole fifteen decades.

William Waynflete (1395–1486), Bishop of Winchester, and founder of Magdalen College at Oxford in 1458, says in the statutes of the College:

> We will that the president and each of the fellows of the said college do say in honour and remembrance of the most Blessed Virgin, the mother of our Lord Jesus Christ, with all possible devoutness, on their bended knees, fifty times over, the angelic salutation, together with the Lord's prayer, after every ten rehearsals of the salutation aforesaid.

Thus Waynflete obliges the president and fellows to say each day the five decades.[13] A century earlier, Archbishop Islip, in the statutes of Canterbury Hall (1362), ordered that those who did not say Mass 'should recite fifty "Hail Marys", with "Our Father" and Creed, as is the custom'.

The repetition of a sequence of *Paters* and *Aves*, and the use of a set of beads, embraced a far wider range of devotions in the early sixteenth century than what we should now recognize as rosary devotions. The Lady Margaret, mother of Henry VII, who was famous for her piety, said the Bridgettine rosary or the 'Crown of Our Lady' daily on her knees. It was still in use at the end of the century, for Lady Anne Hungerford's customary meditation on these beads was set out in pictures and verses at the end of John Bucke's *Instruction for the Use of the Beads* in 1589, and it was included in Fr Garnet's *The Societie of the Rosarie*, 1593.

Sir Thomas More

Bridgett recounts a cautionary tale attributed to Sir Thomas
More which demonstrates a certain attitude to the rosary which
is, to say the least, unhelpful – the rosary is not a magical
formula. The story has relevance even today:

There was at Coventry a Franciscan friar of the reformed sort. This
man preached in the city, the suburbs, the neighbourhood, and
villages about, that whosoever should say daily the Psalter of the
Blessed Virgin [i.e. the fifteen decades of the rosary] could never be
lost. The people listened greedily to this easy way of getting to
heaven. The pastor there, an excellent and learned man, though he
thought the saying very foolish, said nothing for a time, thinking
that no harm would come from it, since the people would become
the more devout to God from greater devotion to the Blessed
Virgin. But at last he found his flock infected with such a disease
that the very worst were especially addicted to the rosary for no
other reason than that they promised themselves impunity in
everything; for how could they doubt of heaven, when it was
promised to them with such assurance by so grave a man, a friar
direct from heaven? The pastor then began to warn his flock not to
trust too much in the rosary, even though they said it ten times a
day; that those who should say it well would do an excellent thing,
provided they did not say it with presumption, otherwise they
would do better to omit the prayers altogether, on condition that
they omitted also the crimes which they were committing more
easily under the shelter of these prayers.

When he said this from the pulpit he was heard with
indignation, and everywhere spoken of as an enemy of Our Lady.
Another day the friar mounts the pulpit, and to hit the parish priest
harder takes for his text the words, *Dignare me laudare te, Virgo
sacrata, da mihi virtutem contra hostes tuos* ['Permit me the honour to

praise you, sacred Virgin; grant me valour against your foes']. For they say that Scotus used this text at Paris when disputing on the Immaculate Conception, having been transported there, as they falsely allege, in a moment, from a distance of 300 miles, as the Virgin otherwise would have been in danger. Of course our friar easily convinces men so willing to listen to him that the pastor was as foolish as he was impious.

While the matter was at its hottest, it happened that I arrived at Coventry on a visit to my sister. I had scarcely got off my horse when the question was proposed also to me, whether any one could be damned who should daily recite the rosary? I laughed at the foolish question, but was at once warned that I was doing a dangerous thing; that a most holy and most learned father had preached against those who did so. I pooh-poohed the whole matter as no affair of mine. I was immediately invited to a dinner, and accepted the invitation and went. There enters also an old friar, grave, sour, funereal; a boy follows him with books. I saw that I was in for a quarrel. We sat down, and no time was lost; the question was one proposed by the host. The friar answered just as he had preached. I said nothing; I do not like to meddle in odious and fruitless disputes. At last they asked my opinion. As I was obliged to speak I told them what I thought, but only in a few words and without emphasis. Then the friar pours out a long prepared speech which might have made two sermons. His whole argument hung on certain miracles which he read out from a Mariale and from other books of that kind, which he had had brought to table for greater authority. When at last he had come to an end, I modestly replied that he had said nothing in his whole discourse capable of convincing those who should not admit the truth of those miracles, which they might perhaps deny without abjuring the Christian faith, and that even if they were perfectly true, they did not prove his point. For though you may easily find a king ready to pardon something in an enemy at the prayers of his mother, yet there is nowhere one so great a fool as to promulgate a law by which to encourage the audacity of his subjects against himself by a promise of impunity to traitors, on condition of their paying a certain homage to his mother. Much was said on both sides, but I only succeeded in getting laughed at while he was extolled. The matter reached at last such a height through the depraved dispositions of men who, under colour of piety, favoured their own vice, that it could hardly be calmed down, though the bishop strove to do so with all strength.

I have not related this in order to impute crime to any body of religious, since the same ground produces herbs both wholesome and poisonous, nor do I wish to find fault with the custom of those who salute our Lady, than which nothing can be more beneficial, but because some trust so much in their devotions that they draw from them boldness to sin. It is such things as these that Erasmus censures; if anyone is indignant against him for it, why is he not also indignant with St Jerome?[14]

Cardinal John Fisher

Bridgett also records part of a sermon given by Cardinal John Fisher on the occasion of the funeral of the Lady Margaret, Countess of Richmond and mother of Henry VII:

Every day at her uprising, which commonly was not long after five of the clock, she began certain devotions, and so after them, with one of her gentlewomen, the Matins of our Lady, which kept her to then she came into her closet; where then with her chaplain she said also Matins of the day; and after that, daily heard four or five Masses upon her knees, so continuing in her prayers and devotions unto the hour of dinner, which, of the eating day, was ten of the clock, and upon the fasting day, eleven. After dinner full truly she would go her stations to the altars daily; daily her Dirges and

Commendations she would say, and her Evensong before supper, both of the day and of our Lady, beside many other prayers and Psalters of David throughout the year; and at night before she went to bed she failed not to resort unto her chapel, and there a large quarter of an hour to occupy her devotions. No marvel though all this long time her kneeling was to her painful, and so painful that many a time it caused her back pain and disease. And yet nevertheless daily, when she was in health, she failed not to say the Crown of our Lady, which, after the manner of Rome, containeth sixty-and-three *Aves*, and at every *Ave* to make a kneeling.[15]

A Time of Transition

With the coming of the Reformation, attitudes began to change, as Jan Rhodes[16] tells us. The promise of pardons attached to devotions like the Lady psalter, the repetition of a single prayer – and that in a 'foreign' language – and the use of prayer beads which were often 'special' because they were indulgenced or had been blessed, all these were branded by the Reformers as superstitious.

The Royal Injunctions of 1538 sought to purify the English Church of such abuses. They condemned the 'saying over a number of beads, not understood or minded on'. The reference here is not specifically to the rosary, 'beads' were simply prayers, but rather to the mindless, inattentive repetition of prayers, which was not peculiar to the 1530s: Julian of Norwich had criticized such prayer nearly two centuries earlier. But taken with the other provisions of the 1538 Injunctions, which included condemnation of pilgrimage and the veneration of images and relics, this was an indirect attack on the form of prayer used in the rosary. They also attacked the whole underlying principle of devotion to Our Lady, which was regarded as derogating from the honour due to Christ alone.

A direct consequence of these Injunctions, with their condemnation of images and relics, was the destruction of the best-known English shrines of Our Lady: Walsingham, Willesden, Caversham and many others. They effectively brought to an end all public devotion to Our Lady in England, apart from the brief five-year respite under the Catholic Queen Mary.

In the years following the Royal Injunctions of 1538 the rosary continued to be used by Catholics. In 1570, for instance, a Durham woman was cited before the courts for saying her rosary. She replied 'that she occupied her gaudes as many thousand did'.[17] In more remote areas government legislation made little headway against traditional Catholic practices. Rosaries continued to be used in public in parts of Lancashire in the 1590s, and in 1604 eight people were reported for using them at Eccleston. However, public attitudes hardened against Catholics during 1569–70. They were implicated in the Northern Rising of 1569 and at the same time the flight of Mary Queen of Scots into England gave focus to a potential Catholic rebellion. Then, in 1570, Pope Pius V excommunicated Elizabeth, technically freeing her Catholic subjects from allegiance to her and making them all potential traitors in the eyes of the government.

The anti-Catholic legislation passed by Parliament the following year threatened confiscation of all property and imprisonment during the queen's pleasure for anyone found guilty of bringing into the country prayer beads and other religious objects such as an *Agnus Dei* (these were tokens of the Lamb of God, blessed by the Pope and worn by many Catholics, even in penal times). It was the discovery of an *Agnus Dei* medal that led to the arrest and subsequent martyrdom in 1577 of the first of the seminary priests, Cuthbert Mayne. In 1580 the High Commission sitting at Beverley wanted to know: 'whether any person or persons have brought into this realm any *Agnus Dei*, or any crosses, pictures, beads or such like vain or superstitious [things]', or whether 'any such like thing with intent to be worn' had been received from Rome. When the Vaux house in Warwickshire was raided by government pursuivants in 1593 Fr Garnet reported that they were searching particularly for rosaries, *Agnus Dei* medals, pictures and books, which would have been taken as proof positive of illegal Catholicism.

It was in defiance of the law and in full awareness of the consequences that English Catholics continued to honour Our Lady in her rosary. In some of the larger Catholic establishments there was comparative freedom, intermittently at least. For instance, at Battle in Sussex, Lady Magdalen Montague was accustomed to say three rosaries each day, and she kept the beads by her bedside to use if she woke during the night. Rosaries, together with the Office of the Blessed Virgin Mary and the Jesus psalter, were evidently freely available in the Inglebys' house at Ripley, for the young Mary Ward gave all of them to a young Protestant visitor, who later became a seminary priest. Further evidence of covert proselytism in a recusant household was given by a Durham man, John Nicholson, in 1606. He reported that he had been given crosses, pictures, the Jesus psalter and certain beads to say his prayers with while employed by the Catholic Pudseye family. The danger and the constant threat of betrayal did not apparently deter Catholics from attempting to win converts whenever the circumstances allowed.

English Catholics on the Continent did a good deal to keep their friends in England supplied. Fr Persons SJ spent large sums of money on books, chalices and other religious objects, which he had smuggled into the country. In *A Poor Man's Mite* (1639), the English Benedictine Anthony Batt recalled how he had sent his sister a plain rosary and instructions on how to use it. But English Catholics were not entirely dependent on the Continent for their supplies of rosaries and books. In 1595 an old man named Green, 'who maketh all the beads that lie in little boxes [i.e. rosaries]', was cited at Rowell in Northamptonshire. A couple of years later, Fr John Gerard SJ, while imprisoned in the Tower of London, exercised his hands (damaged by torture) by cutting orange peel into the shape of crosses and stringing them together to make rosaries. There was even a little traffic in the opposite direction. In 1595 Fr Garnet reported that he had in his possession the rosary which Fr Southwell SJ had thrown from the scaffold at his execution. This he would send, together with a fragment of the martyr's knee-bone, to Rome as relics as soon as occasion offered.

With the official silencing of devotion to Our Lady, the rosary acquired a new significance. 'The beads', wrote Fr Garnet, 'must be to our afflicted brethren instead of all manner of armour or weapons.'

The rosary offered some substitute for the Roman Liturgy, which was not available on any regular basis in most places, and enabled Catholics to follow in spirit the seasons of the liturgical year. It could be used in a family group or said privately. Its doctrinal teaching and instruction on prayer and meditation could be extended in books of rosary devotions. But one of the greatest strengths of the rosary was that it was not dependent on books. It could be 'read' by the blind and the illiterate and, as the recusant authors recognized, it was especially suited to the instruction of the 'simpler sort'. It could be used by anyone whenever he wished and nobody was excluded from the benefits conferred by this devotion. The beads must have helped to give the threatened and widely scattered members of the Catholic Church in Elizabethan England a sense of *communitas* and identity: 'Christ's faithful people do use them now commendably as a manifest badge or token of the Roman religion.'

Rosary Books

Two printed rosary books[18] in English survive from before the Reformation, both following the Carthusian model. In *The Rosary of Our Lady* all the prayers were addressed to Our Lady, under a different title in each decade, and sought her intercession.

> It was praise by accumulation in the manner of the fifteenth-century lyric writers such as Lydgate; her titles and 'types' were simply poured forth in a profusion of praise. The final *gaude* began:
>
> > Hail most glorious Virgin, most marvellous in meekness, Princess peerless of true love and kindness; the Queen of heaven, the Lady of the world, the Empress of hell, the contemplation of Angels, the light of grace, the gleaming star of glory, the delectation of hearts ...
>
> and so it continued. It ended with the author's act of personal dedication to Our Lady:
>
> > my heart, dear Lady, under God, most desireth to love thee, which faithfully I offer to thee with whole desire every moment to salute thee.[19]

The other pre-Reformation book was *The Mystic Sweet Rosary of the Faithful Soul*. The 'original' text was published in Antwerp in 1533, under the name of Lanspergius. A later version was edited to make it less offensive to the Reformers.

The prayers were addressed to Christ and the *Ave* was omitted.

The *Paternoster* at the end of each decade was given in English, the only instance of its translation in the sixteenth-century rosary. Scripture quotations were added before all the prayers, even the salutations to the Five Wounds which marked the decades. The only textual references to Our Lady were those demanded by the Gospel narrative. Consequently the articles on her Assumption and Coronation were altered. Yet the magnificent Dürer-like wood-cuts which illustrated each article retained these two mysteries and generally gave far more prominence to her than the text; they had survived from the 'original' edition of Lanspergius. According to the title-page of *The Mystic Sweet Rosary* the illustrations were provided 'that the inward mind might savour the thing that the outward eye beholdeth'.

The Rosary of Our Lady, printed in 1600, was also fully illustrated with good-quality woodcuts. In his preface the editor, Fr Worthington, expressed the hope that 'by diligently viewing and beholding the pictures here placed, everyone may better conceive and consider the Mysteries by them represented, and be perhaps more moved to devotion by sight thereof, than by only reading'. Medieval popular religious instruction had relied heavily on visual representation for a largely illiterate and bookless audience.

The legislation passed under Edward VI and Elizabeth had banished nearly all distinctively Catholic art from the churches where it had been available to public view; Our Lady and the saints were obvious targets for the iconoclastic zeal of the Reformers. Books were the only place where specifically Catholic art could be maintained – illegally. Since the recusant rosary books were particularly intended for the 'simpler sort', illustrations were of great importance.

Wherever possible, the later Elizabethan rosary books were illustrated. In *A Method to Meditate on the Psalter or Great Rosary of our Blessed Lady* (1598), the pictures were made part of the meditation. Each of the fifteen illuminations was to be used to help recall the mystery. John Bucke extended the concept to a more imaginative 'composition of place':

> It is an ancient exercise of devout Christians in time of prayer, and specially in the use of the beads, to set before the eyes of the soul some conceit or imagination of one or other matter contained in the life of our Saviour, or of the Blessed Virgin Mary. And this conceit well imprinted in mind, will keep it from wavering in the vain thoughts, and will make it more attentive and heedful; whereby devotion is sooner kindled, without which prayer yieldeth small fruit.

It was a practice recommended by many sixteenth-century spiritual writers, including St Teresa of Ávila.

The earliest surviving post-Reformation rosary book in English was *A Brief Directory and Plain Way How to Say the Rosary* by one I.M. (perhaps the Carthusian John Mitchell). According to the title-page, it was printed in Bruges in 1576. In fact, it was printed illegally, and at great risk, in London by William Carter. He is known to have printed another ten recusant books. ... It was not long before the government tracked him down and he was put to death in 1584: a reminder of the dangers facing anyone who dared to disseminate Catholic literature in England at that time. ... [importance of these books] to the scattered and persecuted Catholics of Elizabethan England can hardly be exaggerated. Without the doctrinal and spiritual instruction they provided, and the type of personal devotion kindled by the rosary books, the Catholic faith would hardly have survived the sixteenth century under such adverse conditions. ...

Fr Worthington's *Rosary of Our Lady* (1600) offered instruction of another kind. It consisted of 150 sentences, most of them drawn from scripture; there were no imaginative meditations and no prayers. The decades were linked by a biblical narrative and each was accompanied by a good-quality illustration. The preface claims that this 'method' was devised by a priest imprisoned in the Tower of London and deprived of books and beads. This type of scriptural rosary may have appealed to those for whom the English scriptures were still an exciting novelty.[20]

Rosary Confraternities

The rosary confraternities first established in Douai in c. 1470 and Cologne in 1475 met with a great popular response. They were less exclusive, and less spiritually demanding, than some of the religious Third Orders tended to be, but still more spiritual than some of the old religious guilds had become. Their greatest strength was that membership was open to all, men and women, rich and poor, clerics, religious and lay people. It must have been one of the few officially approved Church organizations to have escaped the usual clerical domination of the period. The Society of the Rosary was more than just another local pious association; Fr Garnet described it as 'a general corporation over all the world'. That universality was particularly important to the isolated Catholics of Elizabethan England. Branded as traitors and forced to live as social outcasts, it gave them tangible proof that they were yet members of the Church universal. More immediately it gave a social dimension to what was still largely a private devotion. It is not clear how far the Society of the Rosary was established in England before the Reformation. Fr Garnet suggests that it was not widely known. Perhaps the Marian guilds were more alive than their continental counterparts, and better able to provide for the spiritual and social needs of their members. But in any case, Marian associations were virtually outlawed in England after 1538, apart from the brief respite under Mary Tudor.

In Elizabeth's England the rosary became the 'badge of Catholics', being produced by martyrs on the scaffold and by such intrepid witnesses to the Catholic faith as Mary Ward. Many ordinary men and women were willing to face the risk – an almost certain risk – of being cited before the courts for daring to continue to use their rosaries in public. It is unlikely that it was ever recited in common except behind locked doors, or in the comparative security of one of the great Catholic houses: the Montagues' at Battle or the Inglebys' at Ripley, for example. There it perhaps served as a substitute for the regular liturgical round. In a letter to his sister, Fr Garnet stated that the rosary enabled English Catholics to follow in spirit the calendar of the Roman Church, even though they were so often deprived of Mass.

Fr Henry Garnet SJ

Fr Garnet was one of the most important figures in the propagation of the rosary among the Catholics of Elizabethan England. He had been in Rome when, in 1573, Pope Gregory XIII had refounded the Feast of the Rosary that had been established the previous year in thanksgiving for the Christian victory over the Turks at Lepanto in 1571. During his time in Europe he had observed many confraternities of the rosary among the laity, associations among the clergy, and in colleges. Before leaving Rome for the English Mission in 1587, he had received from the Dominican Master-General faculties (normally reserved to that order) to establish rosary confraternities and admit English members. He also gained dispensations from some of the regulations, notably that the name of each member should be inscribed in the society's book, as it would have been invaluable evidence in the hands of the government. 'This manner of enrolling being not convenient in our country for respects too well known: it sufficeth that after the names be once taken of such as enter, they be torn [up].'

From the beginning, the rosary had been recognized as a

powerful weapon against heresy. Fr Garnet wrote from his own experience of England: 'How general a deluge of heresy and of all manner of iniquity our miserable country hath these late years sustained, we yet feel by the experience of the calamity thereof; and it is pitiful to remember how many souls have already perished thereby.' It was out of concern for the salvation of his countrymen and the desire to strengthen Catholics in their faith that Fr Garnet sought to promote the Society of the Rosary.

He compiled what is in effect a handbook for the society, called *The Societie of the Rosarie* (1593). A summary life of Our Lady served to explain Marian traditions and doctrines. There were several chapters on the origins, rules, obligations and privileges of the society. The main part of the book was about the rosary, explaining what it was and outlining the many different ways of performing the devotion.

Those who wrote, compiled, printed and distributed the illegal rosary books in Elizabethan times had a great love for their country and a great concern for their countrymen's eternal salvation. During this period of history, the rosary proved to be one of the Catholic Church's most effective weapons. Individual devotion was aroused and Catholic truth and practice maintained. For many the simple string of beads became a lifeline, uniting them to the Church and bringing them into a living relationship with Christ and his Mother Mary.

Indulgences

We learn of another book from Thomas Bridgett:[21] *A Chayne of Twelye Links*, a treatise on indulgences translated from the Italian. It appeared in 1617 with the Preface dated 20 October

1605, but without name of writer or place of printing. The translator says in his Preface that

> whereas Pope Gregory XIII of blessed memory seeing the desolation of our country, granted certain Indulgences to Grains [rosary beads], Crosses, and Medals, thereby to animate not only the remnant of Catholics which were left in England, but also to stir up the Catholic people in other countries to pray for the reduction of the said Island and reunion thereof with the See Apostolic, from whence we first received the faith; and for that the same Indulgences have ever since continued and have been now lately confirmed by word of mouth by him that sitteth in St Peter's Chair, Paulus the Fifth, this very year 1605, the 30th of May. For this cause it seemed to me convenient to translate this little sequent discourse.

The indulgences are said to have been granted 'at the request of the English Seminary'. As these grants are very interesting and little known, the first three are given by way of example:

1. They that have any of these grains, in what place so ever they be, gain all the Indulgences granted unto the Society of the Blessed Trinity in Rome, if they do fulfil that which is there commanded. But those who do obtain the Indulgences following that have devoted themselves to the restoring of the Catholic faith in England, or labour any way for that cause, or pray for England.

2. Whosoever having one of these hallowed grains, and being contrite, with a full purpose at the least to confess and communicate as soon as he can commodiously, shall recite the Corone or Rosary of our Blessed Lady; or shall read the Passion of our Saviour, or the seven Psalms, or the Litanies, praying for the Pope's Holiness, or for the state of the Catholic

Church, or for the propagation of the Catholic faith, or for the conversion of England, Ireland, and Scotland, or of heretics, shall gain, for so often as he doth this, a Plenary Indulgence.

3. Plenary Indulgence for those who communicate on certain great feasts, including those of St Thomas, the Archbishop of Canterbury, of St Edmund, of St Gregory the first, Apostle of England, or in the feast of the patrons of the diocese or place.

The Reformation in England

The seeds of the Reformation[22] in England begin with the Statutes of Provisors and Praemunire. The Provisors Act of 1351 provided that 'the King and other lords shall present unto Benefices of their own, and not the Bishop of Rome'. The second Act, passed in 1353, imposed the penalties of 'Praemunire for suing in a foreign realm, or impeaching of Judgment given [*sc.* in the English courts]'. 'Praemunire' is the title given to those statutes designed to protect the rights claimed by English Crown against the Papacy (repealed by the Criminal Law Act of 1967). So it was the beginning of a struggle for power against the Papacy which was to become a major issue when Henry VIII wished to have his own way in his matrimonial affairs. During the second half of the fourteenth century, the Lollards, followers of John Wycliffe (1330–84), proposed reform, basing their teaching on personal faith, divine election and the fact that the scriptures were the sole authority in religion. They attacked the priesthood and the Papacy, and denied transubstantiation and other Catholic teachings. The first complete English translation of the Bible was published in 1382–84 under the influence of Wycliffe.

Henry VIII, a convinced traditionalist in both doctrine and Church government, accomplished the overthrow of Papal Supremacy and the dissolution of the monasteries largely in support of short-term political ends and the extension of royal controls. Despite his opposition, reforming continental doctrines and native heresy became more widespread. During the reign of Edward VI the political calculation and influence of Thomas Cranmer led to a greater alteration of doctrine and liturgy, culminating in the Prayer Book of 1552 and the Forty-Two Articles of 1553. During the reign of Elizabeth I, Calvinist doctrinal views came to be widely held, but demands for institutional reform were resisted by the Crown and its advisers. The English Reformation thus grafted elements of Reformed theology and worship onto a traditional Church structure.

There was a strong antipathy to those things which had their origin in Papal teaching and appeared not to be in conformity with scripture. Among those things was the rosary, and we can turn to Thomas Bridgett for an insight into how this affected the Catholics of England during the Reformation. The use of the beads in England was universal in the fourteenth and fifteenth centuries. It survived the Reformation and was, with the greatest difficulty, abolished.

> The attachment of the people to the use of the beads appears in the articles exhibited against Ferrar, Bishop of St Davids. This man, who suffered as a Protestant under Mary Tudor, was accused as a favourer of superstition under Edward. Among other charges, 'Whereas superstitious praying upon beads is not only ungodly, but reproved in the king's majesty's injunctions, the said bishop, meeting many with beads in their hands, never rebuked any of them.' To which he answered:
>
>> That in the time of the rebellion in Devonshire and Cornwall threatening to come into Wales, he teaching the people the true form of prayer according to God's holy Word, and declaring the prayer upon beads to be vain and

superstitious, yet durst not, for fear of tumult, forcibly take from any man his beads without authority. And touching the not reproving such as he should meet wearing beads, he remembereth not that he hath so done, unless it were in the rebellion-time, at which time he durst not rebuke such offenders.

[. . .]

When the Catholic religion had been restored for a few days in the churches of Durham in the year 1569, by the Earls of Northumberland and Westmoreland, proceedings of the most barbarous character were instituted against even the simple people who had taken no further part than to join in the reinstated worship.

> That by the laws of England, not only Mass, Matins, song, private confession, procession, hallowing of water, bread, and other superstitious Latin services, etc., devised *of late years* (!) by the Bishop of Rome, *ancient* (!) enemy to the crown of England, with all his usurped authority, for most just cause is utterly abolished, but also all books and ornaments belonging to the same service is or ought to be defaced and rent, and especially all altar, holy-water stones, and beads, as monuments of idolatry and superstition, so that no memory of the same do remain in walls, pavements, or elsewhere, within any church or house within this realm.

Yet, notwithstanding this,

> by the instigation of the devil and open contempt of the queen's majesty's godly proceedings, divers evil-disposed persons did unlawfully erect an altar and holy-water stone, and came to Mass, Matins, Evensong, procession, and like idolatrous service, thereat kneeling, bowing, knocking, and showing suchlike reverent gesture, used praying on beads,

confession or shriving to a priest, took holy water and holy bread, etc., etc., to the peril and damnation of their own souls and slander of God and Christian people: therefore by reason of these premises A. B. is a stubborn and rebellious hinderer of God's word and Christ's religion and the queen's proceedings, and a notorious favourer of idolatry, superstition, and popish Latin service. [Surtees Society Public. for 1845, p. 131, in Bridgett, pp. 211–12.]

From the deposition of various witnesses it appears that immense crowds flocked to the Mass, delighting to sign themselves with holy water once more, to taste blessed bread, and to be reconciled with the Church of Rome. One poor woman acknowledges that 'she occupied her gauds as many thousands did'.

But the laws then in force were not considered stringent enough. Two years later by statute (13 Elizabeth c. 2) the pains of praemunire were extended to all who should import or receive any *Agnus Dei*, crosses, or beads, etc., blessed by the Pope or by any one holding authority from him – these penalties being, that after conviction the defendant should be out of the sovereign's protection, and his lands and tenements, goods and chattels, forfeited to the sovereign, and his body remain in prison at the sovereign's pleasure. Nor was the statute left as a dead letter.

In 1577 Mr Tregian was condemned to perpetual imprisonment for having received an *Agnus Dei* from the martyred priest Cuthbert Maine. Lastly, in 1616 Thomas Atkinson was convicted of being a priest, on no other evidence than that of beads found in his possession, and executed at York. This venerable man was more than 70 years old when he was hanged, disembowelled and quartered. Challoner adduces contemporary evidence that God glorified His confessor by visible miracles during his imprisonment, and also that Our Blessed Lady appeared to him, and revealed to him the death by which he should glorify her Son, as he made known to some fellow prisoners. Notwithstanding all this, the rosary continued a favourite devotion during the penal times; indeed, confraternities of the rosary were founded and maintained.[23]

The Rosary in England during the Eighteenth and Nineteenth Centuries

Little seems to have been written about the rosary in eighteenth-century England. Rosaries would have been found in the homes of recusant families, and the practice was certainly known to Richard Challoner (1691–1781). The devotion was in regular use among the English Catholics at Douai in 1712. The two popular devotions, Benediction and the rosary, were included in Challoner's spiritual classic, *The Garden of the Soul*, written in 1740. Challoner was probably the most notable English Catholic of the age. A convert from Presbyterianism at the age of thirteen, he entered Douai in 1705 where he spent the next 25 years. In 1730 he returned to London and in 1741 was consecrated coadjutor bishop to Dr Petre in the London District. The next three years were spent visiting the five counties that constituted the district, but he did not attempt to visit the overseas missions, namely Maryland, Pennsylvania and some of the West Indian islands. He wrote on the English martyrs, but he will be remembered for his revision of the Douay Bible and Rheims New Testament. He succeeded Dr Petre as Vicar Apostolic in 1758. Much of his life was spent in hiding, owing to the state of the law, and often he had hurriedly to change his lodgings to escape the Protestant informers, who were anxious to earn the government reward of a hundred pounds for the conviction of a priest. He and the London priests were continually harassed in this way. This was remedied by the Catholic Relief Act of 1778, by which priests were no longer liable to imprisonment for life. Reaction to this concession led to the Gordon Riots two years later. Challoner's private life was marked by extraordinary mortification. He had the gift of prayer in a marked degree, and on two occasions at least he spoke prophetic words, which later events verified. For these reasons, as much as for the office he held so long, he has been venerated by English Catholics. He died following a stroke, and was buried in the vault of his friend Bryan Barrett, at Milton in Berkshire.[24]

The French Revolution (1789) was to bring great difficulties for the clergy in France, and eventually lead to the closure of Douai College and the other Catholic institutions in 1793–94. The migration of Catholic priests, religious and students to England was to influence and strengthen Catholic life in nineteenth-century England. The Emancipation Act of 1829 allowed for Irish and English Catholics to enter Parliament and began a new phase in religious freedom. The Oxford Movement (1833–45), led by John Keble and John Henry Newman, marked an Anglican religious revival. (Newman converted to Rome in 1845, but others converted to bear the torch.) The Irish potato famine of 1845–49 caused 1.5 million Irish people to emigrate, many to Britain, with a profound effect on English Catholic Church life. From about this time, though not specifically caused by the Irish immigration, there was an upsurge in Catholic devotional practice. This was manifest in the popularity of the *Quarant' ore* (the Forty Hours devotion), Stations of the Cross, recitation of the rosary, novenas and Corpus Christi processions. Undoubtedly the two most popular devotions were Benediction of the Blessed Sacrament and Public Rosary: they grew in parallel and were often combined in the same service – a practice that would last through to the 1960s as 'Rosary, Sermon and Benediction', it being the common Sunday evening service.

The Catholic hierarchy was re-established in 1850, with Wiseman as its first Metropolitan. During the fifteen years of his episcopacy the number of priests increased from 500 to 1500, and 55 monasteries were established. The English hierarchy sought a devotional middle ground, a compromise between popular feeling on the one hand and some clerical over-enthusiasm on the other. There was a marked contrast between the spiritual stance of Newman, who reflected the restrained attitude of the old Catholic recusant families of England, and Fr Faber, who enthusiastically welcomed a more exuberant practice typical of the Italian Church. It has sometimes been supposed that such Catholic devotions were imposed on a reluctant English people by ultramontane clergy, but there is little evidence for that.[25]

John Henry Newman and Frederick William Faber

The writings of those two outstanding converts to Roman Catholicism in the nineteenth century, John Henry Newman and Frederick William Faber, make reference to the rosary and give an insight into the spirituality of the times. It is well to recall that the Anglican Church from which they came taught in Article 22 of the Thirty-Nine Articles: 'The Romish Doctrine concerning Purgatory, Pardons, Worshipping and Adoration, as well of Images as of Reliques, and also invocation of Saints, is a fond thing vainly invented, and grounded upon no warranty of Scripture, but rather repugnant to the Word of God.' Invocation to Mary and the saints was not an acceptable practice for the Anglican Church.

The Venerable John Henry Cardinal Newman (1801–90) had a significant influence on religious life in both the Anglican Church and Roman Catholic Church in England. A Fellow of Oriel College (the House of the Blessed Mary the Virgin in Oxford) and Vicar of St Mary the Virgin (the University

THE USE OF PRAYER BEADS IN ENGLAND

Church), Newman was noted for his preaching and his spirituality. He and John Keble were the leading lights of the Oxford Movement, which grew out of a progressive decline in Church life and a spread of 'liberalism' in theology. The Emancipation Act of 1829 allowed Irish and English Catholics to enter Parliament and inaugurated a new phase in religious freedom. This together with the Reform Act of 1832 gave rise to anxiety in the Anglican Church, provoking Keble to preach on 'National Apostasy' in Oxford, July 1833. In September of the same year John Henry Newman published the first of the *Tracts for the Times* in defence of the Church of England and 'against Popery and Dissent'. These two were joined by E. B. Pusey and others. Their initiatives began an Anglican revival identified as the Oxford Movement (1833–45). Newman's patristic studies led him to an appreciation of the development of doctrine and eventually he was received into the Roman Catholic Church in 1845 by Blessed Dominic Barberi at Littlemore. He was ordained in Rome in 1847 and joined the Oratory of St Philip Neri. On his return to England he founded an Oratory at Maryvale in 1848 which moved to Birmingham in 1849 and to Edgbaston in 1852. If Newman had any initial difficulties in adopting Roman devotional practices it would seem from the following two quotations that he did come to appreciate the rosary.

In mid-June 1848 Newman pointed out to the Marquise de Salvo that no Marian devotion was strictly obligatory, but that he himself had found great spiritual pleasure in reciting the rosary: 'for my own feelings nothing is more delightful than the contemplation of the mysteries of the Incarnation, under the invocation, so to call it, of her who was the human instrument of it so that she who ministered to the Gracious Dispensation itself, should minister also to our adoring thought of it.'[26] On Sunday, 5 October 1879, Newman preached to the boys at

Oscott College from the text: 'They found Mary and Joseph, and the Infant lying in a manger':

You know that today we keep the Feast of the Holy Rosary, and I propose to say to you what occurs to me on this great subject. You know how that devotion came about; how, at a time when heresy was very widespread, and had called in the aid of sophistry, that can so powerfully aid infidelity against religion, God inspired St Dominic to institute and spread this devotion. It seems so simple and easy, but you know God chooses the small things of the world to humble the great. Of course, it was first of all, for the poor and simple, but not for them only, for everyone who has practised the devotion knows that there is in it a soothing sweetness that there is in nothing else. It is difficult to know God by our own power, because He is incomprehensible. He is invisible to begin with, and therefore incomprehensible. We can in some way know him, for even among the heathens there were some who had learned many truths about Him; but even they found it hard to conform their lives to their knowledge of Him. And so in His mercy He has given us a revelation of Himself by coming amongst us, to be one of ourselves, with all the relations and qualities of humanity, to gain us over. He came down from Heaven and dwelt amongst us, and died for us. All these things are in the Creed, which contains the chief things that He has revealed to us about Himself. Now the great power of the rosary lies in this, that it makes the Creed into a prayer; of course, the Creed is in some sense a prayer and a great act of homage to God; but the Rosary gives us the great truths of His life and death to meditate upon, and brings them nearer to our hearts. And so we contemplate all the great mysteries of His life and His birth in the manger; and so too the mysteries of His suffering and His glorified life. But even Christians, with all their knowledge of God, have usually more awe than love of Him, and the special virtue of the Rosary lies in the special way in which it looks at these mysteries; for with all our thoughts of Him are mingled thoughts of His Mother, and in the relations between Mother and Son we have set before us the Holy Family, the home in which God lived. Now the family is, even humanly considered, a sacred thing; how much more the family bound together by supernatural ties, and, above all, that in which God dwelt with His Blessed Mother. This is what I should most wish you to remember in future years.[27]

Fr Frederick William Faber (1814–63), theologian and prolific writer, is remembered today for his hymns, but he too had a marked influence on Victorian Catholic devotional practice. He was born at Calverley, a small town in West Yorkshire, and educated at Harrow and Oxford, where in 1837 he was elected to a Fellowship at University College. His upbringing was Calvinist, but at Oxford he came under the influence of John Henry Newman. On 17 November 1845 he was received into the Roman Catholic Church, a few weeks after Newman. With other converts he formed a small community, the 'Brothers of the Will of God', at Birmingham. In 1847 he was ordained priest, and in 1848 (with his companions) joined the Oratory of St Philip Neri, recently introduced into England by Newman. In 1849 Faber became head of the London Oratory.

Faber wrote a book concerning the Seven Sorrows of Mary, to which he was deeply devoted: *At the Foot of the Cross or Mary's Dolours*. That he had a devotion to the rosary is shown by the following quotation from his work on the spiritual life, *Growth in Holiness*:

I cannot conceive a man being spiritual who does not habitually say the Rosary. It may be called the queen of indulgenced devotions. First consider its importance, as a specially Catholic devotion, as so peculiarly giving us a Catholic turn of mind by keeping Jesus and Mary perpetually before us, and as a singular help to final perseverance, if we continue the recital of it, as various revelations show. Next consider its institution by St Dominic in 1214, by revelation, for the purpose of combating heresy, and the success which attended it. Its matter and form are not less striking. Its matter consists of the Pater, the Ave, and the Gloria, whose authors are our Blessed Lord Himself, St Gabriel, St Elizabeth, the council of Ephesus, and the whole Church, led in the west by St Damasus. Its form is a complete abridgment of the Gospel, consisting of fifteen mysteries in decades, expressing the three great phases of the work of redemption, joy, sorrow, and glory. Its peculiarity is the next attractive feature about it. It unites mental with vocal prayer. It is a devotional compendium of theology. It is an efficacious practice of the presence of God. It is one chief channel of the traditions of the Incarnation among the faithful. It shows the true nature of devotion to our Blessed Lady, and is a means of realising the communion of saints. Its ends are the love of Jesus, reparation to the Sacred Humanity for the outrages of heresy, and a continual affectionate thanksgiving to the Most Holy Trinity for the benefit of the Incarnation. It is sanctioned by the Church, by indulgences, by miracles, by the conversion of sinners, and by the usage of the saints. See also how much the method of reciting it involves. We should first make a picture of the mystery, and always put our Blessed Lady into the picture; for the Rosary is hers. We should couple some duty or virtue with each mystery; and fix beforehand on some soul in Purgatory to whom to apply the vast indulgences. Meanwhile, we must not strain our minds, or be scrupulous; for to say the Rosary well is quite a thing which requires learning. Remember always, as the Raccolta teaches, that the fifteenth mystery is the coronation of Mary, and not merely the glory of the saints. Our beads land us and leave us at the feet of Mary Crowned.[28]

Faber's understanding of the rosary is summed up in his *Notes on Doctrinal Subjects* derived from his sermon notes for Rosary Sunday:

I. The position which the Rosary occupies in the Church.
    1. It is not a special devotion, but unites all devotions.
    2. It distinguishes no order, but all orders.
    3. It is to the laity almost what office is to the clergy.
    4. A true Catholic mind can hardly now be formed without it.
    5. It is distinguished above all other devotions by the approbation of the Church.
II. The Rosary viewed as an instrument of power in itself.
    1. Its peculiar power on earth in forming character, so that it is a Catholic touchstone.
    2. Its influence in Heaven shewn from its being revealed.
    3. Its influence in Purgatory from the immensity of its indulgences.
    4. As a profession of faith also.
    5. As a shield against many temptations.
III. It is also an instrument of power as a teacher.
    1. It illustrates the position of Our Lady to Our Lord, and is another way of looking at their Mysteries.
    2. It teaches also how she is a way to Him.
    3. Also it is what she did all her life herself: she rose to great heights by incessant meditation of Jesus.
    4. Therefore it shows us what she wishes us to do; it is her testament, as the Holy Eucharist is the testament of Jesus.
    5. Hence it is the truest means of loving her; for love consists, (1) in obedience; and (2) in imitation.

In consequence of all these blessings the devil makes the rosary a special subject of temptations, weariness, contempt, and the like. Persevere in it, and it will itself be the chain of your own final perseverance.[29]

133

Notes

1. Edmund Waterton, Old English Devotions, *The Month*, 20 (April 1874): 515.
2. Jan Rhodes, The Rosary in Sixteenth-Century England (I and II), *Mount Carmel*, 31/4 (1983): 180–91; 32/1 (1984): 4–17.
3. Thomas E. Bridgett, *Our Lady's Dowry: How England Gained that Title*, 3rd edn (London: Burns & Oates, 1903), p. 204.
4. Book of Common Prayer, Article 22.
5. Jan Rhodes, The Rosary in Sixteenth-Century England (I and II).
6. Catherine Oakes, The Scales: An Iconographic Motif of Justice, Redemption and Intercession, *MARIA: A Journal of Marian Studies*, 1 (August 2000): 11–31.
7. Andrew Breeze, The Virgin's Rosary and St Michael's Scales, *Studia Celtica*, 24 (1991): 91–8.
8. Peter Huyck, personal communication.
9. Bridgett, *Our Lady's Dowry*, pp. 205–8.
10. Edmund Waterton, *Pietas Mariana Britannica*, p. 166. See also p. 162, note 156: *Memorials of London and London Life in the Thirteenth, Fourteenth, and Fifteenth Centuries: Extracted from Early Archives of the City of London* by H. T. Riley (published by the Corporation of London, 1868), p. 20.
11. Waterton, *Pietas Mariana Britannica*, p. 166.
12. Herbert Thurston, The Rosary amongst the Carthusians, *The Month*, 96 (1900): 516.
13. Daniel Rock, *The Church of Our Fathers*, Vol. 3, ed. G. W. Hart and W. H. Frere (London: John Murray, 1903), p. 267. Originally published 1849.
14. Bridgett, *Our Lady's Dowry*, p. 144. See footnote: 'Not found in the Latin works of Sir Thomas More. It was published in 1520 by Froben, and has been reprinted by Josten in the Appendices to his Life of Erasmus (iii 387).'
15. Bridgett, *Our Lady's Dowry*, p. 161. See note 17: *A Mornynge Remembrance had at the Months Mind of the noble Princess Margaret &c.*, by the Right Revd Father in God John Fisher, Bishop of Rochester.
16. Jan Rhodes, The Rosary in Sixteenth-Century England (I).
17. *'Gaudes'*, derived from the Latin *gaudia*, meaning 'joys', and often used of the five large beads of the rosary.

18. Jan Rhodes, The Rosary in Sixteenth-Century England (II).
19. Ibid., p. 6.
20. Ibid., pp. 7–13.
21. Bridgett, *Our Lady's Dowry*, pp. 491–2.
22. Reformation; Provisors; Lollardy, *Oxford Dictionary of the Christian Church*.
23. Bridgett, *Our Lady's Dowry*, pp. 210–13.
24. Edwin Burton, Challoner, *Catholic Encyclopedia*, Vol. III (1908) and Bernard Ward, Douai, *Catholic Encyclopedia*, Vol. V (1909).
25. Mary Heimann, *Catholic Devotion in Victorian England* (Oxford: Clarendon Press, 1995).
26. Stanley L. Jaki, *Newman Challenge* (Grand Rapids, MI: Eerdmans, 2000), p. 92. See ref.: Letters and Diaries, Vol. II, 11 June 1848, pp. 217–18.
27. John H. Newman, *Sayings of Cardinal Newman* (Dublin: Carraig Books, 1976; facsimile reprint), pp. 44–6.
28. Frederick W. Faber, *Growth in Holiness* (London: Richardson, 1855), pp. 274–6.
29. Frederick W. Faber, *Notes on Doctrinal Subjects*, Vol. I (London: Richardson, 1866), p. 307.

9

The Rosary in Ireland

Early Years

The rosary has been dubbed the 'Irish catechism', suggesting that it was of considerable importance to the people of Ireland during the troubles of the Reformation period when the Catholic faith was under attack. Peter O'Dwyer O. Carm. has made a detailed study of the history of devotion to Mary in Ireland. In his monograph: *Towards a History of Irish Spirituality*, he gives an overview of Irish history, and in his book *Mary: A History of Devotion in Ireland*, traces the development of Marian devotion.

Dealing with the history of Christianity in Ireland from the earliest times, O'Dwyer shows how conflict with England grew from the time of the Norman invasion. In respect of the Reformation, he suggests that it had little success in Ireland. The religious conservatism of the people, the fact that the new religion was associated with an alien government and efforts of the preachers of the Counter-Reformation all helped to make both Anglo-Irish and Gaelic Irish stronger in their adherence to Catholicism. The Reformation was noticeable only in towns and in the Pale in its early years. This is not to say that the Irish did not experience persecution. They suffered and many were martyred. The situation in northern Ireland was made particularly difficult by the policy of colonization or plantation. Presbyterianism in Ireland began in 1610 with the plantation of Ulster by King James I, whose aim was to build a strong Protestant population that would support his policies. He therefore provided land that had belonged to the Irish for Scottish and English settlers. Thousands of Scots responded to the offer of land, but their situation in Ireland was often difficult. They were resented by the Irish Catholics, and the English government's policies towards them were inconsistent. The southern counties remained faithful to the Catholic religion.

According to O'Dwyer, the years 1560–1600 seem to be the decades when the rosary became widely practised in Ireland.[1] That it was known in Ireland before that date is suggested by a sculpture at Jerpoint (c. 1400) showing a figure with a rosary. It is said that the Anglo-Norman community used little rosaries of eleven beads (one *Pater* and ten *Aves*). There is a record of a clandestine Mass celebrated by Fr Henry Fitzsimons SJ in a house in Dublin in 1598. After the Mass, the family were received into the Sodality of Our Lady, which he established there and in other homes. Perhaps it was the spread of the Sodality which gave grounds for the belief that the family rosary grew in popularity in Ireland during the period 1560–1600.[2]

The Seventeenth and Eighteenth Centuries

Indications of the spiritual life may be found in many texts. Fr Geoffrey Keating's *Saltair Mhuire* (1610–12) elaborates on the value and manner of saying the rosary. Each of the fifteen mysteries is to be preceded by a short meditation, and each Hail Mary by a short enlightening scriptural sentence. By way of example, before the tenth *Ave* of the first Joyful Mystery: 'the consecrated virgin answered: "I am the servant of the Lord, let

what you have said be done to me." And then the word was
made man and God and man lived with us in one divine
Person.' This would seem to indicate that the scripture rosary
was well known in the seventeenth century.[3] Each set of
mysteries finishes with the Creed and a prayer.

Following the destruction of statues of Our Lady by decree
of the Royal Commission of 1639 the people came to rely even
more on the rosary beads. Father Thomas Aquinas ODC was
led to his execution (c. 1640) with a crucifix and rosary in his
hand, and he chanted the litany as he prepared for death.
Brother Angelus Haly ODC did likewise. Brother Peter of the
Mother of God, while in prison, invited his fellow-prisoners to
say the rosary and litanies with him. In 1641 Conor Maguire,
who was condemned to death, had a rosary in his prison. The
Provincial Council of Armagh, which was held at Kells in 1642,
directed that the people say the rosary every evening for the
needs of the country for the following year.[4] The decrees of the
Council of Trent were beginning to influence the clergy, and a
considerable effort to re-educate the people was made in the
first half of the seventeenth century to make up for the lack of
preaching and instruction during the time of persecution. The
title 'Rosary Fathers', given to the Dominicans, seems to date
from around the middle of the seventeenth century. Some old
Irish amber beads with their silver tubular crosses, often called
Galway rosaries, also date from this time. Galway, Limerick,
Cork, Waterford, Dublin and Kinsale are known to have been
centres of rosary manufacture. The amber probably came from
Spain. All these ports, except Kinsale, had a Dominican
monastery.[5]

An oath of abjuration was prescribed by the government in
1658. Part of the oath involved rejection of devotion to Mary:
'I firmly believe and avow that no reverence is due to the
Virgin Mary or to any other saint in heaven, and that no

petition or adoration can be addressed to them without idolatry.'[6] In 1680 Oliver Plunkett, Archbishop of Armagh, was imprisoned, but was allowed retain his missal and rosary. In his last speech before his execution at Tyburn, on 11 July 1681, he said: 'I beseech your divine majesty by the merits of Christ and the intercession of His Blessed Mother and all the holy angels and saints to forgive me my sins and to grant my soul eternal rest.'[7]

An Act of 1704 to prevent the further growth of 'Popery' declared that the invocation or adoration of the Virgin Mary, as used in the Church of Rome, was idolatrous. Despite this and the prohibition of Mass, which was also incorporated in the Act, Sister Conception Martin, a Poor Clare nun in Galway, made a set of vestments in 1712 with a picture of the Immaculate Conception on them. These are still preserved.[8]

In his references to the Church in Ireland in the eighteenth century Fr John Brady cites an interesting incident in 1745 which relates that the Pretender's eldest son was burned in effigy at Youghal 'with a bundle of rosarys (or padareens) hung on his nose' to show his obedience to the Pope.[9] Rosaries were on sale publicly from about 1750, and rosary confraternities were also developing. In 1747 some churches had sung Vespers and Benediction in the afternoon on Sundays. In 1761 the Dominicans in Dublin had a sermon in Irish at the 7 a.m. Mass and one in English at the 10 a.m. Mass. There was Benediction at noon and in the afternoon Vespers and the rosary and sermon. By this time, owing to the lessening interest in religious matters in the eighteenth century, opposition to Catholic faith and practice was somewhat half-hearted and a more *laissez-faire* attitude prevailed.

During the 1798 Rising, the rosary was said by the old men, girls and children while the battles were being fought. While being hotly pursued in 1801, Michael Dwyer went to some of his friends in Wexford. He managed to return to his father's house on Christmas Eve. Luke Cullen ODC takes up the story: 'When the family prepared for night-prayer, he [Michael Dwyer] as usual read the litanies and gave out the Rosary, and this was his custom particularly in Lent and Advent, and on other vigils of all the principal feasts of the Church.'[10]

The Nineteenth Century

Just as the nineteenth century saw a development and propagation of devotion to Our Lady in Europe it was natural that ideas and practices would be brought back to Ireland by Irish Catholics who visited or lived on the Continent. By 1814 we find Fr Young promoting devotion to Mary on the first Saturday of the month in the parish of St Michan's in Dublin. It was known as the devotion in honour of her Immaculate Heart and was popular in France during the preceding century. The following year he was stationed in Francis Street, where he introduced a daily rosary and evening prayers at 7 p.m. and the Office of Our Lady on Wednesday evenings.[11]

When Daniel O'Connell was elected to Parliament he appeared before the House on 13 April 1829 and was presented with the old oath denying transubstantiation and the invocation of the Blessed Virgin and other saints. O'Connell refused to take the oath. The objectionable sections were taken out and in February 1830 he took the new oath and his seat in Parliament. Sometimes he said his rosary in the precincts of the House before an important debate on an Irish matter.[12]

After Catholic emancipation external forms of devotion to Mary could more easily be practised. We find a sodality and procession in her honour in the monastery and grounds of the Christian Brothers at Mount Sion in Waterford in c. 1831–32. We also possess the Minute Book of the Belfast Rosary Society from 1831 to 1858. The society had been formed in May 1794, under the guidance of Fr Hugh O'Donnell, parish priest of Belfast. Its members met every Sunday evening in St Mary's, the only Catholic church in the city, for the purpose of saying the rosary in common.[13]

Daniel O'Connell fixed the date for his Tara Monster Meeting for the Repeal of the Union on 15 August 1843. Six altars were erected and a succession of priests said Mass throughout the morning. During his imprisonment in 1844, subsequent to the Clontarf meeting, the rosary was frequently offered in public for his release. In fact he attributed his liberation to the novena held throughout the country for the Marian feast day of 8 September 1844.[14]

Marian devotion, which had always been strong, became more personal and developed very appreciably after the apparition at Lourdes in 1858, and was perhaps further enhanced by the events at Knock in 1879. In 1867 Fenian outlaws said the rosary. Speaking of the capture of Peter O'Neill Crowley in Kilclooney Wood near Mitchelstown, County Cork, A. M. Sullivan in *The Story of Ireland* writes:

The fugitives defended themselves bravely, but eventually Crowley was shot down, and brought a corpse into the neighbouring town. Around his neck (inside his shirt) hung a small silver crucifix and a medal of the Immaculate Conception. A bullet had struck the latter and dinged it into a cup shape. Another had struck the crucifix. It turned out that the fugitives, during their concealment in the wood, never omitted compliance with the customary Lenten devotions. Every night they knelt round the embers of their watch fire, and recited aloud the Rosary, and at the moment of their surprise by the soldiery they were at their morning prayers.[15]

The Easter Rising and its Aftermath

O'Dwyer indicates[16] that there is abundant evidence of a continuing devotion among the Irish people to Mary during the early part of the twentieth century in prose and in poetry, in prayer and in action. Just as devotion to Mary was strong in the difficult days of persecution, so we find a tremendous reliance on the rosary in the days of the war of independence. He quotes from the book *Ireland's Loyalty to Mary* by Fr Augustine OFM Cap, who was active at that time, giving instances of how those involved in the Easter Rising (24 April 1916) in Dublin had recourse to the rosary:

> When all hope was practically gone they still turned to the Rosary. In a scene described by Julia Grennan, just before the Volunteers in the GPO surrendered, she says: 'A number of men gathered in the back drawing-room [of a house in Moore Street] and knelt to say the Rosary. This is a picture that will never fade from my memory. They knelt, holding the rifles they were so soon to surrender in their left hands, their beads in their right. Tears ran down many a cheek and the responses were said chokingly ... We then marched out. The GPO was still burning fiercely.'[17]

And further:

> In May 1918 the Irish hierarchy recommended a novena of prayer in honour of Our Lady of Lourdes to secure general and domestic peace. The Rosary was to form part of the appeal to the mother of God. Joe Kenny, who was arrested in 1920, wrote:
>
> > In the middle of June 1920, when arrested by the English military, I was taken to Cork gaol. There the Rosary was recited daily, in the evening, by all the prisoners, each standing at the window where they could all join in the

responses. It was given out and answered in Irish on all occasions, and during the day most prisoners carried their beads around their necks. Later, during the hunger-strike, large crowds assembled at the gaol gate, extending, I believe, as far as the Western Road, and recited the Rosary in a very loud voice so that we could hear and respond to it inside the prison ... This gave the greatest comfort to the prisoners.

The Anglo-Irish war ended on 11 July 1921. Recalling the occasion, William O'Brien wrote: 'When at 12 o'clock, the first stroke of the Angelus bell sounded from the village church tower, the IRA took off their caps and put up their guns.' The continuous Rosary offered for the people brutally murdered in 1921–22 was the comfort of the widows. The saying of a decade of the Rosary in Irish at gravesides may stem from this time.[18]

The Legion of Mary

A notable event in the history of Irish Marian devotion took place on 7 September 1921, when the Legion of Mary was founded in Dublin by Frank Duff and a number of people interested in the lay apostolate and devotion to Mary. It was Ireland's response to the call of the Church for the involvement of the laity in the apostolate. In addition to a simple and regular prayer life, members of the Legion began visiting the poor in the South Dublin Union Hospital. Their guiding principle in this matter was that their apostolate should be performed in a spirit of faith and in union with Mary, in such a way that the person of Our Lord is seen and served by Mary, his mother. The Legion spread quickly, first to the cities and then throughout the country. In a relatively short time it had been established world-wide.

Notes

1. Peter O'Dwyer, *Mary: A History of Devotion in Ireland* (Dublin: Four Courts Press, 1988), p. 210.
2. Ibid., p. 210.
3. Ibid., pp. 212–14.
4. Ibid., p. 218.
5. Ibid., p. 222.
6. Ibid., p. 222.
7. Ibid., p. 226.
8. Ibid., p. 233.
9. Ibid., p. 243.
10. Ibid., p. 249.
11. Ibid., p. 258.
12. Ibid., p. 259.
13. Ibid., p. 260.
14. Ibid., p. 261.
15. Ibid., p. 266.
16. Ibid., p. 297.
17. Ibid., p. 299.
18. Ibid., p. 300.

The Marian Movement and the Twentieth Century

The Marian Movement

The nineteenth century is notable for the Marian movement, which reached its climax in the mid twentieth century. The movement was marked by an upsurge of devotion to the Blessed Virgin, together with congresses, pilgrimages and a vast literature on the subject. During the same period there began a series of Marian apparitions, the first of these being the apparition of the Blessed Virgin to Catherine Labouré at the Rue de Bac (Paris) in 1830 (see Chapter 11, p. 156). This was followed by the issuing of the Miraculous Medal and a growing devotion to the Immaculate Conception, leading up to the definition of the dogma on 8 December 1854 by Pius IX in the Apostolic Constitution *Ineffabilis Deus*:

We declare, pronounce and define that the doctrine which holds that the most Blessed Virgin Mary, in the first instant of her conception, by a singular grace and privilege granted by Almighty God, in view of the merits of Jesus Christ, the Saviour of the human race, was preserved free from all stain of original sin, is a doctrine revealed by God and therefore to be believed firmly and constantly by the faithful.

The Marian movement continued its momentum in the late nineteenth century, when during 1883–98 Pope Leo XIII promoted the rosary as the 'most glorious and effective prayer' for those who want to reach Jesus through Mary. He encouraged the family rosary and advocated the beads as an antidote to rationalism and liberalism.

The movement continued through the first half of the twentieth century, reaching its peak with the definition of the Assumption on 1 November 1950 by Pope Pius XII in the Apostolic Constitution *Munificentissimus Deus*:

> By the authority of Our Lord Jesus Christ, of the blessed Apostles Peter and Paul, and by our own, we proclaim and define it to be a dogma revealed by God, that the Immaculate Mother of God, Mary ever Virgin, when the course of her earthly life had finished, was taken up body and soul into the glory of heaven.

The Church in the Twentieth Century

The twentieth century witnessed the most profound, widespread and rapid changes in all spheres of human endeavour since history was recorded. There were great scientific, technological and social changes. The Catholic Church too underwent great changes, with the liturgical, scriptural, Marian and ecumenical movements, and theological scholarship, all of which came to fruition with the dogmatic definition of the Assumption and the Second Vatican Council.

The Church itself is undergoing a radical reform initiated by the Second Vatican Council, but this is as yet unfulfilled. In real numbers the Church is growing, but is it keeping pace proportionately with the dramatic growth in world population? In the last 50 or so years, the Church has been blessed by exceptional papal leadership. We may not agree with everything each individual Pope has said or done, but they have been outstanding men.

The Second Vatican Council

The ecclesial event of the twentieth century was the Second Vatican Council (1962–5), called by Pope John XXIII under the inspiration of the Holy Spirit. In the course of the Council there was intense debate as to how the Church should formulate its teaching on the Blessed Virgin. By a narrow majority it was decided not to have a separate schema but to include her within the Dogmatic Constitution on the Church. Article 54 says:

> Wherefore this sacred synod, while expounding the doctrine on the Church, in which the divine Redeemer brings about our salvation, intends to set forth diligently both the role of the Blessed Virgin in the mystery of the Incarnate Word and the mystical body, and the duties of the redeemed towards the Mother of God, who is mother of Christ and mother of humanity, and especially of all those who believe. It does not, however, intend to give a complete doctrine on Mary, nor does it wish to decide those questions which the work of theologians has not yet fully clarified.

This was a providential document, giving a balanced teaching on Mary. There followed what has been described as a Marian eclipse, during which attention to Marian theology and devotion declined. This may well have been because the energies of the whole Church were directed to the liturgical and scriptural renewal which flowed from the Council.

The documents of the Second Vatican Council reflect the work of scholars in the fields of patristic, liturgical, biblical and ecumenical studies which had evolved during the course of the twentieth century. The first fruit of these deliberations was the promulgation of the Constitution on the Sacred Liturgy in December 1963. In 1964 Paul VI set up a commission to implement the Constitution and revise the liturgical books. The *Missale Romanum* was published in March 1970, followed by the *Liturgia Horarum,* 'The Liturgy of the Hours' (in four volumes), in April 1971. A most significant development was the introduction of the use of the vernacular in the Eucharistic Liturgy, bringing with it the problems of translation. During the same period new versions of the Bible appeared, reflecting the renewed interest in scripture. *La Bible de Jérusalem* (the *Jerusalem Bible*) was first printed in 1956. The English version was published in 1966 and adopted for use in the English Liturgy. Ecumenical dialogue was progressing, and significantly, on 7 December 1965, in a joint declaration, Pope Paul VI and Patriarch Athenagoras I lifted the anathemas between Rome and Constantinople which had existed since 1054.

This preoccupation with the renewal of the Church's official and public prayer life had in some way deflected the faithful from more traditional devotions. Pope Paul VI, being aware of this, issued his Apostolic Exhortation *Marialis cultus* on 2 February 1974. He begins by saying how he has constantly striven to enhance devotion to the Blessed Virgin Mary because 'this devotion forms a very noble part of the whole sphere of that sacred worship in which there intermingle the highest expressions of wisdom and of religion and which is therefore the primary task of the people of God'.

Pope John Paul II, whose whole life is dedicated to Mary, has constantly promoted devotion to the Blessed Mother by word and example, such as publicly leading the rosary. His Encyclical Letter *Redemptoris Mater* (25 March 1987) is an extended teaching on Mary.

THE MARIAN MOVEMENT AND THE TWENTIETH CENTURY

The Present Situation

The Marian movement reached its apogee with a Marian year in 1954; thereafter it began to wane. Similarly, the public recitation of the rosary has been less common in parish settings during the last forty or so years, but it still holds a prominent place at Marian shrines. At parish level it is frequently prayed in small groups and remains the most popular personal devotion among Catholics, and, interestingly, to an increasing degree among members other Churches.

It is a prayer at once simple and profound, easy and yet supremely difficult. It is adaptable to the needs of people of widely different levels of intellectual ability or degrees of spiritual development, enabling all people to pray together without distinction. Generally the classical method is adopted, but new versions of the mysteries are now available, often with the addition of scriptural passages if variety is desired. Pope Paul VI emphasized 'the Gospel inspiration of the Rosary' (*Marialis cultus*, 44), and encouraged the use of scripture together with the rosary, but allowed that 'the faithful should feel serenely free in its regard'. The old adage 'pray as you can, not as you can't' is very apt. We should also avoid the notion that the rosary is a magical formula. To be effective we must pray from the heart, saying the rosary slowly and with concentration.

The rosary may have begun as a psalter of *Paternosters* or as Marian *Ave* psalters, a substitute for the prayer of the Church. The revised Divine Office – the Liturgy of the Hours – has become more accessible to the laity, and perhaps we should be giving a greater priority to this type of prayer. Still, the rosary will always hold a special place in the spiritual life of most Catholics.

In response to the call to 'pray at all times' the rosary may be used in many situations. Peter Batty, a journalist, once wrote

that during the night of the great storm of 16 October 1987 in
England, he kept to his bed and slipped into 'automatic *Ave*
mode'. I recall that, as a small boy at school, I noticed that Sister
Elizabeth – a rather diminutive nun who was our cook – always
walked to and from the convent with one hand in her pocket.
We were told that Sister Elizabeth was always praying the
rosary. It can be fruitful to pray the rosary when out walking,
waiting at the bus stop or doing the housework, even though it
may be in 'automatic *Ave* mode'.

11

Marian Apparitions and the Promotion of the Rosary

Since 1830 there has been a great increase in the frequency of reported apparitions of the Blessed Virgin Mary, and this has had a pronounced influence on Marian devotion in the life of the Church. The rosary has featured in many of the apparitions and that is the justification for including this chapter. Indeed, a modern history of the rosary would be incomplete without some consideration of the matter.

The 'Mary page' on the University of Dayton's website[1] provides an interesting statistical analysis of Marian apparitions over the centuries (see Figure 11.1). Reported apparitions were frequent from the twelfth through to the fifteenth century, after which there was a significant drop. They reached a peak in the thirteenth century, with a record of 772 apparitions. (These figures would have applied to Europe only.) It was during this era that Marian devotion was growing and the rosary prayer evolved.

Figure 11.2 is a chart by Fr Edward D. O'Connor[2] based on Robert Ernest's *Lexikon der Marienerscheinungen* (1989). It is based on different criteria to those of Figure 11.1 and gives a very different picture. This work by Ernest attempts to list all seriously attested Marian apparitions since the beginning of the Church. O'Connor comments that Ernest has been historically uncritical in that he has included some legendary material from

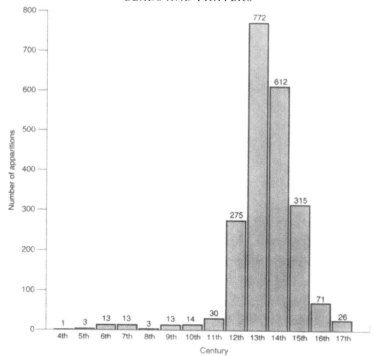

Fig 11.1 Early Marian apparitions
Source: University of Dayton, Marian Library

early times and some very doubtful apparitions in the modern era. The most obvious discrepancy is in the late Middle Ages. Ernest records far fewer alleged apparitions than the Dayton material. Clearly one cannot be very scientific about these claims.

In the twentieth century, the age of global coverage, there were at least 386 reported apparitions, though more could be added. The Church has made 'no decision' about the supernatural character regarding 299 of the 386 cases. It has made a 'negative decision' about the supernatural character in 79 of the 386 cases. The Church, through the local bishop, has decided that there is a supernatural character in only eight cases: Fatima (Portugal); Beauraing (Belgium); Banneux (Belgium);

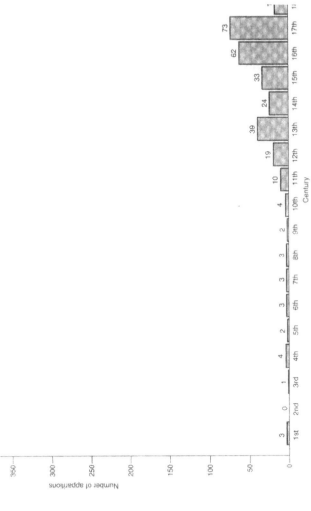

Fig 11.2 Marian apparitions until 1989

Source: Edward D. O'Connor, *Marian Apparitions Today: Why So Many?*

Akita (Japan); Syracuse (Italy); Zeitoun (Egypt); Manila (Philippines); and Betania (Venezuela). In addition there are eleven sites which have received the approval of the local bishop as an expression of faith, permitting prayer and devotion at the site without deciding on the supernatural character of the events.

The Meaning and Significance of Apparitions

Visions and apparitions are nothing new in the history of the People of God. In the Old Testament, God spoke to mankind through the medium of angels and prophets. At the time of the coming of Christ, God sent an angel to Zechariah in the Temple, the Archangel Gabriel to the Virgin of Nazareth and an angel in a dream to Joseph. These angels carried messages from God concerning the Redeemer. After the birth of Christ, angels were sent to assist the Apostles Peter and Paul. And now in our own times, God continues to send angels with his messages. He sent them at Fatima and Akita. But the principal bearer of his messages in recent times is Mary, the Mother of the Redeemer.

The position of the Catholic Church on the matter of apparitions is quite clear. The Catechism of the Catholic Church expresses it thus:

66. 'The Christian economy, therefore, since it is the new and definitive Covenant, will never pass away; and no new public revelation is to be expected before the glorious manifestation of our Lord Jesus Christ' (*Dei Verbum*, n. 4) . . .

67. Throughout the ages, there have been so-called 'private' revelations, some of which have been recognized by the authority of the Church. They do not belong, however, to the deposit of faith. It is not their role to improve or complete Christ's definitive Revelation, but to help live

more fully by it in a certain period of history. Guided by the Magisterium of the Church, the *sensus fidelium* knows how to discern and welcome in these revelations whatever constitutes an authentic call of Christ or his saints to the Church.

Apparitions can add nothing to the 'deposit of faith', which ended with the death of the last Apostle. We are not required to believe in any message given in a 'private' revelation. The Church has always been very cautious about apparitions. The Fifth Lateran Council (1512–17) – which was dealing primarily with prophetic utterances rather than apparitions[3] – issued an edict encouraging bishops to take a critical view of such revelations:

> We wish that ... such revelations should henceforth be reserved for examination by the Apostolic See before being made public or preached to the people. If this were to involve a risk of delays, or should some other circumstance dictate a different procedure, then the local Ordinary ought to be informed ... The latter, with the advice of three or four learned men, will subject the matter to diligent scrutiny. If, in their view, all things seem proper, and let this be for them a serious matter of conscience, then permission may be granted.[4]

The Code of Canon Law of 1917 (canon 1385) banned all books and publications describing new apparitions, revelations, visions, prophecies and miracles, or proposing new devotions, even under the pretext that they were private. This situation changed when Paul VI abolished this canon on 14 October 1970.[5] Apparitions may now be discussed openly, and as they inevitably attract much attention are now frequently reported in the media. The institutional Church remains very cautious, and whatever approval it may give, it is never an exercise of its infallible gift of discernment. The Church does no more than give its official permission that Mary (in the case of a Marian apparition) may be venerated in a special way at the place where the apparition has occurred.

The Miraculous Medal

The apparitions of the modern era began with the apparition of the Blessed Virgin to a young nun, Catherine Labouré, at her convent in the Rue de Bac, Paris, in 1830. This resulted in the production of the Miraculous Medal and an increase in devotion to the Immaculate Conception. The dogma of the Immaculate Conception was defined on 8 December 1854 by Pius IX with the Apostolic Constitution *Ineffabilis Deus*, and seemed to be affirmed by the apparitions at Lourdes beginning on 11 February 1858.

Lourdes

On 25 March 1858 the apparition, in response to Bernadette's request – 'Mademoiselle, would you be so kind as to tell me who you are, if you please?' – replied in the local patois: '*Que soy era Immaculada Councepciou*' – 'I am the Immaculate Conception.' Bernadette tells us of her response to the first apparition:

> I put my hand in my pocket and I found my rosary there. I wanted to make the Sign of the Cross. I couldn't raise my hand to my forehead. It collapsed on me. Shock got the better of me. My hand was trembling.
>
> The vision made the Sign of the Cross. Then I tried a second time, and I could. As soon as I made the Sign of the Cross, the fearful shock I felt disappeared. I knelt down and I said my rosary

in the presence of the beautiful lady. The vision fingered the beads of her own rosary but she did not move her lips. When I finished my rosary, she signed for me to approach; but I did not dare. Then she disappeared, just like that.[6]

It is interesting to note Bernadette's almost automatic recourse to the rosary, and the fact that the apparition had her own rosary. Bernadette prayed the rosary each time she presented herself at the Grotto. The Virgin did not request the rosary to be said. It was said because that was Bernadette's normal mode of prayer and the Virgin acknowledged this action by silently fingering her own beads. The apparition called for penance, for processions and the building of a chapel.

Pontmain

The last officially approved Marian apparition of the nineteenth century occurred at Pontmain in France on 17 January 1871 to the twelve-year-old Eugène Babbette. The parish priest was called and immediately ordered the recitation of the rosary. The seer reported that as they began to recite the rosary, 'The stars on her [the apparition's] navy-blue gown grew larger and larger until she appears clothed in gold.' When the Magnificat was intoned there appeared in block letters under the feet of the apparition 'But pray my children.' Curiously, the chaplet recited was the small red rosary in honour of the 26 Japanese martyrs. Following this event, the invading army of Prussia withdrew. It is reported that some enemy soldiers on the outskirts of the city saw the Virgin, as it were, guarding the country and preventing them from advancing.

Knock

At the village of Knock in the west of Ireland, on the evening of 21 August 1879, fifteen people found themselves in the presence of the Blessed Virgin together with St Joseph and St John. To the left of St John was a full-sized altar on which stood a six-week-old lamb and a cross without a corpus. The Lady did not speak, but her silent mission gave hope and comfort to a people who had in the recent past been afflicted by the deadly potato famine. Those who experienced the apparition responded by praying the rosary.[7]

Fatima

In the spring of 1916 an angel appeared to three shepherd children from the village of Aljustrel in the parish of Fatima, Portugal, and taught them to pray. On 13 May 1917 a Lady with a rosary in her hand appeared to them. She would subsequently identify herself as 'the Lady of the Rosary', and encouraged the children to 'Say the rosary every day, to obtain peace for the world and an end to the war.' She asked them to accept suffering for the conversion of sinners. The request to say the rosary every day was repeated in the apparitions that followed on the 13th of each month until October.[8] It had been the habit of the children to say the rosary, but they had only been saying the words 'Hail Mary' and 'Our Father' on their beads, henceforth they were to recite the rosary in full and with great devotion.

Banneux

At Banneux, a small hamlet in the Ardennes, Belgium, apparitions took place from 15 January to 2 March 1933. The visionary was twelve-year-old Mariette Beco. The Lady was dressed in white with a blue belt, a rosary on her arm and a rose on her right foot. On the evening of 18 January, Mariette went into the garden to pray the rosary and again the vision appeared. The following night the apparition told Mariette that she was the Virgin of the Poor and led her to a stream, telling her that it was for all the people for the relief of the sick.

Akita

The events in Akita, Japan (1969–81) seemed to be a continuation of the Fatima message, but the manifestations were of a different kind. Brilliant lights from the tabernacle and multitudes of angels adoring the Blessed Sacrament were a confirmation of the true Presence. A statue of the Blessed Virgin wept 101 times, and the messages from Our Lady seemed to come from the statue. Sister Agnes of the Handmaids of the Eucharist was taught the Fatima prayer in 1969. She was in hospital in Myoko saying her rosary when her guardian angel appeared to her and told her to pray at the end of each decade: 'O my Jesus, forgive us our sins; save us from the fires of hell; lead all souls to heaven, especially those most in need of thy mercy.' At that time this prayer had not been published in Japan.

Medjugorje

The evening of 24 June 1981 saw the beginning of a series of reported apparitions of Our Lady, Queen of Peace, to six teenagers at Medjugorje. Here the Blessed Virgin makes a most insistent call to 'Pray, pray, pray.' The youngsters respond first by praying a traditional Croatian chaplet of seven Our Fathers, Hail Marys and Glory Be's, plus the Creed. (This is now recited each evening after Mass in the church.) It was in July 1981 that Our Lady gave a specific message to Jakov Colo that she wished that all should say the rosary daily as a group. The rosary is said each evening in the church: the Joyful and Sorrowful Mysteries before Mass and the Glorious Mysteries after Mass. The Blessed Virgin has said that the Mass is the greatest prayer, but emphasizes that every prayer is pleasing to her.

Reading the accounts of the many apparitions that have occurred in recent times one comes to the conclusion that there is one basic message: the world is in a mess owing to sin and is heading for a great disaster unless it changes its behaviour by a renewal of faith, repentance, prayer and penance. The disaster, or the chastisement, may be man-made or it may be some extraordinary event sent by God as an expression of his justice. However, by prayer and penance we can change the course of history. Pope John XXIII, speaking in a radio message for the close of the Lourdes centenary year (1958–9), shows how that might be:

And if, beside these public manifestations, we evoke the silent work of grace, our gratitude grows all the more: how many in darkness received light at Lourdes! How many tepid or hardened hearts have got the grace to return to God! How many unsteady wills have received the strength to persevere! In the silence of wordless prayer, or in the midst of eucharistic or marian acclamations, generous people have received the joy of a more generous gift of themselves. The sick received, if not always a cure, at least resignation and serenity in offering their sufferings, whilst the dying learned there to make peacefully the sacrifice of their lives. How wonderful in the eyes of God is this secret history engraved on people's hearts; a history of the victory of God, 'who has rescued us from the ruling force of darkness and transferred us to the kingdom of the Son that he loves' (Colossians 1.13–14).[9]

Fr Edward O'Connor, after reviewing the apparitions of Mary since 1830, sees that the Blessed Virgin presents herself in three modes: as the caring Mother who comes to comfort, encourage and heal her children; as an anxious weeping Mother coming to warn her children that if they persist in their sinful ways God's justice will prevail and they will be punished; and finally she offers her Immaculate Heart as a refuge from the dangers that threaten.[10]

The rosary features in many of the apparition stories. I have the impression that the Blessed Virgin takes people where they are and encourages the form of prayer they are familiar with. At Lourdes and at Fatima Our Lady appears with a rosary on her arm and specifically encourages its use – in Fatima in particular she asks for the recitation of the rosary and identifies herself as Our Lady of the Rosary. There can be no doubt that the rosary as a popular devotion has increased greatly through the cult that has developed from these two series of apparitions.

A Theological Reflection

Though there is no new revelation to be found in these apparitions, they do serve to remind us of aspects of the Gospel message and of the development of doctrine that derives from the scriptures. In the Gospel we learn of Mary's virginal conception of Jesus (Luke 1.26–38), which was accepted and taught by the Magisterium of the Church as an historical fact from the earliest times. That she is the mother of the Lord was proclaimed by Elizabeth (Luke 1.43), the full implication of which became clear at the Council of Ephesus in 431 when the Fathers of the Church, in considering who and what Jesus Chirst is, accepted that Mary is rightly called the *Theotokos*, the

God-bearer, because the son she gave birth to was one Person with two natures, God and man. Being mother of the one Person who is God, we may then know her as the Mother of God in his humanity.

'They have no wine' (John 2.3) is Mary's first recorded act of intercession. The earliest recorded prayer to the Blessed Virgin is that of the *Sub tuum praesidium* from about AD 300 showing that the early Church recognized Mary's role as intercessor:

> Under your mercy, we take refuge, Mother of God [*Theotokos*], do not reject our supplications in necessity. But deliver us from danger, [You] alone chaste, alone blessed.[11]

John tells us that

> standing by the cross of Jesus were his mother, and his mother's sister ... When Jesus saw his mother, and the disciple whom he loved standing near, he said to his mother, 'Woman, behold, your son!' Then he said to the disciple, 'Behold, your mother!'
>
> (John 19.25–27)

Mary had chosen to share in the Passion and redemptive suffering of her Son. After this, Jesus commissions Mary to be our Mother, to be our Mother in the order of grace, and we, as did the beloved disciple, must accept her motherly role.

That Mary was immaculately conceived was an understanding that gradually evolved in Catholic tradition, though it had no explicit scriptural foundation. Luke tells us that Mary was the 'highly favoured' one (Luke 1.28), and from the earliest times she was recognized as being free from all personal sin. That she could have been conceived without stain of original sin became a possibility when it was realized that she is the perfectly redeemed creature, of a perfect redemption, by the perfect Redeemer. Thus it was that she could respond to the Angel 'Behold, I am the handmaid of the Lord; let it be to me according to your word' (Luke 1.38) and so cooperate perfectly with the Father in the salvation of mankind. If Mary was conceived free of all stain of original sin, then she is free of the propensity to personal sin and free from the corruption of the grave. Therefore the Church teaches that 'when the course of her earthly life had finished, [she] was taken up body and soul into the glory of heaven',[12] a doctrine we know as the Assumption.

The vision of the Miraculous Medal given to Catherine Labouré in November 1830 is symbolic. On one side is the Blessed Virgin standing on the globe of the world, on which crawls the serpent, symbolic of Genesis 3.15: 'I will put enmity between you and the woman, and between your seed and her seed; he shall bruise your head, and you shall bruise his heel.' The hands of the Virgin are held downwards, opening out, and from them come streams of light representing the graces Mary dispenses to all who ask for them and reminding us that the Lord from the cross gave us the 'Woman', the new Eve, to be our spiritual Mother and Mediatrix of grace. The inscription around the edge of the oval medal reads: 'O Mary, conceived without sin, pray for us who have recourse to you', thus identifying the apparition as Mary Immaculate. On the reverse side is Mary's monogram, the letter M surmounted by the cross and below it the hearts of Jesus and Mary – the one surrounded by a crown of thorns and the other pierced by a sword. Encircling the whole are twelve stars. Mary stood at the foot of the cross suffering and cooperating with her Divine Son in the redemptive sacrifice. She is a redeemer with Christ in a significant though utterly subordinate way. Now assumed into heaven, the united hearts of Jesus and Mary still bear the wounds of the Passion. The twelve stars suggest the Woman of the Apocalypse: 'And a great portent appeared in heaven, a woman clothed with the sun, with the moon under her feet, and on her head a crown of twelve stars' (Revelation 12.1). The 'woman' may be interpreted as Mary who is the type of the Church. The Miraculous Medal (distributed in 1832) was widely accepted, leading to an increase in devotion to the Immaculate Conception, thus preparing the faithful for the definition of the dogma of the Immaculate Conception in 1854. This was beautifully confirmed to Bernadette at Lourdes on 25 March 1858 by the apparition, who said: 'I am the Immaculate Conception.'

Mary Immaculate is the perfect model of discipleship who cooperated with Christ in the redemptive sacrifice of the cross. At Fatima the three young visionaries were asked:

> Would you like to offer yourselves to God, to accept all the sufferings which He may send you in reparation for the countless sins by which He is offended and in supplication for the conversion of sinners?

The children did accept. They did suffer much, resulting in many blessings and graces.

What is the relevance of all this for us? St Paul, writing to the Corinthians, said: 'For we are God's fellow workers' (1 Corinthians 3.9). He was indicating that, as Christians, we have a mission to become co-workers with Christ for the sake of the Kingdom. That is, God invites us to cooperate in the work of salvation/redemption as fellow workers with Christ. This work involves a renunciation of self and often much suffering. So in a mystical way we can say with St Paul:

> Now I rejoice in my sufferings for your sake, and in my flesh I complete what is lacking in Christ's afflictions for the sake of his body, that is, the church.

> (Colossians 1:24)

Mary is our role model. Mary has shown us what we have to do. By offering all our prayers, works, sufferings and joys each day to Jesus with Mary, in a spirit of sacrifice, we are able to cooperate, in a subordinate way, in the ongoing work of redemption. We become 'God's fellow workers' and 'complete what is lacking in Christ's afflictions for the sake of the church'.

The ordinary magisterium of the Church holds that Mary is Co-redeemer with Christ, Mediatrix and Advocate. Perhaps the recent series of apparitions which portray Mary's sorrow through her tears and her call to prayer and penance are a preparation for a more definitive understanding of her universal mediation and role as Co-redeemer.

Notes

1. *www.udayton.edu/mary/*
2. Edward D. O'Connor, *Marian Apparitions Today – Why So Many?* (Santa Barbara: Queenship, 1996), p. 76.
3. Ibid., p. 136.
4. Fifth Lateran Council, Session 11, 19 December 1516, in *Conciliorum Oecumenicorum Decreta* (Bologna: Herder, 1962), p. 637, in René Laurentin, *The Apparitions of the Blessed Virgin Mary Today,* 2nd edn (Dublin: Veritas, 1991), p. 22.
5. Decree of the Congregation for the Doctrine of the Faith, *Acta Apostolicae Sedis (AAS)*, 29 October 1970, p. 1186.
6. René Laurentin, *Bernadette of Lourdes* (London: Darton, Longman & Todd, 1979), Chapter 2.
7. Fr James, *The Story of Knock* (Knock: Knock Shrine Annual, 1950).
8. Francis Johnston, *Fatima: The Great Sign* (Chulmleigh, Devon: Augustine Publishing, 1980), pp. 27ff.
9. *Acta Apostolicae Sedis,* 51 (1959): 144–5.
10. Edward D. O'Connor, *Marian Apparitions Today*, p. 33.
11. Michael O'Carroll, The Hail Mary, *Theotokos*: 165–6.
12. Pius XII, *Munificentissimus Deus,* 1 November 1950.

The Symbolism of the Rose, Rose Garland and Rose Garden

The strong symbolic potency of the rose has a long history. In Greek mythology the rose, a flower with five petals, became the five-pointed star of Aphrodite, which later became associated with the Roman cult of Venus. The Woman of the Apocalypse crowned with twelve stars is a reference to Venus. Since the rose was already a pre-Christian symbol of beauty, love, wisdom and mystery, it is not surprising that it was from very early on used as a symbol of the beautiful, wise and mysterious Virgin, Bride and Mother, Mary – the Rose without a Thorn, the Peerless Rose, the Rose of Sharon, the Rose of Jericho.[1] St Ambrose referred to her as the '*rosa pudoris*', the Rose of Modesty. In the earliest Greek litanies she appears as the 'Mystic Rose', a name which reappears in the twelfth-century Litany of Loreto. Floral titles of Mary are found in many Latin hymns and sequences: Noble Rose, Fragrant Rose, Chaste Rose, Rose of Heaven, Rose of Love, etc.

As a symbol of blood and suffering the five-petal rose became associated with the Five Wounds of Christ, and hence a symbol of the Resurrection, so that rose bushes came to be planted on graves. The dark red rose is inseparable from the symbolic cup of wine and blood, and the blood of the suffering God is not wholly distinct from the hymeneal blood of consummated marriage, which again symbolizes the union of immortality.

Christ weds his Church by means of his dying blood and this blood is then drunk by the faithful as consecrated wine.

In ancient Rome the Rosalia was a spring festival honouring the dead that was celebrated when the roses began to bloom. In many parts of Europe the May celebrations are associated with the May Lady who was called *Maia*, a Roman title for Venus. We have 'the May', May Day, May Tree, May Pole, Queen of the May, May Bride, Maid Marian (*Mariam* is the Greek form of the Hebrew *Miryam* – hence 'Mary').

The Rose Garland

In the Middle Ages the May celebrations featured hoops of roses suspended on maypoles and the wearing of garlands of roses. There is a precedent for this in Wisdom 2.6–8: 'Come, therefore, let us enjoy the good things that exist, and make use of the creation to the full as in youth. Let us take our fill of costly wine and perfumes, and let no flower of spring pass by us. Let us crown ourselves with rosebuds before they wither.'

On every festive occasion it was the invariable custom, when the season admitted, to provide great quantities of rose blossoms. Rose garlands were woven and worn by both men and women. The *chappelliers de fleurs* in Paris were among the most important of the trade guilds and were allowed to work even on Sundays at making rose garlands when the roses were in blossom. Thurston[2] stressed how essential it is to grasp this point in order to understand the conditions which influenced both the development of the rosary devotion and the name by which it was most commonly called.

Popular poetry frequently referred to the practice of wearing rose garlands. In a thirteenth-century ballad, 'The Knight and the World', the World bids the Knight give up his serious pursuits and join the merry dance:

> This is my rede, disport thee now,
> Weave thee a rose-wreath for thy brow.

But the Knight protests:

> The dance I have forsworn and chaplets gay,
> Come weal or woe, I stand by what I say.[3]

In 'The Flower and the Leaf', a poem once attributed to Chaucer, we are told that every lady:

> ... had a chaplet on her head
> Which did right well upon the shining hair
> Made of goodly floures, whyte and red.
> The knights eke, that they in hande led,
> In sute of them wore chaplets everyone.[4]

In contrast, St Louis forbade the young princes to wear garlands on a Friday, out of respect for the Saviour who wore a crown of thorns on that day. The Dominican Stephen of Bourbon (c. 1250) appealed to the devout: 'just as lovers, striving to compass the object of their passion, adorn their heads with flowers, so Christ our Lord, in order to gain souls, bedecks Himself in the guise best fitted to win their love. After the manner of a hat of roses, He wears a crown of thorns, all purple with His Blood.'[5]

An extract from the diary of Le Bourgois de Paris (c. 1418) reads:

> Also the people decided to erect the confraternity of St Andre in the parish of St Eustache, and they did it on a Thursday, the 9th of June, and everyone who joined had a wreath of crimson roses (*un chappeau de rose vermeilles*). And so many people of Paris joined, that

the officers of the confraternity stated and declared that they had
had more than sixty dozen wreaths made, but that before twelve
o'clock the supply of wreaths had given out. The minster church of
St Eustache was crowded with people, but there was hardly one
person present, man, priest, or anyone else, who had not upon his
head a wreath of crimson roses, and there was such a sweet scent in
the minster that it smelt as if it had been washed with rose water.[6]

The Rose Garden

Eithne Wilkins, in her book *The Rose-Garden Game*, develops
the symbolism of the rose garden – a garden enclosed by a rose
hedge, which constituted the ideal *locus amoenus* for romantic
encounters. Anne Winston-Allen in *Stories of the Rose* takes up
the same theme. The term 'rose garden' can mean (variously):
the embodiment of joy and delight; a title of the Virgin Mary; a
literary anthology; a burial ground; and in the diminutive form
'*rosengärtlin*', an obscene usage.[7]

It is in the twelfth century that the rose garden becomes the
standard image of Paradise reminiscent of the Persian garden – a
high-walled place, well-watered in contrast to the arid desert
outside. The resurrected Christ walking in the garden, where
Mary Magdalen meets him and takes him to be the gardener, is
a reflection of the Creator walking in Paradise. The Creator is
the Gardener. The Virgin is also depicted as the 'rose garden'
(i.e., the garden that bore Christ, God's rose garden). Dante, in
his *Paradiso,* writes of the 'Rose in which the Word of God
became flesh'.

The Enclosed Garden of the Song of Songs

The primary source of these images is the Song of Songs, which
was the most commented-on book of the Bible in the Middle

Ages. It is a dialogue between the bride and groom. The bride
praises her beloved as the 'rose of Sharon', and the bridegroom
admires his bride as 'a lily among thorns' (2.1–2). The lover
eulogizes the chastity of his virgin bride, likening her to an
enclosed garden and a sealed fountain (4.12). The speakers in
the Song were identified as Christ and his Church or as Christ
and an individual soul. By the twelfth century the bride was
popularly identified with the Virgin Mary as a type of the
Church. Mary is the first bride of Christ and model for each
believer.

In religious typology the 'enclosed garden' became the
symbol of Mary's untainted virginity. Illustrations depict images
of a locked, walled garden representing the *hortus conclusus*. By
the time the Feast of the Immaculate Conception had spread
from England to France (c. 1140), the enclosed garden had
become a standard symbol of Mary's womb. The garden of the
Incarnation, the *hortus conclusus* is contrasted with the Garden of
Paradise. Mary is not only the enclosed garden but is frequently
shown seated in a walled garden, and these images reflect the
heavenly paradise where Mary is now enthroned. In the same
way Mary was contrasted to Eve. Just as the name 'Eva' when
reversed gives '*Ave*', so the sin of Eve is reversed by Mary. The
new Eve is 'The answer to man's Fall and Expulsion, is God's
entrance into the Mary-garden'.[8]

Aves as Roses: the Rose Chaplet

The transformation of the word '*Ave*' into 'rose' comes through
the identification of the rose with Christ and Christ with the
Word. 'The rose is the Word that the first gardener, who
planted paradise in the beginning, sowed and planted in Mary's
earthly womb ... The word from the mouth of God is our
Lord Jesus Christ.' The *Ave* which commemorates this event is

itself a 'rose'. The earliest mention of *Aves* taking the form of roses and comprising a chaplet occurs in the late-thirteenth-century legend 'Aves seen as Roses'. It recounts how a monk who was in the forest reciting 50 *Aves* was seen by two potential robbers to be with a beautiful maiden who plucked from his mouth a series of roses which she made into a chaplet, placed it on her head and disappeared into heaven.

From the thirteenth century the term 'chaplet' designated 50 *Aves*, one-third of an *Ave* psalter. The Beguines of Ghent in 1242 prayed three such chaplets a day. The Latin term *corona* or *sertum* was used at this time for a wreath of roses. From c. 1280 to 1300 the Germans employed the term *Rosenkranz*, which appears to have been translated back into Latin as *rosarium*. Prior to this, *rosarium* was used to designate an anthology of texts – a *florilegium*. The transition from *psalterium* to *rosarium* seems to take place in a work by Engelbert, Abbot of Admont (1297–1331), in which each of the 150 stanzas begins with '*Ave, rosa*'.[9]

Since classical antiquity, collections of poetry by various authors have been called 'anthologies', 'posies' of writings gathered like flowers (*anthos* = a flower, *logia* = a collection). Another word associated with the rosary at this time is *florilegium*. These prayers, 50 or 150, are little poems or thoughts about Mary that rhyme with '*Ave*'. The Hail Mary is then repeated after each. Books of collected items other than poems were called 'flower gardens'. *The Garden of the Soul*, a collection of prayers published by Richard Challoner in 1740, was in use until recent times.

Social and Psychological Aspects of the Rosary

The rosary has both social and psychological significance. According to Eithne Wilkins:

the rosary is both physical and spiritual, sensual and mystical. It may glitter, flash, and tinkle; it is in some legends 'fragrant', and sometimes literally so; it moves, it is to be continually touched and handled; it involves the use of the word and of exact number, which pertains to wisdom, power, and the very nature of being. It is a device to promote detachment of mind, to release the spirit. All 'world' religions have the rosary, and it is found also outside them.

A given number of counters, arranged in a given pattern on a string or metal chain, are either moved along or slid between thumb and finger tip. Generally this can be done with one hand, but the rosary is more often held in both hands, doubtless in order, by having it in a central position, to keep in balance the physical and psychic resources that its use involves.[10]

Certainly the handling of the rosary satisfies some primitive need. One observes the baby reaching out to grasp and then explore with the mouth any object within reach. It is comforting and calming simply to hold and manipulate the beads – the tactile nature of the actual beads being important. The use of 'worry-beads' is a widespread and acceptable custom in the Middle East and elsewhere.

The Rosary: an Object of Beauty, Value and Decoration

The rosary is a very personal object to which one becomes sentimentally attached after a long period of use. To make a gift of a rosary can be very meaningful, hence we often find rosaries left as votive offerings at Marian shrines. The story of Lady Godiva (see p. 95) makes this point.

Rosaries were often displayed or worn about the person, as demonstrated in the many funeral effigies and monumental brasses in England, and described by Chaucer in *The Canterbury*

Tales. As such, they may well have been objects of pious display rather than personal devotion. In c. 1350 it is recorded that an Augustinian canon of Osnabruck outlawed the wearing of coral rosaries around the neck. One presumes that it was the display of wealth that was being condemned. A chronicle from the city of Biberach in Germany of 1530 relates that everyone 'carries a paternoster', or is taken to be non-Christian. Carrying a rosary wrapped around one's hand or upper arm was considered a sign of respectability. For the devout it may have been simply that they wished to have it readily available for use, though one suspects that for many it was a matter of fashion to display a highly decorative and maybe valuable object. Some of the strings of beads seen on monumental brasses are rather large and so would be impractical as an aid to prayer.

The Rosary as Amulet

It could well be that for some the rosary may have become an amulet or charm, that is, an object believed to be endowed with special powers to protect or bring good fortune. Among believers, amulets are thought to derive power from their connection with their religious association. In the case of the rosary, its association with the Mother of God, the all-powerful intercessor, gave great comfort. One must distinguish between religious practice and magic. The term 'magic' essentially refers to an activity that is thought to lead to the influencing of human or natural events by an external and impersonal mystical force beyond the ordinary human sphere, whereas religion acknowledges a personal, conscious and omnipotent spiritual being as the object of its devotion. Amulets (charms) have been used for protection in all ages and in all types of human societies, and persist even today. The purpose of most amulets is not so much religious as protective (i.e., against danger, sickness

Figure 12.1 (Left) Monumental brass of Geoffrey Kidwelly (d. 1483), Little Wittenham parish church. From the rubbing by Henry Trivick. (Right) Lettys Terry (from the bracket brass to the memory of her and her husband John Terry, 1524), St John Maddermarket, Norwich. Both reproduced by permission of Henry H. Trivick, RBA, and John Baker Ltd

Source: Wilkins, E., The Rose-Garden Game (1969), p. 176

and bad luck). Venus figurines dating from about 25,000 BC may be among the earliest of man-made amulets. The MacGregor papyrus of ancient Egypt listed 75 amulets, one of the commonest of which was the scrab beetle, symbol of life, worn by the living and dead alike.

In the Middle Ages Christian amulets included the relics of saints, crosses or crucifixes, and rosaries – either *Paternoster* or *Ave* beads. The Orthodox Jewish male wears the 'phylactery' or 'tefillin' on the left forearm and the forehead during the morning and afternoon service. Each contains a written text from Deuteronomy 6.8, as a reminder of Shaddai (God) and of the obligation to keep the Jewish Law. Muslims today often carry verses from the Qur'an, the names of God, or associated sacred numbers within small satchels.[11] Hastings quotes several examples in Hindu culture of the use of strings of beads as charms to protect or cure snake-bite, or to ward off the effects of the evil eye. Nearer home, Hastings suggests that in southern Italy the rosary has, among other things, been used by witches to break spells, or cure male impotence.[12] (An inverse affirmation of the power of the beads!)

Notes

1. Anne Winston-Allen, *Stories of the Rose*, p. 115.
2. Herbert Thurston, The Name of the Rosary (I), *The Month*, 111 (1908): 518–29.
3. Ibid., p. 524.
4. Ibid., p. 523.
5. Ibid., p. 525.
6. Ibid., pp. 525–6.
7. Grimm's *Deutsches Wörtenbuch*, as quoted by Winston-Allen in *Stories of the Rose*, p. 84.
8. Winston-Allen, *Stories of the Rose*, pp. 89–92.

9. Ibid., pp. 100–3.
10. Eithne Wilkins, *The Rose-Garden Game*, p. 28.
11. Magic and Religion; Phylactery; Amulet, *Encyclopaedia Britannica CD* 2000.
12. Winifred S. Blackman, Rosaries, *Encyclopaedia of Religion and Ethics*, ed. James Hastings (Edinburgh: T. & T. Clark, 1918).

13

The Rosary in Papal Documents

Leo X was the first Pope to give the rosary approbation, in 1520. This was confirmed and officially approved in 1569 by Pope Pius V (Apostolic Letter *Consueverunt Romani Pontifices*). Christopher O'Donnell has summarized the teaching of Pius V: 'the necessity of prayer to overcome the difficulties of wars and other calamities; the simplicity of the rosary as a prayer within the reach of all; the help the rosary has been against heresies; the instrumentality of the rosary in many conversions. The recitation of the rosary is therefore commended to all.'[1] (It was Pius V who attributed the decisive victory of the Christian fleet over that of the Turks at Lepanto in 1571 to Our Lady of Victory through the prayer of the rosary.)

The Popes of modern times have continued to promote the rosary as an important devotion. Four Popes in particular stand out: Leo XIII, Pius XII, Paul VI and John Paul II.

Leo XIII

Pope Leo XIII (1878–1903) wrote many significant Encyclicals.[2] The rosary was the subject of twelve Encyclicals and five Apostolic Letters. Beginning in 1883 and concluding in 1898, an Encyclical on the rosary appeared almost every year, usually in preparation for the month of October.

The rosary Encyclicals can be divided into two main groups: 1883–85 and 1891–98. The first group established the rosary as a public devotion. The first Encyclical (1883) prescribed the public recitation of the rosary and the Litany of Loreto in Catholic churches and chapels as a special observance for the month of October.

The Encyclicals of 1884 and 1885 directed that October devotions be continued. The Feast of the Most Holy Rosary was given a higher liturgical standing, and the invocation 'Queen of the Most Holy Rosary' was added to the Litany of Loreto. The rosary was officially encouraged as a public devotion.

From 1891 Leo XIII dwelt on the value of the rosary and on its role within the life of the Church and of society. He made frequent reference to the perilous situation in which the Church found itself: anticlerical governments and forces opposed to religion threatened its existence. In response to these trying times, Leo XIII followed the example of Pius V, who had proposed the rosary as a 'weapon' in the fight against the Turkish forces in 1571. The rosary would be 'balm for the wounds of society' and it would make possible the two great goals of Leo's papacy: the renovation of Christian life and the reunion of Christendom.

There were no specific indications on how the rosary was to be prayed. The essence of the rosary was 'to recall the mysteries of salvation in succession, [while] the subject of meditation is mingled and interlaced with the Angelic Salutation and prayer to God the Father' (1883). Meditation on the mysteries of salvation was a short and easy method to nourish faith and to preserve it from ignorance and error (1895).

The rosary was presented both as a 'school of faith' and a 'school of charity'. Meditation on the mysteries of salvation was to lead to conversion of heart and change of conduct.

Contemplation of the mysteries was essentially a loving act of gratitude (1894), through which the heart was 'filled with love ... hope enlarged, and the desire increased for those things which Christ has prepared for such as have united themselves to Him in imitation of His example and in participation in His sufferings' (1891).

Attentive consideration of the 'precious memorials' of our Redeemer led to 'a heart on fire with gratitude to Him' (1892). The rosary was an expression of faith in God, the future life, the forgiveness of sins, 'the mysteries of the august Trinity, the incarnation of the Word, the Divine Maternity and others' (1896).

The rosary, the Pope believed, would also influence society as a whole. The 1893 Encyclical spoke of the social consequences, or the effects on society, that meditation on the mysteries of the rosary could produce. The three sets of mysteries were an antidote for the errors afflicting society.

The Joyful Mysteries, centred on the 'hidden' life of Christ and the Holy Family at Nazareth, stood in contrast to the contemporary disdain for poverty and simplicity of life. The Sorrowful Mysteries, depicting Christ's acceptance of the cross, stood opposed to the attitude of fleeing from any hardship and suffering. Finally, the Glorious Mysteries – which include the Resurrection, the Ascension, the Descent of the Spirit and the Assumption of the Virgin Mary – were a reminder that this life is a prelude to a future life with God.

Even when prayed privately, the rosary had a social and ecclesial dimension. Similar to the Divine Office, the Psalter of Our Lady was part of the Church's 'public, constant and universal prayer' (1897). The Encyclicals frequently encouraged the sodalities or confraternities whose purpose was to promote the rosary through meetings, religious services and processions. The last Encyclical (1898) was followed by an Apostolic Letter, with a charter for the sodalities and confraternities of the rosary. The 1897 Encyclical encouraged the development of the 'Living Rosary', a movement started earlier in the century by Pauline Jaricot (the founder of the Society for the Propagation of the Faith). Jaricot's Living Rosary was a group of fifteen individuals, each pledged to say one decade of the rosary a day. 'The prayers and praises, rising incessantly from the lips and hearts of so great a multitude, will be most efficacious' (1897).

In all the Encyclicals, the rosary is not so much presented as a devotion directed to Mary. Instead, it is Christ, in all the facets of his life — hidden, public, final suffering and resurrection — who 'stands forth' in this prayer (1896). The rosary is principally an instrument 'to expand the kingdom of Christ'. It is a prayer that has been 'wonderfully developed at the close of the century, for the purpose of stimulating the lagging piety of the faithful' (1897).

The rosary Encyclicals show a great confidence in Mary's power and her intercession for the Church (1892). As 'guardian of the faith', Mary is able to 'ward off the errors of the times' (1895). She is a powerful intercessor before God, a 'worthy and acceptable Mediatrix to the Mediator' (1896).

The Encyclicals of Leo XIII are the first papal documents to speak of Mary's universal motherhood; she is the mother of all peoples — 'our mother' — and the one who could bring about the unity of the Church (1895). Through the intercession of Mary, the zeal of the Christian people would be renewed and a deeper unity produced.

The legacy of Pope Leo's Encyclicals was that the rosary was established as a central devotion in Western Catholicism.

Pope Pius XII

In his Encyclical *Ingruentium malorum* (On Reciting the

Rosary), Pius XII writes in anticipation of the month of October 1951 with its rosary devotion. He stresses the urgent needs of the time and advocates supplication to the Mother of God by means of the rosary and in particular the family rosary. Armed with the rosary, we become 'strong like David with his sling'. He writes in *Ingruentium malorum*

> You know well, Venerable Brethren, the calamitous conditions of our times. Fraternal harmony among nations, shattered for so long a time, has not yet been re-established everywhere ... To this, one must add the violent storm of persecution, which in many parts of the world, has been unleashed against the Church ... Nor can We pass over in silence a new crime to which, with utmost sorrow, We want earnestly to draw not only your attention, but the attention of the clergy, of parents, and even of public authorities. We refer to the iniquitous campaign that the impious lead everywhere to harm the shining souls of children ... mindful of that Divine teaching: 'Ask and it shall be given to you; seek and you shall find; knock, and it shall be opened to you' (Luke 11.9), fly with greater confidence to the Mother of God. There, the Christian people have always sought chief refuge in the hour of danger, because 'she has been constituted the cause of salvation for the whole human race' (St Irenaeus) ... We look forward with joyful expectation and revived hope to the coming month of October, during which the faithful are accustomed to flock in larger numbers to the churches to raise their supplications to Mary by means of the Holy Rosary (nn. 4–7)[3].

Pope Paul VI

The Second Vatican Council (1962–5) did not intend to give a complete doctrine on Mary but restated the role of the Blessed Virgin Mary in the plan of salvation, and placed her firmly within the Church. It encouraged devotion to Mary, saying:

> The sacred synod ... admonishes all the sons of the Church that
> the cult, especially the liturgical cult, of the Blessed Virgin, be
> generously fostered, and that the practices and exercises of
> devotion towards her, recommended by the teaching authority
> of the Church in the course of centuries, be highly esteemed, and
> that those decrees, which were given in the early days regarding
> the cult images of Christ, the Blessed Virgin and the saints, be
> religiously observed.
>
> *(Lumen gentium*, n. 67)

Following this Council there was a falling away in Marian
devotion, perhaps because the main focus of the Church was
on, and its energy directed towards, liturgical renewal and the
faithful were enabled to participate more actively in the
Church's official worship. No longer was the rosary a necessary
vehicle for entering into and focusing on the mysteries of
salvation as depicted in the life of Christ and the Virgin Mary.

In an attempt to enhance devotion to the Blessed Virgin,
Paul VI published his Apostolic Exhortation *Marialis cultus*, on 2
February 1974. The first part deals with devotion to the Blessed
Virgin in the Liturgy, while the second is concerned with the
renewal of devotional practice. In Article 25 the Pope says: 'it is
supremely fitting that exercises of piety directed towards the
Virgin Mary should clearly express the Trinitarian and
Christological note that is intrinsic and essential to them'. He
goes on to give four guidelines for devotion to the Blessed
Virgin:

a. All forms of worship should have a scriptural basis (n. 30).
b. Our devotions should be in harmony with the sacred
liturgy and the liturgical seasons (n. 31).

c. Devotion to the Mother of the Lord should have an ecumenical aspect (n. 32).

d. Mary should be seen as the model of the perfect disciple – she heard the word of God and acted upon it (n. 34).

Part III considers the Angelus and the rosary: 'We wish now . . . to dwell for a moment on the renewal of the pious practice which has been called "the compendium of the entire Gospel": the Rosary' (n. 42). Pope Paul went on to emphasize 'the Gospel inspiration of the Rosary' (n. 44), and then how 'the Rosary reflects the very way in which the Word of God, mercifully entering into human affairs, brought about the Redemption' (n. 45). He continued: 'As a Gospel prayer, centred on the mystery of the redemptive Incarnation, the Rosary is therefore a prayer with a clearly Christological orientation' (n. 46). In the next article he introduced the element of contemplation.

> Without this the Rosary is a body without a soul, and its recitation is in danger of becoming a mechanical repetition of formulas and of going counter to the warning of Christ: 'And in praying do not heap up empty phrases as the Gentiles do; for they think that they will be heard for their many words' (Matthew 6.7). By its nature the recitation of the Rosary calls for a quiet rhythm and a lingering pace, helping the individual to meditate on the mysteries of the Lord's life as seen through the eyes of her who was closest to the Lord. In this way the unfathomable riches of these mysteries are unfolded. (n. 47).

There followed a consideration of the relationship between the Liturgy and the rosary:

> Once the pre-eminent value of liturgical rites has been reaffirmed

it will not be difficult to appreciate the fact that the Rosary is a practice of piety which easily harmonizes with the liturgy. In fact, like the liturgy, it is of a community nature, draws its inspiration from Sacred Scripture and is oriented towards the mystery of Christ ... the Rosary is an exercise of piety that draws its motivating force from the liturgy and leads naturally back to it, if practised in conformity with its original inspiration. It does not, however, become part of the liturgy. In fact, meditation on the mysteries of the Rosary, by familiarizing the hearts and minds of the faithful with the mysteries of Christ, can be an excellent preparation for the celebration of those same mysteries in the liturgical action and can also become a continuing echo thereof. However, it is a mistake to recite the Rosary during the celebration of the liturgy, though unfortunately this practice still persists here and there. (n. 48).

The Pope goes on (n. 49) to analyse the various elements of the rosary:

a. Contemplation, in communion with Mary, of three series of mysteries of salvation, expressing the joy of the messianic times, the salvific suffering of Christ and the glory of the Risen Lord.
b. The Lord's Prayer, which is at the basis of Christian prayer.
c. The litany-like succession of the Hail Mary, which is made up of the Angel's greeting to the Virgin (Luke 1.28) and of Elizabeth's greeting (Luke 1.42), followed by the ecclesial supplication Holy Mary. The 150 Hail Marys, characteristic of the rosary, is analogous with the Psalter and goes back to the very origin of the exercise of piety.
d. The 'Glory be to the Father' concludes the prayer with the glorifying of God who is one and three, from whom,

through whom and in whom all things have their being (Romans 11.36).

The rosary may be recited privately, in community, in the family or in groups, or publicly, in assemblies to which the ecclesial community is invited (n. 50).

One could 'insert into the ordinary celebration of the Word of God some elements of the Rosary, such as meditation on the mysteries and litany-like repetition of the angel's greeting to Mary. In this way these elements gain in importance, since they are found in the context of Bible readings, illustrated with a homily, accompanied by silent pauses and emphasized with song' (n. 51).

The Pope strongly recommends the recitation of the family rosary. There has to be 'a concrete effort to reinstate communal prayer in family life if there is to be a restoration of the theological concept of the family as the domestic Church' (n. 52). He went on:

But there is no doubt that, after the celebration of the Liturgy of the Hours, the high point which family prayer can reach, the Rosary should be considered as one of the best and most efficacious prayers in common that the Christian family is invited to recite (n. 54).

In concluding these observations, which give proof of the concern and esteem which the Apostolic See has for the Rosary of the Blessed Virgin, we desire at the same time to recommend that this very worthy devotion should not be propagated in a way that is too one-sided or exclusive. The Rosary is an excellent prayer, but the faithful should feel serenely free in its regard. They should be drawn to its calm recitation by its intrinsic appeal (n. 55).

These last two sentences should be emphasized. The rosary is indeed an excellent prayer, but the Liturgy of the Church takes first place.

On the 30 April 1965 Paul VI wrote an Apostolic Exhortation on 'The Month of May'. He recalls that the month of May is specially dedicated to Our Blessed Lady. He declared that: 'We have compelling reasons for believing that the present hour is especially grave; that it makes a call for united prayer from the whole Christian people more than ever a matter of urgency.' Peace, he reminds us, is a gift from God. 'We shall do our utmost to obtain this incomparable blessing by prayer ... And in a special way calling on the intercession and protection of the Virgin Mary, who is the Queen of Peace.' He ends by exhorting his brother bishops: 'And since this is a fitting occasion do not fail to lay careful stress on the saying of the Rosary, the prayer so dear to Our Lady and so highly recommended by the Supreme Pontiffs.'

In his Encyclical *Christi Matri* (15 September 1966), Pope Paul VI called for prayers to Mary for peace. He said:

It is a solemn custom of the faithful during the month of October to weave the prayers of the Rosary into mystical garlands for the Mother of Christ. Following in the footsteps of Our predecessors, We heartily approve this, and We call upon all the sons of the church to offer special devotions to the Most Blessed Virgin this year. For the danger of a more serious and extensive calamity hangs over the human family and has increased, especially in parts of eastern Asia where a bloody and hard-fought war [the Vietnam War] is raging. So We feel most urgently that We must once again do what We can to safeguard peace.

Again, in his Apostolic Exhortation *Recurrens Mensis* (7 October 1969), Paul VI reminds the Church that: 'It is a solemn custom of the faithful during the month of October to weave with the prayers of the Rosary a spiritual garland to the Mother of Christ. This we heartily approve ... and this year we call upon all the children of the Church to perform these special exercises of devotion to the same Most Blessed Virgin.'

Pope John Paul II

The devotion of Pope John Paul II to the Blessed Virgin is well known. He has made a special point of promoting devotion to the Blessed Mother. In his Angelus address on the last Sunday of October 1978 the Pope drew attention to the rosary. He describes the rosary as

> my favourite prayer. A marvellous prayer! Marvellous in its simplicity and in its depth. In this prayer we repeat many times the words that the Virgin Mary heard from the Archangel, and from her kinswoman Elizabeth. The whole Church joins in these words. It can be said that the Rosary is, in a certain way, a prayer commentary on the last chapter of the Constitution *Lumen Gentium* of the Second Vatican Council, a chapter that deals with the wonderful presence of the Mother of God in the mystery of Christ and the Church.[4]

On 6 June 1987 international television showed the Holy Father publicly reciting the rosary.

After the celebration of the Mass and beatification of Padre Pio in May 1999, Pope John Paul II quoted Padre Pio's last wish: 'Love Our Lady and help others to love her. Always recite the Rosary.' The Pope, mindful the troubles in former Yugoslavia, went on to say: 'With all my strength I invite you, brothers and sisters, to pray intensely throughout the month of May, imploring Our Lady for the gift of peace in the Balkans and in all the many places in the world where violence reigns.'[5]

Once again, we have the example of the Pope calling on the Church in time of grave threat to seek intercession on the part of the Virgin Mary.

The Catechism

The following extracts from the Catechism[6] adequately reflect the official position of the Church on Marian devotion and popular piety in relation to the Liturgy and its official prayer life:

(971) *'All generations will call me blessed'*: 'The Church's devotion to the Blessed Virgin is intrinsic to Christian worship.' The Church rightly honours 'the Blessed Virgin with special devotion. From the most ancient times the Blessed Virgin has been honoured with the title of "Mother of God", to whose protection the faithful fly in all their dangers and needs ... This very special devotion ... differs essentially from the adoration which is given to the incarnate Word and equally to the Father and the Holy Spirit, and greatly fosters this adoration.' The liturgical feasts dedicated to the Mother of God and Marian prayer, such as the rosary, an 'epitome of the whole Gospel', express this devotion to the Virgin Mary.

(1674) Besides sacramental liturgy and sacramentals, catechesis must take into account the forms of piety and popular devotions among the faithful. The religious sense of the Christian people has always found expression in various forms of piety surrounding the Church's sacramental life, such as the veneration of relics, visits to sanctuaries, pilgrimages, processions, the stations of the cross, religious dances, the rosary, medals, etc.

(1675) These expressions of piety extend the liturgical life of the Church, but do not replace it. They 'should be so drawn up that they harmonize with the liturgical seasons, accord with the sacred liturgy, are in some way derived from it and lead the people to it, since in fact the liturgy by its very nature is far superior to any of them'.

(2678) Medieval piety in the West developed the prayer of the rosary as a popular substitute for the Liturgy of the Hours. In the East, the litany called the *Akathistos* and the *Paraclesis* remained closer to the choral office in the Byzantine Churches, while the Armenian, Coptic and Syriac traditions preferred popular hymns and songs to the Mother of God. But in the *Ave Maria*, the *theotokia*, the hymns of St Ephrem or St Gregory of Narek, the tradition of prayer is basically the same.

(2708) Meditation engages thought, imagination, emotion and desire. This mobilization of faculties is necessary in order to deepen our convictions of faith, prompt the conversion of our heart and strengthen our will to follow Christ. Christian prayer tries above all to meditate on the mysteries of Christ, as in *lectio divina* or the rosary. This form of prayerful reflection is of great value, but Christian prayer should go further: to the knowledge of the love of the Lord Jesus, to union with him.

Notes

1. Christopher O'Donnell, *At Worship with Mary: A Pastoral and Theological Study* (Wilmington, DE: M. Glazier, 1988), see 'Our Lady of the Rosary', p. 190.
2. I am indebted to Fr Thomas A. Thompson, of the International Marian Research Institute, University of Dayton, for his work on the rosary Encyclicals of Leo XIII. The summary I offer here is based on his article, 'The Rosary Encyclicals, *The Priest*, 12 (October 1998): 39–41.
3. Pius XII, Letter to the Archbishop of Manilla, '*Philipinas Insulas*': *AAS*, 38 (1946), p. 419.
4. *L'Osservatore Romano* (weekly English edition), 9 November 1978.
5. Ibid., 5 May 1999.
6. *Catechism of the Catholic Church* (1994).

14

A Method for Praying the Rosary

The usual pair of rosary beads is a circlet of 50 small beads divided into decades by a larger bead. One of the larger beads is replaced by a 'centre medal' to which is attached a pendant of three small beads with two large beads and a crucifix.

It is customary to recite a rosary of five decades while meditating on one of the three sets of five of the fifteen mysteries of the rosary. However, one is free to recite a single decade or the full rosary of fifteen decades.

The Mysteries

The five Joyful Mysteries of the rosary
The Annunciation
The Visitation
The Birth of Jesus
The Presentation in the Temple
The Finding of the Child Jesus in the Temple

The five Sorrowful Mysteries of the rosary
The Agony in the Garden
The Scourging at the Pillar
The Crowning with Thorns
The Carrying of the Cross
The Crucifixion

The Five Glorious Mysteries of the rosary
  The Resurrection
  The Ascension
  The Descent of the Holy Spirit
  The Assumption of the Blessed Virgin
  The Crowning of the Blessed Virgin as Queen of Heaven.

Method

Begin by making the sign of the cross, saying:

In the name of the Father, and of the Son, and of the Holy Spirit.
Amen.

Let us contemplate the five Joyful/Sorrowful/Glorious Mysteries
of the most holy rosary.

Using the pendant say:

(on the crucifix):	the Creed
(on the first large bead):	Our Father
(on the three small beads):	Hail Mary
(on the second large bead):	Glory be to the Father.

This would be for the intentions of the Holy Father and to gain
the indulgence associated with this prayer.

Before each decade pause to meditate on the specific
mystery. Alternatively, read an appropriate passage of scripture,
or use one of the many books with printed meditations and
pictures. Then say:

(on the large bead):	Our Father
(on each small bead)	Hail Mary
(on the next large bead)	Glory be to the Father.

Many people now add the Fatima prayer between decades:

Lord Jesus Christ, forgive us our sins, save us from the fires of hell.
Lead all souls to heaven, especially those most in need of Thy
Mercy.[1]

Prayers Following the Recitation of the Rosary

Hail Holy Queen, mother of mercy –
Hail our life, our sweetness and our hope.
To thee do we cry, poor banished children of Eve.
To thee do we send up our sighs,
mourning and weeping in this vale of tears.
Turn then most gracious advocate,
thine eyes of mercy towards us, and after this our exile,
show unto us the blessed fruit of thy womb, Jesus.
O clement, O loving, O sweet Virgin Mary.

Pray for us, O holy Mother of God.
That we may be made worthy of the promises of Christ.

Let us pray
O God, whose only-begotten Son,
by His life, death and resurrection
has purchased for us the rewards of eternal life,
grant, we beseech Thee, that meditating on these mysteries
of the most holy Rosary of the Blessed Virgin Mary,
we may imitate what they contain and
obtain what they promise.
Through the same Christ our Lord. Amen.[2]

Queen of the most holy Rosary, pray for us.

O Mary, conceived without sin,
pray for us who have recourse to thee.

May the Divine assistance remain always with us.

May the souls of the faithful departed,

through the mercy of God, rest in peace. Amen.

These prayers are not essential to the rosary, but have become customary. They are subject to wide variation. The form of the rosary presented here is in common use in England today and is what most Catholics would recognize as 'The Rosary'. We might call it the Dominican rosary to acknowledge its origins and to distinguish it from the many historical variations.

There are indeed many variations in the practice of the rosary. We may say the rosary alone or in company when the prayers are said in an antiphonal fashion. A verse of a Marian hymn may be sung between decades. At one time the rosary was chanted, particularly in procession, but this practice seems now to have dropped out of fashion.[3]

The Scripture Rosary

The rosary is a meditation on the life of Christ in the company of his Mother who 'kept all these things in her heart'. So what better way to meditate than by incorporating the scriptures. The scripture rosary is said in the standard fashion, but a verse of scripture is inserted between each Hail Mary. There are many booklets available giving an appropriate selection of readings. The public life of Christ is not included in the usual fifteen mysteries but there is nothing to prevent us meditating on any scene in the Gospel. (Again, one can find booklets with suggested meditations.)

It is as well to remember what Paul VI said in *Marialis cultus*: 'we desire ... that this very worthy devotion should not be propagated in a way that is too one-sided or exclusive. The Rosary is an excellent prayer, but the faithful should feel serenely free in its regard. They should be drawn to its calm recitation by its intrinsic appeal.' He showed his awareness of new forms of prayer, recommending the insertion into the rosary of scripture readings, 'illustrated with a homily, accompanied by silent pauses and emphasized with song'.

For those who find the rosary difficult or unhelpful, be reassured by Pope Paul's statement that 'the faithful should feel serenely free in its regard'. Yes, it is an excellent prayer and maybe we have to work at it to derive the full benefit. However, we should pray in the way that best suits our temperament and aptitude. There are other ways of giving honour to the Mother of God – remember that 'the eucharistic sacrifice, [is] the source and summit of the Christian life' (*Lumen gentium*, 5) and that the scriptures are the word of God.

Further Reading

The following booklets give excellent examples of how one might vary the recitation of the rosary. They focus on the scriptures and bring new life to this adaptable prayer form.

Hans Urs von Balthasar, *The Three-Fold Garland* (San Francisco: Ignatius Press, 1982). A reflection on the mysteries of the rosary by one of the leading Catholic theologians of the twentieth century. Scholarly, yet accessible.

Peter Huyck, *Rosary Psalms* (New York: Alba House, Society of St Paul, 1994). In this small book Peter Huyck has put together a scripture rosary based on the standard fifteen mysteries, applying a line from the psalms to each *Ave*.

Peter Huyck, *A Scripture Rosary – 1596* (New York: Alba House, Society of St Paul, 1999). This is a scripture rosary covering the fifteen mysteries of the rosary taken from the second edition, published in about 1596 of a rosary book, *The Societie of the Rosarie*. It was compiled by Fr Henry Garnet SJ, who was martyred in 1606. This modern copy is beautifully produced and has some interesting historical notes.

Kevin A. Laheen, *Pondering with Mary* (New York: Alba House, Society of St Paul, 2000). Contains fifteen sonnets on the mysteries of the rosary, fifteen four-line verses on the same themes and seven four-line verses on the Sorrows of Mary. Each sonnet is followed by a scripture reference.

Domenico Marcicci, *Through the Rosary with Fra Angelico* (New York: Alba House, Society of St Paul, 1988). Each mystery is illustrated with a painting by Fra Angelico, and has a scriptural citation and a prayer intention. The prayer format uses a Jesus clause in the style of Dominic of Prussia. A brief but accurate account of the origins of the rosary is given in the Forward.

Alan Robinson, *The Six Chaplet Rosary* (New York: Alba House, Society of St Paul, 1994). Alan Robinson has composed six chaplets. The Opening Mysteries, Prophetic Mysteries, Joyful Mysteries, Sorrowful Mysteries, Glorious Mysteries and Continuing Mysteries. For each mystery he has chosen a short passage of scripture, followed by a prayer and five meditation points. He begins with Creation, call of Abraham, Moses, Samuel and David, then introduces the prophets from Elijah to John the Baptist. After the Resurrection we are asked to meditate on the saints, martyrs, angels, Christ the High Priest and, finally, the Second Coming.

Roland Walls, *The Royal Mysteries* (London: Darton, Longman & Todd, 1990). This helpful booklet suggests five 'mysteries' covering the public ministry of Christ. The Baptism, Temptation, Transfiguration, Entry into Jerusalem and, finally, Institution of the Eucharist. With each mystery we are offered a meditation and ten verses of scripture.

Notes

1. Authorized by Rome, 4 February 1956, Office of Indulgences, 878: 567.
2. This prayer is the Collect from the Mass of the Feast of the Most Holy Rosary, prior to the recent reform of the Missal.
3. Franz M. Willam, *The Rosary: Its History and Meaning*, pp. 62 and pp. 204–5.

15

Meditating on the Rosary

But Mary kept all these things, pondering them in her heart.

(Luke 2.19)

It is customary to begin the rosary with the words: 'Let us contemplate the five Joyful [Sorrowful or Glorious] Mysteries of the most holy rosary.' We are about to join with our Blessed Mother in considering the mighty things God has done for her and to reflect on the life, death and resurrection of her Divine Son.

In combining vocal, mental and bodily prayer the rosary attempts to open up the inner world. The idea that we might just contemplate the mysteries is not new. Fr Gabriel Harty quotes extensively from the studies of Père Bernard of Toulouse, *Le triple Rosaire* (third edition, 1679), a large manual written for directors of rosary confraternities.[1]

Fr Bernard speaks of the 'three ages of the Rosary', or three stages of rosary mental prayer: 'The meditated Rosary for beginners, the Rosary of the affections for proficients, and the Rosary of union with God for the perfect.' The following is a summary of his teaching on each of these areas.

The Rosary of Meditation

At this stage we engage in serious reflection on the mysteries of the Rosary, in order to know, love and imitate the virtues of Jesus and

Mary. [There is] No need to be frightened of the idea of meditation. The merchant meditates seriously his business, seeking ways of profit; the student meditates on his studies; while even the wicked meditates evil in his heart. Nothing more is required than goodwill and the aid of the Holy Spirit, together with some simple method.

The Rosary of Affection

Father Bernard then treats of the discernment needed to know when a soul is moving into the stage of intimacy with God, and so looking to the Lord more as friend than servant.

The Rosary now becomes simpler and more profound. One makes acts of love, adoration, thanks, and petition; one listens and praises following the attraction of the moment. There may be darkness, one prays: 'Lord, open my lips and my tongue shall declare your praise.' There may be heaviness, one prays: 'Heal me, Lord, for I have sinned against you.'

The author is conscious of the fact that some might at this stage abandon the rosary. He advises that 'one should pause in the recitation of the private Rosary and follow the lead of the Holy Spirit, taking it up at a later stage'. He is concerned about the manner in which certain souls have been forced to remain in crude straitjackets unsuited to their present stage of rosary prayer.

The Rosary of Union

Father Bernard continues:

Embrace then, devout souls, this Confraternity, in such fashion that those who pray the Rosary with a high degree of simple contemplation be not constrained to make complicated meditations, for that would be to pay their spiritual debts in silver, when they should be trading in gold!

What I wish to stress is that a person who has arrived at a high degree of contemplation and unitive prayer would find meditation as such almost impossible. Having arrived at a passive kind of prayer, and already receiving the fruits of the Rosary, he is no longer helped by that searching which is peculiar to meditation. He must use the talent God has given him in restful prayer, applying it for the intentions of the fraternity.

This kind of prayer is often compared to that of an infant asleep on its mother's breast, or like the drop of water lost in the ocean. One is lost in God. It may be an active or passive state, or a mixture of both, demanding purity of heart and the quieting of the passions.

Practical Advice

Father Bernard goes on to offer the following advice:

Keep yourself in the presence of God, listening rather than speaking, quieting even thoughts and affections and all discursive meditation. You are no longer listening to the preacher, the director, or the holy books, but hearing God in the depths of your heart; for he speaks more effectively, more sweetly and more intelligently than any of these. God knows better the proper times and dispositions.

The author does not deny the need for preaching and meditation and study, but he does insist that, at the actual time of praying the rosary, a person in this state leaves aside all anxiety about carefully worked out mental images or desires.

These things dispose us for the Divine presence, but at prayer-time they no longer occupy the forefront of our minds.

The preaching, the books, the meditation, have helped you, dear Rosarian, on your way, but now you must direct yourself to God alone, no longer striving to figure things out in the mind or stir up the affections. This work has already been done; now you are invited to rest in the Lord himself.

Imagine a King who summons his two sons to reveal to them the secrets of his heart. One passes quickly through the anterooms to hasten to the throne room; the other dallies on the way looking at the works of art, and never reaches the King. How much better to see the King than to be dazzled by his treasures.

Many of those called to be contemplatives, in the rosary act like this second son. Their rosary should be one of simple union, but they weary themselves in the labour of meditation.

With a final word of encouragement, Father Bernard says:

Freely, then, enter into this Brotherhood of the Mother of God, and you will increase your merits, gain many indulgences, and share in the prayers of all the members and of the whole Dominican Order; and win the favour of the Queen of the Most Holy Rosary.

In a note for people obliged to pray a certain number of rosaries, Father Bernard remarks:

Those who do not wish to leave their practice of the simple presence of God and their prayer of union, may spend their Rosary Hour by simply applying their accustomed prayer for the intentions of the Rosary Hour. They should say one *Ave* at the beginning and one at the end for this purpose. When it happens

that they are not drawn to say the full Rosary during the time
allotted to them, they may say it in parts at various other times.

St Louis-Marie Grignion de Montfort (d. 1716) in his classic
The Secret of the Rosary stresses that 'the Rosary is made up of
two things: mental prayer and vocal prayer. In the Holy Rosary
mental prayer is none other than meditation of the chief
mysteries of the life, death and glory of Jesus Christ and His
Blessed Mother.'[2] St Louis-Marie in his time did a great deal to
popularize the rosary devotion, but the common sense and
sound practical advice of Père Bernard probably has more
appeal in our day.

The Rosary: Meditation and its Physiological Benefits

Meditation is an integral part of the Dominican rosary. This
mode of meditation is an active process of thinking and
reflection. With time and practice this may reduce to a simple
idea or phrase which occupies the forefront of the mind, while
the Hail Marys continue in the background in a mantra-like
fashion. This form of prayer may lead on to a desire to pray in
the manner of meditative contemplation, when the beads
become superfluous. This is a silent form of meditation without
active thought.

Contemplative meditation is a technique which may be
learned. It differs from 'infused contemplation', which is a
sovereign gift of God. Meditation techniques have been used in
all the major religions, but have been popularized in our age by
the practice of yoga and transcendental meditation (TM).
Christian meditation has a long and authentic history typified
by the Jesus Prayer and the Hesychast tradition. The technique
in itself is spiritually neutral, but there is a fundamental
difference between what we might call 'cosmic' and 'Christian'

meditation. Whereas in cosmic meditation there is an awareness of the underlying being of the universe, in Christian meditation the awareness is of Christ and his redemptive love. Such meditation opens the person to spiritual influence. In the case of the Christian, one attempts to be present, alert and receptive to the presence of the loving God. Christian meditation is nothing less than a love affair between two free agents.[3]

The practice of meditation has been found to have beneficial physiological effects and has been demonstrated to be a useful adjunct to the treatment of stress-related conditions such as hypertension (high blood pressure). Dr Herbert Benson of the Harvard Medical School examined a number of people who regularly practised TM. He found that during meditation the resting heart-rate was reduced, on average, by three beats per minute; in those with an initial high blood pressure, this was reduced to normal levels; the rate of breathing, oxygen consumption and blood lactate levels were all reduced; electroencephalography revealed a pattern of brain activity which is associated with relaxation rather than sleep or hypnosis. Dr Benson concluded that he had demonstrated an integrated response which was the opposite of the 'fight or flight' response normally associated with a stressful situation. This he called 'the relaxation response'. It is not unique to TM and can be demonstrated with other classical methods of relaxation. The basic requirements are a quiet environment, a comfortable posture, an object for the attention to dwell on and, most importantly, a passive attitude.[4]

An international team of physicians led by Luciano Bernardi reported in the *British Medical Journal* in December 2001 their serendipitous discovery that reciting the *Ave Maria* prayer in Latin as in the rosary or repeating a yoga mantra enhances and synchronizes the inherent cardiovascular rhythm because it slows respiration to almost exactly six respirations per minute, which is essentially the same timing as that of our basic circulatory rhythm. The control of these rhythms is influenced by respiration, arousal and activity. It has been shown that a slow respiratory rate of six per minute has beneficial effects on cardiovascular and respiratory function, and increases the arterial baroreflex, which is a favourable prognostic factor in cardiac patients.

The investigators were surprised to find that when the rosary was recited in Latin, with a leader saying one part and the others the second part, each cycle was completed within a single slow respiration, in almost exactly ten seconds. They expressed their belief that the rosary may have in part evolved because it synchronized with the inherent cardiovascular rhythms, thus giving a feeling of well-being and perhaps an increased responsiveness to the religious message.

Similar beneficial effects were found with the use of the yoga mantra 'om-mani-padme-om', and also with respiration controlled by a metronome. It may be no coincidence that the use of repetitive prayer in Christianity originated in Egypt, where it may well have been learned from eastern religious practice. If so, this practice introduced – consciously or not – a new and previously unrecognized element of oriental health practice into Western culture. The rosary might be viewed as a health practice as well as a religious practice.[5]

From personal observation I have found that the Hail Mary, recited quickly, takes approximately ten seconds, and I have used it to time certain biochemical tests for the presence of sugar in a specimen.

If, however, one prays the Hail Mary silently and in the mind, as it were, dividing it as follows:

(with inspiration)	Hail Mary, full of grace, the Lord is with you,
(with expiration)	blessed are you among women, blessed is the fruit of your womb, Jesus
(with inspiration)	Holy Mary, Mother of God
(with expiration)	pray for us sinners, now and at the hour of our death, Amen

then it is perfectly possible to control the breathing to a rate of six respirations per minute, that is three Hail Marys per minute. The expiratory phase is a bit too long for comfort and is not as good as using the ideal phrase: 'Lord Jesus Christ, Son of God – have mercy on me a sinner', where each inspiration and expiration is an equal seven syllables.

Notes

1. Gabriel Harty, *Rediscovering the Rosary* (Dublin: Veritas, 1979), Chapter 12.
2. Louis-Marie Grignion de Montfort, *The Secret of the Rosary* (New York: Montfort, 1965), Part I, 'The First Rose', p. 17.
3. Matthew McGetrick, *Meditation for Modern Men and Women* (Dublin: Dominican Publications, 1983), p. 1.
4. Herbert Benson, *The Relaxation Response* (London: Collins, 1976).
5. Bernardi, L., Sleight, P., Bandinelli, G., *et al.*, Effect of Rosary Prayer and Yoga Mantras on Autonomic Cardiovascular Rhythms: A Comparative Study, *British Medical Journal*, 323 (22–29 December 2001): 1446–9.

16

Other Rosaries and Chaplets

In this chapter we will look at three important and historically significant variants of the Marian rosary: the Bridgettine rosary; the Franciscan corona; and the scripture rosary of the Servites. We will then go on to consider other chaplets of Jesus and Mary.

The Bridgettine Rosary

Historically, the greatest rival in popularity to the Dominican rosary was the so-called Bridgettine rosary. Fr Thurston has investigated the origins of this chaplet.[1] He quotes from the official publication of the Sacred Congregation of Indulgences (*sic*), *Raccolta di orazioni e pie opere*:

> The chaplet called after St Bridget, because she first devised it and propagated it, is recited in honour of the most holy Virgin Mary, in order to commemorate the sixty-three years which, as it is said, she lived on this earth. It consists of six divisions, in each of which are said the Our Father, the Hail Mary ten times and the Apostles' Creed once. After these six divisions another Our Father is added to make up the number of her seven dolours, or seven joys; and the Hail Mary is said three times to make up the number of her sixty-three years.

In spite of this tradition and Papal authority there is no hard evidence to support the idea that this rosary originated with St Bridget. She may well have used a string of beads, then commonly called a paternoster, but there is no evidence that she or any of her followers invented a new method of praying the beads. The first documentary evidence is a decree of the Congregation of Indulgences issued in 1714 which quotes a Brief of Pope Leo X from 1515 (this Brief is now lost) granting an indulgence of one hundred days for each *Ave* to those reciting the *coronas S. Birgittae*. Then there is the Brief of Pope Clement XI of 1714 giving a plenary indulgence to those who make a daily practice of reciting at least five decades.

There is no question that St Bridget did assign the term of 63 years for Our Lady's life in her *Revelations*. It is therefore reasonable to postulate that the name of St Bridget became associated with the 63 *Ave* corona to distinguish it from the Franciscan corona of 72 *Aves*. The Franciscans attribute the period of 72 years to a revelation made to a young friar of the order in 1422. The corona of Our Lady or 'Bridgettine' rosary was almost as popular as the rosary properly so-called in the sixteenth and seventeenth centuries. The little pendant of three small beads now almost universally attached to all rosaries, has been transferred, with a lack of any understanding of its significance, from the six-decade corona (60+3) to the five-decade chaplet, where no meaning can be assigned to them.

A dozen seventeenth-century rosaries were shown at the Limoges Exposition in 1891, of which half had six decades. The big crowned outdoor statue of Our Lady at Lourdes has a six-decade rosary over her right arm. Some might think that the sculptor made an error, but it may well be that he used a Bridgettine rosary as his model.

According to Richard Gribble, an interesting variant of the Bridgettine rosary, a survival of the sixteenth century perhaps, is still in use in the village of Schrocken, in the Alps.[2] It has a circle of 60 beads with a pendant of three beads on which are recited the first part of the Hail Mary, together with a *clausula* which is read by a member of the congregation. The final three *clausulae*, said on the three beads of the pendant, are:

1. Grant that we may hear with devotion the word of God.
2. Grant that we may keep the word of God in our hearts.
3. Grant that we may attain the happiness of heaven through Jesus Christ.

The Franciscan Corona: the Rosary of the Seven Joys of Mary

This fifteenth-century devotion is recited like the rosary. It consists of seven decades of *Aves* separated by a *Pater* and completed with the *Gloria Patri*, after which two *Aves* are added (making 72 *Aves* in all, the traditional years of Our Lady's life as revealed in a vision to St James of the March) and a *Pater*, *Ave* and *Gloria* for the Pope's intentions.

St Francis of Assisi is known for his love of Lady Poverty and Christ Crucified, but less well known for his deep devotion to the Mother of Jesus. Thomas of Celano, the first biographer of Francis, tells us that:[3]

> Towards the Mother of Jesus he was filled with an inexpressible love because it was she who made the Lord of majesty our brother. He sang special praises to her, and poured out prayers to her, offered her his affections, so many and so great that the tongue of man cannot recount them . . .[4]

St Bonaventure confirms this, in his later biography of Francis, when he says:

He embraced the Mother of Our Lord Jesus Christ with indescribable love because, as he said, it was she who made the Lord of majesty our brother, and through her we found mercy. After Christ he put all his trust in her and took her as his patroness for himself and for his friars. In her honour he fasted every year from the feast of Saints Peter and Paul until the Assumption ...[5]

Francis salutes the Mother of Christ as follows:

> Hail, His Palace!
> Hail, His Tabernacle!
> Hail, His Home!
> Hail, His Robe!
> Hail, His Servant!
> Hail, His Mother![6]

As Mary chose to follow her Son by choosing the poor and lowly state, so too did Francis:

I, brother Francis, the little one, wish to follow the life and poverty of our most high Lord Jesus Christ and of his most Holy Mother and to persevere in this until the end.[7]

For St Francis of Assisi the Passion and death of Christ were the glorification of the Lord and the source of joy. In conversation with Brother Leo, Francis explained perfect joy thus:

Suppose, Brother Leo, we are suffering intensely from hunger and the painful cold. We knock on the door of a Franciscan Friary in Assisi. The porter fails to recognise us. He becomes so enraged that he takes a club, grasps us by the cowl, throws us to the ground, rolls us in the mud and beats us severely. If we endure all those evils and insults and blows with joy and patience – O Brother Leo that is perfect joy![8]

The Seven Joys of Mary: Method

1. *The Annunciation* (*Pater*, ten *Aves*, *Gloria*)
   Virgin Mother of our Saviour,
   Who didst bear, at Heaven's favour,
   God's own Word, as Gabriel said:
   Make us through thy Son's great power,
   Fruitful in our final hour.
   Keep us safe and comforted.

2. *The Visitation* (*Pater*, ten *Aves*, *Gloria*)
   Mary, by thy visitation,
   When thou sangst in exultation
   Of the works God wrought in thee:
   Fill us, poor, with heavenly graces;
   Guide our footsteps, turn our faces
   Ever towards eternity.

3. *The Birth of Jesus in Bethlehem* (*Pater*, ten *Aves*, *Gloria*)
   Hail, thou Mother of thy Maker,
   Purest virgin, yet partaker
   Of the joys of motherhood.
   Grant thy servants, gentle Mother,
   To desire nothing other
   Than the peace that flows from good.

4. *The Adoration of the Magi* (*Pater*, ten *Aves*, *Gloria*)
   Mary, by the adoration
   Which the kings of eastern nation
   Offered to thine infant Son,
   Make us now to love and serve him,
   Hope in him and so deserve him
   Whom, through faith, the Magi won.

5. *The Finding in the Temple* (*Pater*, ten *Aves*, *Gloria*)
   Jesus lost, in deepest sorrow
   Thou didst seek, and on the morrow
   Find, 'mid doctors of the Law.
   Mary, refuge of the sinful,
   Grant that those who, blind and wilful,
   Follow evil may withdraw.

6. *The risen Saviour appears to his Mother on Easter Morning*
   (*Pater*, ten *Aves*, *Gloria*)
   Mother by the joy that filled thee,
   When the glorious vision thrilled thee
   Of thy resurrected Son,
   Fill us with a shame all-burning,
   And our hearts from evil turning,
   Make us seek the Eternal One.

7. *The Blessed Virgin Mary is assumed into Heaven and crowned*
   Queen of the Universe (*Pater*, ten *Aves*, *Gloria*)
   O rejoice! 'Mid stars enthroned,
   Queen of men and angels owned,
   Sharer of Christ's regal might,
   Grant that, 'mid the thrones of Heaven,
   E'er through thee may we be given
   Joys of everlasting light.

   AMEN. ALLELUIA.

The Scripture Rosary: the Seven Sorrows of Mary

This chaplet originated with the Servites in the fourteenth century and was actively promoted by them during the Black Death plague of 1347–51.

Fr William M. McLoughlin OSM, writing of Our Lady of Sorrows,[9] tells us that the sorrows of Mary, standing under the cross of Christ, have had a prominent place in the spirituality of the Servite Order. There is no episode relating to Mary in the Gospels which cannot be read in terms of the mystery of the Passion of Mary's Son, since 'everything is relative to Christ and dependent on him' (Paul VI, *Marialis cultus*, II, 25). The sufferings of Christ define the Marian sorrows and give them their significance and salvific value in the life of the Church and individual Christians.

Devotion to Our Lady of Sorrows found expression in the Servite Order, which sees itself as 'a community of men reunited in the name of the Lord Jesus. Moved by the Spirit, we engage ourselves, like the first Fathers, in giving witness to the Gospel in fraternal communion and in being at the service of God and man, taking constant inspiration from Mary, Mother and Servant of the Lord' (OSM Constitutions, article 1). The text goes on to say: 'In this bond of service, let the figure of Mary at the foot of the Cross be our guiding image' (article 290).

In the Servite tradition, the black habit of Mary's widow-hood was given on Good Friday 1239 by the Mother of God to the founders of that order, and this particular Good Friday coincided with the Feast of the Annunciation. The Blessed Virgin Mary's *fiat* was to conceive the Redeemer. Mary's unique cooperation in what happened at Calvary was a fulfilment of her active consent then and at every stage of her life.

Devotion to the Sorrowful Mother developed gradually, popular tradition seeing her as 'the Mother dressed in black'. There is an oratory at Herford, Paderborn, dedicated to Our Lady at the Foot of the Cross, dated c. 1011. During the twelfth and thirteenth centuries, a growing awareness of the significance of the humanity of Jesus and his sufferings led to an awareness of the human dimension of Mary's Sorrows. McLoughlin continues:

The middle ages saw a parallel development of devotion to the joys of Mary and to the sorrows of Mary. Before the settled convention of seven sorrows was arrived at, we know that there are occasional references to five sorrows to complement five joys, but also of nine joys, fifteen sorrows or twenty-seven sorrows. Over and above historical considerations, the choice of the number seven was related to its symbolic value. In the biblical symbolism so widely accepted during the middle ages, seven was seen as suggesting fullness, completeness and abundance. Medieval writers, therefore, did not, in listing seven sorrows, intend a limit of the sufferings of the mother of Christ to seven particular episodes but rather wanted to assert that she was truly 'full of sorrows' as was often written in the devotional literature of the time. As the symbolic value of the number seven became less obvious, it came to be seen as a limit and authors often had to specify that these were only the 'principal sorrows'.

The sorrow of the Virgin found its first and ultimate meaning in the mystery of the cross of Christ, but it was also extended back from Calvary to embrace the other events of the life of the Son in which the mother took part personally according to explicit mention or where tradition has deemed it likely that she did.

From the first half of the fourteenth century, when the number of the sorrows was already firmly established, there were two ways of beginning the series of sorrows:

- in those devotions in which the seven sorrows of the blessed Virgin were strictly tied to the events of Christ's passion, the first sorrow was the arrest of Jesus in the Garden of Olives;

- in other devotions in which the sorrows of Mary were extended to include episodes of the Lord's infancy, the first sorrow was the prophecy of Simeon;

- very rarely is found a list of seven sorrows beginning with the circumcision of Jesus (as in that issued at the General Dicta OSM at Reggio Aemelia of May 1660) and as yet no pontifical document has been produced which prescribes beginning the series of sorrows with that suffered by Mary at the circumcision of her Son.[10]

Eventually the Seven Sorrows as set out in the responsories of Matins for the feast granted to the Servite Order in 1668 were accepted as the popular form of the devotion.

In modern times this chaplet has lost its general popularity, but is kept alive in Servite devotions. Very recently it has received endorsement and encouragement in Kibeho, Rwanda, where it is reported that the Blessed Virgin, the Mother of the Word, has been appearing to a group of young people since 28 November 1981. On 27 March 1982 Marie-Claire Mukangango was instructed to inform the bishop that the Blessed Virgin wished Christians to recite the Chaplet of the Seven Sorrows, since the world was in revolt. On 31 May 1982 Our Lady is reported to have said to Marie-Claire: 'What I am asking of you [the world] is to repent. If you recite this chaplet, duly meditating upon it, you will receive the strength to truly repent.'[11]

The Seven Sorrows of Mary: Method

Begin with the Our Father and follow each verse with the Hail Mary.

1. The Sword of Sorrow

1 And behold, there was in Jerusalem a man named Simeon and this man was just and devout, looking for

the consolation of Israel (Luke 2.25).

2 And Simeon blessed them and said to Mary His Mother, 'Behold this Child is destined for the fall and the rise of many in Israel, and for a sign that shall be contradicted' (Luke 2.34).

3 'And thy own soul a sword shall pierce, that the thoughts of many hearts may be revealed' (Luke 2.35).

4 And He shall be a sanctification to you: but a stone of stumbling and a rock of offence to the two houses of Israel, a snare and a ruin to the inhabitants of Jerusalem (Isaiah 8.14).

5 Behold I lay in Sion a stumbling-stone and rock of scandal: and whoever believes in Him shall not be disappointed (Romans 9.33).

6 A stone which the builders rejected, the same has become the head of the corner (1 Peter 2.7).

7 And when they had fulfilled all things prescribed in the law of the Lord, they returned to Galilee, into their own town of Nazareth (Luke 2.39).

2. The Flight into Egypt

1 Behold, an angel of the Lord appeared in a dream to Joseph, saying: 'Arise and take the Child and His mother, and flee into Egypt' (Matthew 2.13).

2 'And remain there until I tell you. For Herod will seek the Child to destroy Him' (Matthew 2.13).

3 So he arose, and took the Child and His mother by night, and withdrew into Egypt (Matthew 2.14).

4 And remained there until the death of Herod; that what was spoken by the Lord through the prophet might be fulfilled (Matthew 2.15).

5 'Out of Egypt I called My Son' (Matthew 2.15).

6 But when Herod was dead, behold, an angel of the Lord

appeared in a dream to Joseph in Egypt, saying: 'Arise, and take the Child and His mother, and go into the land of Israel' (Matthew 2.19–20).

7 But hearing that Archelaus was reigning in Judea in the place of his father Herod, he was afraid to go there; and being warned in a dream, he withdrew into the region of Galilee (Matthew 2.22).

3. Jesus is Lost for Three Days

1 And when He was twelve years old, they went up to Jerusalem according to the custom of the feast (Luke 2.42).

2 The boy Jesus remained in Jerusalem, and his parents did not know it (Luke 2.43).

3 And not finding Him, they returned to Jerusalem in search of Him (Luke 2.45).

4 'Son, why have You done this to us? Behold, in sorrow Your father and I have been seeking You' (Luke 2.48).

5 'Did you not know that I must be about My Father's business?' (Luke 2.49).

6 And they did not understand the word that He spoke to them (Luke 2.50).

7 And He went down with them and came to Nazareth, and was subject to them; and His mother kept all these things in her heart (Luke 2.51).

4. The Meeting On the way to Calvary

1 And so they took Jesus and led Him away (John 19.16).

2 And bearing the cross for Himself, He went forth to the placed called 'The Skull' (John 19.17).

3 There was following Him a great crowd of people, and of women who were bewailing and lamenting Him (Luke 23.27).

4 But Jesus turning to them said, 'Daughters of Jerusalem, do not weep for Me, but weep for yourselves and for your children' (Luke 23.28).

5 Now as they went out, they found a man of Cyrene named Simon; him they forced to take up His cross (Matthew 27.32).

6 'If anyone wishes to come after Me, let him deny himself, and take up his cross, and follow Me' (Matthew 16.24).

7 'Take My yoke upon you, and learn from Me, for I am meek and humble of heart' (Matthew 11.29).

5. *Our Lady Stands at the Foot of the Cross*

1 And they gave Him wine to drink mixed with gall; but when He had tasted it, He would not drink (Matthew 27.34).

2 And after they had crucified Him, they divided His garments, casting lots (Matthew 27.35).

3 And they put above His head the charge against Him, written: 'This is Jesus, the King of the Jews' (Matthew 27.37).

4 Now the passers-by were jeering at Him, shaking their heads, and saying, 'You who would destroy the temple and in three days build it up again, save yourself!' (Matthew 27.39–40).

5 In like manner, the chief priests with the scribes and elders, mocking, said, 'He saved others, himself he cannot save!' (Matthew 27.41–2).

6 And the robbers also, who were crucified with Him, reproached Him in the same way (Matthew 27.44).

7 And Jesus said, 'Father, forgive them, for they know not what they do' (Luke 23.34).

6. The Death of Jesus and His Descent from the Cross

1 When Jesus, therefore, saw His mother and the disciple standing by, whom He loved, He said to His mother, 'Woman, behold, thy son' (John 19.26).

2 Then He said to the disciple, 'Behold, thy mother.' And from that hour the disciple took her into his home (John 19.27).

3 And Jesus cried out with a loud voice and said, 'Father, into Thy hands I commend My spirit.' And having said this, He expired (Luke 23.46).

4 One of the soldiers opened His side with a lance, and immediately there came out blood and water (John 19.34).

5 And behold, the curtain of the temple was torn in two from top to bottom; and the earth quaked, and the rocks were rent (Matthew 27.51).

6 And all the crowd that collected for the sight, when they beheld what things had happened, began to return beating their breasts (Luke 23.48).

7 Joseph of Arimathea, a noble counsellor, who was also himself looking for the kingdom of God, came and went in boldly to Pilate and begged the body of Jesus . . . and he gave the body to Joseph (Mark 15.43–45)

7. The Burial

1 And Joseph, taking the body, wrapped it in a clean linen cloth, and laid it in his new tomb, which he had hewn out of rock (Matthew 27.59–60).

2 And he rolled a great stone to the door of the monument and went his way (Matthew 27.60).

3 And Mary Magdalene and Mary the mother of Joseph saw where He was laid (Mark 15.47).

4 And the next day, which was the one after the Day of

Preparation, the chief priests and the Pharisees went in a body to Pilate, saying (Matthew 27.62):

5 'Sir, we have remembered how that deceiver said, while He was yet alive, "After three days I will rise again"' (Matthew 27.63).

6 'Give orders, therefore, that the sepulchre be guarded until the third day, or else His disciples may come and steal Him away' (Matthew 27.64).

7 So they went and made the sepulchre secure, sealing the stone and setting the guard (Matthew 27.66).

Other Chaplets of Our Lady and Jesus

Other chaplets of Our Lady include the following:

Little Crown of the Virgin

Crown of Twelve Stars

Rosary of Mary's Immaculate Heart

Chaplet in Honour of the Immaculate Heart of Mary

Little Rosary of the Seven Dolours of Mary

Rosary of Our Lady's Tears

Rosary of the Tears of Blood

Rosary in Praise of the Most Blessed Virgin

Chaplet of Our Lady of Guadalupe

Rosary of Our Lady of Consolation

Chaplet of Our Lady of Czestochowa

Chaplet of Our Lady, Star of the Sea

Rosary of Our Lady of Perpetual Help.

Chaplets of Jesus include:

The Crown of Jesus	(33 *Paters* + five *Aves* – 33 years and the Five Wounds)

Chaplet of the Sacred Heart   (five large beads and 33 small – the Five Wounds and the 33 years)

Chaplet of the Dead   (four decades for the 40 hours in the tomb)

Chaplet of the Five Wounds   (five sets of five separated by a large bead or medal).

Anglican Prayer Beads

A novel version discovered on the Internet:[12]

> The 'Anglican Prayer Beads' have 33 beads, grouped in 7s rather than 10s as in the Catholic Rosary. The most usual prayers used with Anglican Prayer Beads are based on Anglican incarnational theology. The prayer sequence begins with the cross, then there is a large bead following the cross on the pendant, which is the Invitatory bead – the invitation to praise and worship (as in the Daily Office). The circle itself is comprised of four sets of seven beads called 'Weeks' to represent the 7 days of creation/7 days of the temporal week/7 seasons of Church year, which are divided by four large beads called 'Cruciform' beads representing the centrality of the cross in our lives and faith. The total number of beads is 33 – the number of years of Jesus' life on this earth.

This is a new tradition, dating from the 1980s, too recent to have developed an 'official' set of prayers for the beads. One can use prayers such as the *Trisagion* (Holy God, Holy Mighty One, Holy Immortal One), the Jesus Prayer, a set of thoughts from Julian of Norwich, or excerpts from the Book of Common Prayer and Common Worship. Others can be used as well.

The Chaplet of Divine Mercy

This chaplet is of recent origin and is now widely accepted and in current use. Sister Faustina, born Helen Kowalska (canonized 30 April 2000), had a vision of the King of Divine Mercy on 13 September 1935, who gave her this powerful prayer to be said on ordinary rosary beads. Begin by saying an Our Father, a Hail Mary and the Creed, then on each of the five larger beads:

> Eternal Father, I offer you the Body and Blood, Soul and Divinity of your dearly beloved Son, Our Lord Jesus Christ, in atonement for our sins and those of the whole world.

And on each of the ten small beads:

> For the sake of his sorrowful Passion, have mercy on us and on the whole world.

To complete the chaplet of prayers, say three times:

> Holy God, Holy Mighty One, Holy Immortal One, have mercy on us and on the whole world.

Notes

1. Herbert Thurston, The So-called Bridgettine Rosary, *The Month*, 100 (1902): 189–203.
2. Richard Gribble, *The History and Devotion of the Rosary*, p. 63, and see note 23, p. 80.
3. The following quotations are from John Harding, The Place of Mary in the Writings of St Francis and St Clare, in *Mary and the Churches*, ESBVM, Chichester Congress Papers 1986, ed. Alberic Stacpoole (Dublin: Columba Press, 1987), pp. 122–8; *The Classics of Western Spirituality, Francis and Clare: The Complete Works*, trans. Regis J.

Armstrong and Ignatius Brady (London: SPCK, 1982) cited as 'AB' with the page number; Marion A. Habig (ed.), *St Francis of Assisi: Writings and Early Biographies: English Omnibus of Sources for the Life of St Francis* (Chicago: Franciscan Herald Press, 1973), cited as 'Omnibus' with page number.

4. Omnibus 521.
5. St Bonaventure, *Major Life* IX, 3, Omnibus 699.
6. AB 150
7. AB 46
8. 'Fioretti' or 'The Little Flowers of St Francis', quoted in John R. H. Moorman, *St Francis of Assisi*, (London: SPCK, 1976), p. 26.
9. William M. McLoughlin, Our Lady of Sorrows – a Devotion Within a Tradition, in *Mary and the Churches*, ESBVM, Chichester Congress Papers 1986, ed. Alberic Stacpoole (Dublin: Columba Press, 1987), pp. 114–21.
10. Ibid., pp. 115–16.
11. Gabriel Maindron, *The Apparitions of Our Lady at Kibeho* (Godstone, Surrey: The Marian Spring Centre, 1996), pp. 39–40.
12. *http://members.ols.net/~michael/PrayerBeads.html*

17
The Jesus Clause

Dominic of Prussia wrote fifty *clausulae* or *formulae* to be recited after the words 'Jesus Christ' and ending with 'Amen' (see above, p. 15). The second part of the Hail Mary was introduced later and replaced the *clausula*. In 1921 the Holy See authorized the introduction of the Jesus clause into the Dominican rosary without prejudice to the attached indulgences.[1] They are of more than historic interest and are given here in English translation so that they may again be used.[2] Additionally some modern variations are offered.

Hail Mary, full of grace, the Lord is with you,
Blessed are you among women and blessed is the fruit of your womb,
  Jesus Christ:
1. Whom you conceived by the Holy Spirit upon the Angel's annunciation. Amen.
2. Whom having conceived, you went up into the hill country, to Elizabeth. Amen.
3. Whom, with joy, you brought to birth, remaining ever a Virgin, holy in mind and body. Amen.
4. Whom you adored as your Creator and suckled at your virginal breast. Amen.
5. Whom you wrapped in swaddling clothes and laid in a manger. Amen. (add 'Amen' each time)

6. Whom the angels praised, singing glory in highest heaven and whom the shepherds found at Bethlehem.

7. Who was circumcised on the eighth day and called Jesus.

8. Who was reverently adored by three Magi, bringing three gifts.

9. Whom you carried in your maternal arms to the Temple and presented to God his Father.

10. Whom the aged Simeon took in his arms and blessed, and the widow Anna recognized.

11. With whom you fled into Egypt away from Herod.

12. With whom after seven years, recalled by an angel, you returned to your own country.

13. Whom you lost in Jerusalem when he was twelve years old and found again in the Temple after searching with sorrow for three days.

14. Who advanced daily in age, and wisdom, and in favour with God and men.

15. Whom John baptized in the Jordan and pointed out the very Lamb of God.

16. Who fasted in the desert for forty days and whom Satan thereupon tempted three times.

17. Who gathered disciples from one place and another and preached to the world the Kingdom of Heaven.

18. Who gave light to the blind, cleansed lepers, healed paralytics and freed all who were oppressed by the devil.

19. Whose feet Mary of Magdala washed with her tears, wiped with her hair, kissed and anointed with perfume.

20. Who raised to life Lazarus four days dead and also others who had died.

21. Who on Palm Sunday, seated on a donkey, was hailed by the people with great glory.

22. Who at his Last Supper instituted the august Sacrament of his Body and Blood.

23. Who went into a garden with his disciples and, praying there at length, sweated drops of blood.

24. Who of his own accord went to meet his enemies and freely delivered himself up to them.

25. Whom the servants of the Jews bound fast and led in bonds to the chief priests.

26. Whom they accused on false testimony, blindfolded, spat upon and struck with hand and fist.

27. Whom before Pilate and Herod they declared guilty of death as a malefactor.

28. Whom Pilate had scourged, naked, long and cruelly.

29. Whom also the servants crowned with thorns and clad in derisory purple, adored in mockery.

30. Whom they unjustly condemned to a most ignominious death and led away with two other wrongdoers.

31. Whom they fastened hands and feet to a cross and to whom they offered wine mixed with myrrh and gall.

32. Who prayed for those who crucified him, saying 'Father, forgive them, for they know not what they do.'

33. Who said to the thief on his right hand, 'Truly, I tell you, today you shall be with me in Paradise.'

34. Who said to you, his most holy Mother, 'Mother, there is your son'; and to John, 'there is your Mother'.

35. Who cried out, 'My God, my God, why have you forsaken me?'

36. Who said, 'It is accomplished.'

37. Who, at the end, said, 'Father, into your hands I commit my spirit.'

38. Who died a most bitter, a most holy, death for us wretched sinners: thanks be to God!

39. Whose side a soldier opened with his lance, and blood and water flowed from it for the forgiveness of sins.

40. Whose most sacred body they took down from the cross and

returned lifeless to your bosom, as is piously said.

41. Whom righteous and holy men anointed with spices, wrapped in a linen sheet and buried.

42. Whose tomb the Jews marked with seals and secured with guards.

43. Whose most holy soul descended into Hell and, consoling the holy fathers, led them out with himself into Paradise.

44. Who rose on the third day and gladdened you with ineffable joy.

45. Who after his Resurrection often appeared to his disciples and his faithful and strengthened their hearts in holy faith.

46. Who before their eyes and with you too present and watching, ascended to heaven and sits at the right hand of the Father.

47. Who on the day of Pentecost sent from heaven to his faithful the Holy Spirit whom he had promised to them.

48. Who at length took you, his dearest Mother, up to heaven to himself, set you at his right hand and crowned you gloriously.

49. Who at your intercession, we pray, will deign to take us up also, his servants and yours, after the course of this wretched life, and establish us in the kingdom of his Father.

50. Who with the Father and the Holy Spirit and with you, his most glorious Mother, lives and reigns, King unconquered and glorious, for all eternity.

Some Modern Examples of the Jesus Clause

In the modern form of the Jesus clause, for each mystery, a single phrase is repeated with each Hail Mary, and concludes with 'Holy Mary, Mother of God [etc.]'.

Joyful Mysteries

Jesus incarnate

Jesus sanctifying

Jesus born in poverty

Jesus sacrificed

Jesus, Saint among saints

Sorrowful Mysteries

Jesus in His agony

Jesus scourged

Jesus crowned with thorns

Jesus carrying His cross

Jesus crucified

Glorious Mysteries

Jesus risen from the dead

Jesus ascending into heaven

Jesus filling Thee with the Holy Spirit

Jesus raising Thee up

Jesus crowning Thee

(St Louis-Marie Grignion de Montfort)[3]

The Source

Jesus, whom you, O Virgin, conceived of the Holy Spirit

Jesus, whom you, O Virgin, took to Elizabeth

Jesus, to whom you, O Virgin, gave birth

Jesus, whom you, O Virgin, offered up in the Temple

Jesus, whom you, O Virgin, found again in the Temple

The Transition

Jesus, who sweated blood for us

Jesus, who was scourged for us

Jesus, who was crowned with thorns for us

Jesus, who bore the heavy cross for us

Jesus, who was crucified for us

The Consummation

Jesus, who rose from the dead

Jesus, who ascended into heaven

Jesus, who sent us the Holy Spirit

Jesus, who took you, O Virgin, up into heaven

Jesus, who crowned you, O Virgin, in heaven

(Hans Urs von Balthasar)[4]

Joyful Mysteries

Jesus, who becomes one of us

Jesus, who brings His Spirit to all

Jesus, who dwells among us

Jesus, who is a light to the gentiles

Jesus, who begins His Father's work

Sorrowful Mysteries

Jesus, who submits to the Father's will

Jesus, by whose wounds we are healed

Jesus, who is humiliated for us

Jesus, who bears our sin

Jesus, who gives Himself to His Father

Glorious Mysteries

Jesus, who is risen and glorified

Jesus, who reigns with the Father

Jesus, who with the Father sends the Holy Spirit

Jesus, who draws Mary, body and soul, into heaven

Jesus, who crowns His Mother, Queen of Heaven

(J. D. Miller)

Notes

1. Herbert du Manoir, Chartreux, Culte de la Virge, in *Maria: Etudes sur la Sainte Virge* (Paris: Beauchesne, 1949–71), Vol. II, p. 675.

2. From Karl-Josef Klinkhammer, *Adolf von Essen und seine Werke: Der Rosenkranz in der geschichtlichen Situation seiner Entstehung und in seinem bleibenden Anliegen*, Frankfurter Theologische Studien, 13 (Frankfurt: Knecht, 1972), trans. Revd Theodore Berkeley OCSO.
3. Gabriel Harty, *Rediscovering the Rosary*, p. 25.
4. Hans Urs von Balthasar, *The Threefold Garland* (San Francisco, CA: Ignatius Press, 1982), pp. 5–6.

18

Indulgences Associated with the Rosary

The teaching of the Church on indulgences is summarized in
The Code of Canon Law (1983):[1]

Canon 992 An indulgence is the remission in the sight of God of
the temporal punishment due for sins, the guilt of which has
already been forgiven. A member of Christ's faithful who is
properly disposed and who fulfils certain conditions, may gain an
indulgence by the help of the Church which, as the minister of the
redemption, authoritatively dispenses and applies the treasury of
the merits of Christ and the Saints.

Canon 993 An indulgence is partial or plenary according as it
partially or wholly frees a person from the temporal punishment
due for sins.

Canon 994 All members of the faithful can gain indulgences,
partial or plenary, for themselves, or they can apply them by way of
suffrage to the dead.

In the early Church from the third century the intercession
of confessors and those awaiting martyrdom was allowed by
ecclesiastical authority to shorten the canonical discipline of
those under penance. With the development of the doctrine of
purgatory in the West, canonical penance came to be
considered as a substitute for temporal punishment in

purgatory. Then came the belief that the prayers and merits of the saints availed to shorten such punishment. The granting of general indulgences dates from the eleventh century and grew in the twelfth century when plenary indulgences were offered to those taking part in the Crusades.

In 1343 Pope Clement VI officially sanctioned the view that Christ and the saints had left a treasury of merits that other members of the Church could draw on for remission of the temporal punishment due to their sins. One obtained a share in these merits by means of a Church indulgence, usually granted by the Pope in exchange for some good work or gift of alms. Official teaching always insisted on an interior repentance on the part of the recipient.

During the Great Jubilee Year 2000 a plenary indulgence was granted to those who visited a designated place of worship, celebrated the sacrament of reconciliation, participated in the Eucharist and said the Creed and other prayers for the intention of the Pope. The principle underlying this formula is that, on our part, a change of heart is required. We must change the focus of our life away from ourselves and towards God. The sacrament of reconciliation helps us towards that end. We should then come into a closer union of love with our Lord Jesus Christ, which is made eminently possible in Holy Communion through the celebration of the Eucharist. And finally we should show our love for, and our unity with, the Mystical Body of Christ, the Church, by praying for the intentions of the Head of the Church, our Pope.

At the General Audience of Wednesday, 29 September 2000, Pope John Paul II said: 'The starting-point for understanding indulgences is the abundance of God's mercy revealed in the Cross of Christ. The crucified Jesus is the great "indulgence" that the Father has offered humanity through the forgiveness of sins and the possibility of living as children in the Holy Spirit.'

He stressed that inner conversion is required in order to benefit from indulgences. Far from being a sort of 'discount' on the duty of conversion, they are instead an aid to its prompt, generous and radical fulfilment. This is required to such an extent that the spiritual condition for receiving a plenary indulgence is the exclusion 'of all attachment to sin, even venial sin'.[2] Therefore, it would be a mistake to think that we can receive this gift by simply performing certain outward acts. On the contrary, they are required as the expression and support of our progress in conversion. They particularly show our faith in God's mercy and in the marvellous reality of communion, which Christ has achieved by indissolubly uniting the Church to himself as his Body and Bride.

During the past 500 years the rosary has been endowed with more indulgences than any other prayer.[3] A radical reform of indulgences was undertaken by Pope Paul VI, and the Enchiridion of Indulgences, published on 1 January 1967, revoked all former indulgences except those contained in the new Enchiridion. Article 48 laid down the conditions for the granting of plenary indulgences for the recitation of the rosary and simply says a partial indulgence is granted in other circumstances (days, years and quarantines are no longer specified). These gifts of the Church are now to some extent neglected and perhaps there is a need to promote them afresh. A fourth edition of the *Enchiridion indulgentiarum* (the official Vatican handbook of indulgences),[4] published in 1999, indicates the indulgences that may be gained for the recitation of the rosary as follows:

A plenary indulgence is granted to the faithful who:
- Say the Marian rosary devoutly in a church or oratory, or in the family, in a religious community, in a meeting of the faithful, and in general, when several people come together

for some worthy reason.

- Say the same prayer with the Supreme Pontiff, joining him through television or radio.

To obtain the plenary indulgence for the recitation of the Marian rosary, the following are specified:

- it is enough to say one-third, but the five decades are to be said continuously;
- meditation on the mysteries is added to the vocal prayers;
- in public recitation the mysteries are to be announced according to the approved local custom;
- in private recitation it suffices that the faithful add meditation on the mysteries to the vocal prayer.

Since 1967 partial indulgences are no longer quantified but simply called partial if they remit only part of the temporal punishment still due for sin after its guilt has been forgiven. If all such punishment is remitted, the indulgence is called plenary.

Additionally we may look to *The Code of Canon Law*, which stipulates the following conditions:

1. To be capable of gaining indulgences a person must be baptised, not excommunicated, and in the state of grace at least on the completion of the prescribed work.

2. To gain them, however, the person who is capable must have at least the intention of gaining them, and must fulfil their prescribed works at the time and in the manner determined by the terms of the grant.

In order to gain a plenary indulgence, there is a presupposition that the sacrament of reconciliation, and the Eucharist with reception of Holy Communion, will be celebrated within a week.

(Canon 996)

Notes

1. The Canon Law Society of Great Britain and Ireland, *The Code of Canon Law* (London: Collins, 1983).
2. Ibid., p. 25.
3. Richard Gribble, *The History and Devotion of the Rosary*, see pp. 173–85 for a summary of indulgences granted by the Roman Pontiffs to Members of the Confraternity of the Most Holy Rosary and to the Faithful in General (collected by W. R. Lawler).
4. *Enchiridion indulgentiarum normae et concessiones*, 4th edn (Vatican City, Rome: Libreria editrice vaticana, 1999), p. 62.

The *Salve Regina*

'*Salve Regina*' is the title and opening words of the Latin version of the most celebrated anthem of the Blessed Virgin Mary. It has been said or sung since the eleventh century and remains as popular today as it was then. In the Divine Office it is recommended as the final anthem to be sung after Night Prayer from Trinity Sunday through to Advent. It is regularly said as a prayer following the recitation of the rosary and often sung as a hymn.

> Hail, holy Queen, Mother of mercy, Hail, our life, our sweetness and our hope.
> To thee do we cry, poor banished children of Eve.
> To thee do we send up our sighs, mourning and weeping in this vale of tears.
> Turn then most gracious advocate thine eyes of mercy towards us,
> and after this our exile show unto us the blessed fruit of thy womb, Jesus.
> O clement, O loving, O sweet Virgin Mary.

The Origins and History of the *Salve Regina*

According to Fr Herbert Thurston SJ, whose scholarly research was first published in *The Month* in 1916, this prayer, as we know it today, differs from the original in only two respects: the title Mother of Mercy was added to the title Queen of Mercy and in the final phrase she is designated 'Virgin Mary' rather than simply as 'Mary'.

This eleventh-century anthem has been attributed to various authors, but general opinion would seem to favour Herimannus Contractus (Hermann the Lame), a monk of Reichenau, who died in 1054. He is known to be the composer of the words and the music of the *Alma Redemptoris Mater*, and it is thought that the musical setting of the *Salve* is contemporaneous.

Another possible author is Adhémar, Bishop of Le Puy, who was appointed by Urban II in 1095 to be his representative on the First Crusade. It is said that 'Before his departure, towards the end of October 1096, he composed the war-song of the crusade, in which he asked the intercession of the Queen of Heaven, the *Salve Regina*.'[1] The shrine of Our Lady of Le Puy was a place of pilgrimage, and it could well be that the anthem was already in use at that shrine and adopted by Adhémar to seek the intercession of the Queen at the outset of this new venture, but it is hardly a 'war-song'. The Spanish favour the claim of William Durandus (1230–96), who, following James de Voragine, ascribed it to Petrus of Monsoro, Bishop of Compostella (d. c. 1000).[2]

A sixteenth-century narrative connects the anthem to St Bernard of Clairvaux. It relates that, while acting as Apostolic Legate in Germany, Bernard entered the Cathedral of Speyer on Christmas Eve, 1146, to the processional chanting of the anthem, and, as the words 'O *clemens, O pia, O dulcis Virgo Maria*' were being sung, genuflected three times. 'Plates of brass were laid down in the pavement of the church, to mark the footsteps of the man of God to posterity, and the places where he so touchingly implored the clemency, the mercy, and the sweetness of the Blessed Virgin Mary.'[3]

None of the evidence is conclusive, but it does seem that the

Salve Regina originated in France before the close of the eleventh century and the most probable author was Herimannus Contractus, on the grounds that he alone had the mastery in composition of the words and music of this type of anthem.

The first documented evidence of the use of the *Salve Regina* for any liturgical purpose is found in the Statutes of Peter the Venerable, Abbot of Cluny, in the year 1135:

> It has been enacted that the antiphon made concerning the Holy Mother of God which begins *Salve, Regina misericordiae* should be sung by the community upon the feast of her Assumption during the procession and also during the processions which take place according to custom from the principal church of the Apostles towards the church of the same Virgin Mother, excepting only those festivals of the saints in which ancient usage prescribes that canticles should be sung commemorating those saints.[4]

Though we do not know for what purpose the anthem was composed, it would seem that the *Salve* was certainly used as a processional chant. Later the Cistercians, who followed Cluniac customs, adopted the *Salve* as an antiphon to the Benedictus and to the Magnificat on the major Marian feast days. The evidence for this is found in a manuscript dated 1150.[5] An antiphoner of 1225 prescribes the *Salve* as antiphon to the Benedictus on the Feast of the Assumption and to the Magnificat on the feasts of the Purification, Annunciation and Nativity. This is firm evidence that the *Salve* was used by the Cistercians as an antiphon within the Divine Office at this period. Later usage seems to suggest that the *Salve* acquired its own identity as a hymn in honour of the Blessed Virgin as a conclusion to the particular liturgical hour. The Cistercian General Chapter of 1218 directed the *Salve* to be sung either after Prime or after the daily chapter. In 1251 it was prescribed for use after Compline, a practice which became general throughout the order by 1335.[6]

In 1228 the Cistercian General Chapter ordered that the *Salve Regina* be sung together with seven psalms every Friday for the Pope (i.e. Gregory IX), for peace in the Roman Church and for many other intentions.[7] In this instance the *Salve* becomes a separate 'rite', a trend which will be taken up and developed by the laity in the secular Church. The Cistercians spread rapidly throughout Europe, ensuring a popularity of the *Salve* at least in the monastic tradition.

In spite of Franciscan support the anthem did not come into general use in the Church until much later. A decree was passed by the Council of Peñafiel in Spain, in 1302, which declared:

> Since human frailty cannot live without sin ... and since for those who have fallen the only recourse, after Our Lord Himself, is to the holy and glorious Virgin to whom we are all bound to address ourselves as the Mother of Mercy with hymns and canticles of gladness, we have therefore thought well to ordain in her honour that every day after Compline the *Salve Regina* be sung aloud in every church with the versicle *Ora pro nobis*, the prayer *Concede nos, famulos tuos*, also *Ecclesiae tuae*, and for His Holiness the Pope, *Deus omnium fidelium*, and for our King *Quaesumus, omnipotens Deus*.[8]

According to the *Chronica XXIV' Generalium*, the Franciscans sang one of the four antiphons of Our Lady: the *Alma*, the *Ave Regina*, the *Regina caeli* and the *Salve*, after Lauds and Compline from 1249. These were adopted for the first time into the Roman Office by Pope Clement VI in 1350. The anthem was especially dear to Blessed Jordan of Saxony, the second General of the Order of Dominicans, who ordered it to be sung in procession at the end of Compline every day, to put an end to the assaults of the evil spirits by which the repose of his brethren was at that time (c. 1230) so much disturbed.

The *Ordinale* of Sibert de Beka (c. 1312) shows the Carmelites marking the *Salve* with special honour. The first words were sung kneeling and two candles were to be lighted. The practice of lighting a special candle during the *Salve*, after Compline, seems to have prevailed in many of the older orders of nuns, and the various observances often associated with this lighting, such as for example the wearing of gloves, are of curious interest.

The Benedictines passed a decree in their General Chapter held at Northampton in 1444 ordaining that the *Salve* should always be said after Compline: 'In order that the wily serpent may not beguile those in the night time whom he is unable to overthrow in their waking hours, we think it necessary that before sleep we should implore her help who crushed the serpent's head.'[9]

The Breviary of Pius V published in 1568 made it obligatory for the whole Church to recite the *Salve Regina* after Compline from Trinity to Advent.

The *Salve Regina* was taken up by the faithful outside the monasteries and convents, becoming popular as an evening service. The early stages of this development are unclear but must have begun in the thirteenth century. Louis IX (1214–70) of France had one of the anthems of Our Lady chanted every night after Compline 'very solemnly and with music'. In due season it would be the *Salve Regina* with its accompanying prayers, all his household and children being required to attend this service.

By the late Middle Ages the *Salve*, which nearly everywhere followed Compline, attracted popular attention, partly, no doubt, from its devotional appeal, partly from its musical setting and the ceremonial with which it was surrounded. The people wishing to have this in their parish churches provided funds in order to have an anthem of Our Lady sung in the evening before some favourite statue or altar or shrine with a display of lights and music. The service may have been a daily one, or confined to Saturdays, or held only on the vigils of Our Lady's feast days. Documents of all kinds, and more especially wills, testify to the prevalence of this institution both in England and abroad. In the will of Nicholas Charleton of London, a skinner, dated 1439 we find the following bequest:

> Also I devise and ordain a c lb. of wax to minister and serve to the use of the Salve of Our Lady chapel in the said church of St Austin's, that is to say two tapers to stand on the altar of Our Lady, each of the two tapers of a pound weight, there to be lighted and to burn at Salve time as long as the same c lb. weight of wax dure . . .

During the fourteenth century we have evidence of the formation of 'confraternities of the Salve Regina' in England, Germany and the Netherlands, in which the principal requirement was attendance at the chanting of the *Salve Regina* on Saturday evenings.[10] In England at the church of St Magnus the Martyr, London Bridge, the *Fraternitas Dominae Nostrae de Salve Regina* was established. In the records of the Tower of London, we learn that its certificate of foundation was issued in 1343, and that it was founded by five parishioners, including William Double, fishmonger, Henry Bosworth, vintner, and Steven Lucas, fishmonger, who, with

> others of the better sort of their great devotion and to the honour of God and the glorious Mother, our Lady Mary the Virgin, began and caused to be made a chantry, to sing an anthem of Our Lady, called *Salve Regina*, every evening; and thereupon ordained five burning wax lights at the time of the said anthem, in honour and reverence of the five principal joys of our Lady aforesaid and for exciting the people to devotion at such an hour, the more to merit

their souls. And thereupon many other good people of the same parish, seeing the great honesty of the said service and devotion, proffered to be aiders and partners to support the said lights and the said anthem to be continually sung, paying to every person every week an halfpenny; and so that hereafter, with the gift that the people shall give to the sustentation of the said light and anthem, there shall be to find a chaplain singing in the said church for all the benefactors of the said light and anthem.[11]

In *Arnold's Chronicle*[12] (c. 1500) is a copy of visitation articles of the church of St Magnus which mentions a service called the *Salve*. Arnold, who was probably a member of the congregation of St Magnus, notes the existence of a body called the 'mastirs of the *Salve*' together with its 'priestis and clarkis'. This fraternity flourished until its suppression during the reign of Edward VI. Happily, it was refounded in 1922 in order to maintain the daily act of devotion and of witness to the Faith in the midst of the City of London. Among its objectives is the public adoration of the Blessed Sacrament and the maintenance of Our Lady's Shrine in dignity and beauty and the burning of seven candles at the time of the Office.[13]

A similar guild founded in the fourteenth century existed in Antwerp. They too sang the *Salve* with music and lights, in a service known as the *lof*. By the end of the sixteenth century, leave was granted to expose the Sacred Host during the service, especially on Saturdays. The practice of venerating the Sacred Host exposed outside the Mass had begun in the fourteenth century, but became more prevalent during the sixteenth century. Thurston notes that in France 'Benediction' is known as '*salut*', a term applied to the *Salve Regina* service. This amalgamation of the *Salve Regina* service and Exposition of the Blessed Sacrament concluding with a blessing with the Sacred Host may well be the origin of our Benediction rite.[14]

In popular usage the *Salve* became the evening prayer of seafarers, though one might have expected the *Ave maris Stella* to have been their choice; here again the attraction may have been the tune. The narrative of Columbus's first voyage supplies more than one reference to the *Salve*. On Thursday, 11 October 1492, the eve of the day on which the land of the New World was first sighted, the Admiral's journal supplies the following entry: 'When they said the *Salve*, which all the sailors are in the habit of saying and singing in their way, and they were all assembled together, the Admiral implored and admonished the men to guard the stern fore-castle well and to keep a good look out for land.'[15] Again, on the return voyage, under the date 16 February 1493, reference is made to 'the time of the reciting of the *Salve*, which is at the beginning of the night'.

The popularity of the *Salve* was such that in the sixteenth century Martin Luther wrote: 'Now the *Salve Regina* is sung throughout the world and the great bells ring full peal for it. Things have reached such a pass that there is hardly a single church which is not richly endowed to have the *Salve Regina* chanted within its walls.'[16]

John Hollybush published a book in London in 1538 which included 'A Confutacion of the Song called *Salve Regina* proving by scriptures laid thereto that it is rather idolatry than lawful to be sung of true Christian men'. He offered an alternative version, which begins: 'Hayle Jesu Christ, Kynge of mercy, oure lyfe, our sweetnesse, and oure hope, hayle.'[17] This need to find a substitute pays tribute to the affection of the people for Our Lady's antiphon. It survived the Reformation and continues to be popular in modern times.

The practice of singing the *Salve* at the conclusion of their conventual Mass was adopted by the Carmelites in 1334,[18] taken up by the Discalced Observance in 1766 and approved for the whole order by Rome in 1854. Leo XIII prescribed the recitation of the *Salve Regina* after Low Mass for the whole Church in 1884 – a practice which was discontinued in 1964. The *Salve* is today widely used by all as a supplementary prayer to the rosary and holds its place in religious congregations as a conclusion to the Night Prayer of the Church.

The Spiritual Significance of the *Salve Regina*

It may well be as Thurston suggests that the popularity of the *Salve Regina* owes much to its attractive musical setting, but the theological and devotional content give it a great depth of meaning. Our Lady is greeted as 'Queen', 'Mother of Mercy', and 'Advocate'. We will now examine these titles.

'Regina'

The symbolism of queenship has lost its immediacy and power in this age of constitutional monarchy and democracy. The title 'Queen' as applied to the Blessed Virgin could only arise out of cultures which recognized empresses and queens, and such was the case in the Christian Church from the beginning but with particular import since the Edict of Milan in AD 313 when the practice of Christianity was formally allowed in the Roman Empire and eventually became the state religion. We are particularly concerned with the situation in the Middle Ages out of which the anthem *Salve Regina* evolved. At that time, society was organized on a feudal system – a system of rights and duties based on land tenure and personal relationships in which land was held in fief by a vassal from the lord to whom he owed specific services and with whom he was bound by personal loyalty.[19] The king had absolute authority and in return for homage invested the lords with office and land.

Likewise the vassal paid homage to his lord offering service in return for his protection and patronage. Thus patronage was important to all at every level of society. A fact which gives meaning to the *Sub tuum*: 'We fly to thy patronage, O Holy Mother of God, despise not our petitions in our necessities, but deliver us from all danger. O ever glorious and Blessed Virgin Mary.'

The royal dignity of Mary is implicit in her Divine Motherhood. At the Annunciation

> the angel said to her . . . you will conceive in your womb and bear a son, and you shall call his name Jesus. He will be great, and will be called the Son of the Most High; and the Lord God will give to him the throne of his father David, and he will reign over the house of Jacob for ever; and of his kingdom there will be no end.[20]

Mary's Son is to inherit the throne of his ancestor David and his reign will last for ever. Elizabeth too greets Mary as 'the mother of my Lord'.[21] The Incarnate Word is to be King and Lord of all things. So with complete justice St John Damascene could write: 'When she became Mother of the Creator, she truly became Queen of every creature.' Likewise, it can be said that the Archangel Gabriel was the first to proclaim Mary's royal office.[22]

Writers in the early Church referred to Mary as 'the Mother of the King' and 'the Mother of the Lord', on the basis of the Annunciation narrative of Luke, signifying that she derived this exalted station from the royal dignity of her Son. St Ephrem makes this prayer to Mary: 'Majestic and Heavenly Maid, Lady, Queen, protect and keep me under your wing lest Satan the sower of destruction glory over me, lest my wicked foe be victorious against me.'[23] St Andrew of Crete attributes the dignity of a Queen to the Virgin Mary: 'Today He transports from her earthly dwelling, as Queen of the human race. His ever-Virgin Mother, from whose womb He, the living God, took on human form.'[24] St Ildephonsus of Toledo gathers together almost all of her titles of honour in this salutation: 'O my Lady, my Sovereign, You who rule over me, Mother of my Lord ... Lady among handmaids, Queen among sisters.'[25]

The Popes have honoured Mary with the title of Queen. St Gregory II (715–31), writing to St Germanus the Patriarch, called her: 'The Queen of all, the true Mother of God', and also 'the Queen of all Christians'.[26] Benedict XIV (1740–58), in his Apostolic Letter *Gloriosae Dominae*, spoke of Mary as 'Queen of heaven and earth', and stated that the sovereign King has communicated to her his ruling power.[27]

The Latin Church has since the Middle Ages regularly used the antiphons *Salve Regina* and *Regina caeli* in the Divine Office. Litanies to Our Lady were formulated in the twelfth century, taken up by the Dominican confraternities of the rosary and became associated with the Shrine of Loreto since about 1558. In today's version we honour Mary as Queen of Apostles, Martyrs, Confessors, Virgins, all Saints, as Queen conceived without original sin, assumed into heaven, of the most holy rosary, and of peace. The fifth glorious mystery of the rosary is a meditation on what 'can be called the mystical crown of the heavenly Queen'.[28]

Following the establishment of the Feast of Christ the King in 1925, there was a popular demand for a parallel feast to celebrate the Queenship of Mary. Pope Pius XII published his Encyclical *Ad caeli Reginam* on 11 October 1954, in which after reviewing the historical and doctrinal foundations he proclaimed: 'by Our Apostolic authority We decree and establish the feast of Mary's Queenship, which is to be celebrated every year in the whole world on the 31st of May'.[29] The Pope concluded:

From the ancient Christian documents, from prayers of the liturgy, from the innate piety of the Christian people, from works of art, from every side We have gathered witnesses to the regal dignity of the Virgin Mother of God; We have likewise shown that the arguments deduced by Sacred Theology from the treasure store of the faith fully confirm this truth. (n. 46)

The Liturgy for the Queenship of Mary, now celebrated on the octave of the Assumption, supports the themes of Mary as Queen and Mother. The Introductory Rite: 'The queen stands at your right hand arrayed in cloth of gold' (Psalm 44.10) reminds us that Mary, assumed into heaven, has taken her rightful place at the right hand of her Son the King. The opening prayer reads: 'Father, you have given us the mother of your Son to be our queen and mother. With the support of her prayers may we come to share the glory of your children in the kingdom of heaven.'

'Mater Misericordiae'

The title 'Mother of Mercy' was well known to Eadmer, St Anselm's pupil and biographer, who died in 1124. In the anthem, Mary is greeted first as Queen then as 'Mother of Mercy'. The first greeting reflects Mary's royal dignity and her Divine Motherhood. The second greeting suggests that she is also our Mother and a source of mercy. By her obedient and free consent at the Annunciation Mary became the mother of the one Mediator between God and man. She was the medium by which the source of all grace was given to us in the person of Christ Jesus. The Gospel tells us that in his dying moment, 'When Jesus saw his mother, and the disciple whom he loved standing near, he said to his mother, "Woman, behold, your son!" Then he said to the disciple, "Behold, your mother!"'[30]

Thus Christ commissioned his mother to take on a maternal responsibility for 'the disciple'. This disciple as the representative of all disciples accepts Mary, on our behalf, as our Mother in the order of grace. It was as a direct consequence of Mary's faithful cooperation in the work of redemption that she was to become our spiritual Mother and Mother of the Church, Mediatrix of the fruits of that redemption and our Advocate.

As Mother of Mercy we may confidently expect her help in our hour of need, for

> the King will say to those at his right hand, 'Come, O blessed of my Father, inherit the kingdom prepared for you from the foundation of the world; for I was hungry and you gave me food, I was thirsty and you gave me drink, I was a stranger and you welcomed me, I was naked and you clothed me, I was sick and you visited me, I was in prison and you came to me.'[31]

At the same time we must bear in mind that Mary is a daughter of Adam, a member of the human race and our sister in need of redemption as we are. Seen in the context of a feudal society Mary is a model for the vassal. Hearing the word of God spoken by the Angel, Mary gives her consent, saying: 'Behold, I am the handmaid of the Lord.'[32] By declaring herself to be 'your *doulos*', 'your slave', 'your servant', Mary opens herself to receive God in person who avails himself of her flesh, assuming a human nature. By Mary's cooperation with her Lord and God the work of salvation can begin. Mary fulfils her maternal mission. She gives birth to the Incarnate Word and shows us the blessed fruit of her womb.

'Advocata'

The word '*advocata*' is used of Mary by Irenaeus and others, in either the sense of '*paracletos*', one who speaks on our behalf, or that of intercession. From medieval times the title of *Advocata* signifies Mary's special power of intercession.[33] This intercession is an aspect of her mediation, and it is an exercise of her spiritual motherhood.[34]

In the Old Testament the Queen-Mother (Hebrew *gebīrah*, literally 'great lady') assisted the king in ruling the kingdom and acted as advocate for the people. King Solomon shows the greatest respect to his mother when

> Bathsheba went to King Solomon, to speak to him on behalf of Adonijah. And the king rose to meet her, and bowed down to her; then he sat on his throne, and had a seat brought for the king's mother; and she sat on his right. Then she said, 'I have one small request to make of you; do not refuse me.' And the king said to her, 'Make your request, my mother; for I will not refuse you.'[35]

In this we see a type of the Mother of Jesus as Advocate for the people of God in her role as Queen and Mother.[36]

The New Testament scene at Cana is often used to illustrate Mary's role as intercessor: 'When the wine failed, the mother of Jesus said to him, "They have no wine." '[37] In the Vatican II document *Lumen gentium*, the Council Fathers affirm that Mary, 'by her intercession brought about the beginning of miracles by Jesus the Messiah' (n. 58). They also refer to Acts 1.14, which describes the Apostles who 'with one accord devoted themselves to prayer, together with the women and Mary the mother of Jesus, and with his brothers', and comment that 'we also see Mary by her prayers imploring the gift of the Spirit, who had already overshadowed her in the Annunciation' (n. 59).

The Council of Trent found it necessary to restate the traditional teaching on the intercession of the saints, which applies pre-eminently to Mary: 'The saints who reign together with Christ, offer up their prayers to God for men; ... it is good and useful to invoke them suppliantly and, in order to obtain favours from God through his Son Jesus Christ our Lord who alone is our Redeemer and Saviour, to have recourse to their prayers, assistance and support.'[38]

The Second Vatican Council neatly sums up Mary's role as Mediatrix and Advocate in a correct relationship to her Son, in *Lumen gentium*:

> This motherhood of Mary in the order of grace continues without interruption from the consent which she loyally gave at the Annunciation and which she sustained without wavering beneath the cross, until the eternal consummation of all the elect. Taken up to heaven, she did not lay aside this saving office but by her manifold intercession continues to procure for us the gifts of eternal salvation. By her motherly love she cares for her Son's sisters and brothers who still journey on earth surrounded by dangers and difficulties, until they are led into their blessed home. Therefore the blessed Virgin is invoked in the Church under the titles of advocate, helper, benefactress, and mediatrix. This, however, is understood in such a way that it neither takes away anything from, nor adds anything to, the dignity of Christ the one Mediator. (n. 62)

Conclusion

The *Salve* arose within a feudal society, its words reflecting the vassal–lord relationship. Mary is both 'Our Lady'[39] and a type of the vassal. The *Salve* proclaims Mary as 'Queen', as 'Mother of Mercy' and as 'Advocate': powerful symbols of her divine maternity and exalted position within the people of God and of her role as intercessor. Her mission is to bring our Saviour and Lord into the world, and so with confidence we cry out to her in our banishment and exile that she turn her 'eyes of mercy towards us' and 'show unto us the blessed fruit of thy womb'.

Notes

1. Migne, *Dictionnaire des Croisades*, s.v. Adhémar, see H. T. Henry, Salve Regina, in *The Catholic Encyclopedia*, Vol. XIII.
2. Herbert Thurston, The Salve Regina, *Familiar Prayers*, p. 121, notes 2 and 3.
3. Ratisbonne, *Life and Times of St Bernard*, American edn, 1855, p. 381, see Henry, Salve Regina, in *The Catholic Encyclopedia*, Vol. XIII.
4. J.-P. Migne, *Patrologia Latina* 189, 1048, in Thurston, The Salve Regina, *Familiar Prayers*, p. 125, note 2.
5. H. Leclercq and F. Cabrol (eds), *Le Dictionnaire d'archéologie chrétienne et de liturgie*, Vol. 15 (Paris: Letouzey et Ané, 1956), pp. 714–23.
6. Archdale A. King, *Liturgies of the Religious Orders* (London: Longmans Green, 1955), p. 112, notes 6, 7 and 8.
7. See Henry, Salve Regina, in *The Catholic Encyclopedia*, Vol. XIII.
8. Hardouin, Concilia, VII, 1156, in Thurston, The Salve Regina, *Familiar Prayers*, p. 128, note 1.
9. Thurston, The Salve Regina, *Familiar Prayers*, p. 129.
10. See Thomas E. Bridgett, *Our Lady's Dowry*, pp. 349–67 for more about the Guilds of Our Lady, of which there were an immense number, whose aims were, 'charity, conviviality and piety'.
11. Fraternity of Our Lady de Salve Regina, *Revised Constitution and Daily Office* (London: Church of St Magnus the Martyr, 1985), p. 3.
12. *Arnold's Chronicle*, Visitacyon of Chirche of St Magnus, p. 277, quoted in Herbert Thurston, Benediction of the Blessed Sacrament, *The Month*, 98 (1901): 275, note 1.
13. Fraternity of Our Lady de Salve Regina, *Revised Constitution and Daily Office*, p. 3.
14. For a full account see Thurston, Benediction of the Blessed Sacrament, *The Month*, 98 (1901): 264–74.
15. J. B. Thatcher's translation in his *Christopher Columbus*, Vol. I, p. 531, in Herbert Thurston, The Salve Regina, *Familiar Prayers*, p. 132, note 1.
16. Thurston, The Salve Regina, *Familiar Prayers*, p. 145.
17. Ibid., pp. 143–4.

18. *Analecta Ord. Carm.*, Vol. III, p. 154, and *Ordin.* (ed. Zimmermann), p. 6, rubr. XLI, see Archdale A. King, *Liturgies of the Religious Orders*, p. 278, note 7 and p. 319, note 1.

19. Cf. Feudalism, *Encyclopaedia Britannica CD 2000*.

20. Luke 1.30–33.

21. Luke 1.43.

22. Pius XII, *Ad caeli Reginam* (1954), n. 34, note 42. S. Ioannes Damascenus, De fide orthodoxa, 1. IV, c. 14; PL XCIV, 1158 s. B.

23. Ibid., n. 10, note 11: S. Ephraem, Oratio ad Ssmam Dei Matrem; Opera omnia, ed. Assemani, t. III (graece), Romae, 1747, p. 546.

24. Ibid., n. 17, note 19: S. Andreas Cretensis, Homilia II in Dormitionem Ssmae Deiparae: PG XCVII, 1079 B.

25. Ibid., n. 21, note 26: Ildefonsus Toletanus, De virginitate perpetua BMV: PL XCVI, 58 A D.

26. Ibid., n. 23, note 29: Hardouin, Acta Conciliorum, IV, 234; 238: PL LXXXIX, 508 B.

27. Ibid., n. 24, note 31: Benedictus XIV, bulla Gloriosae Dominae, d.d. 27 Sept. a. 1748.

28. Ibid., n. 31.

29. Ibid., n. 47. Note: In the revised calendar of 1969 the Queenship of Mary is now kept as a memorial on the octave of the Assumption.

30. John 19.26–27.

31. Matthew 25.34–36.

32. Luke 1.38.

33. Michael O'Carroll, Advocate, *Theotokos*, pp. 5–6.

34. Michael O'Carroll, Mary's Intercession, ibid., p. 186.

35. 1 Kings 2.19–20.

36. Mark I. Miravalle, *Mary, Coredemptrix Mediatrix Advocate* (Santa Barbara, CA: Queenship Publishing, 1993), pp. 58–9.

37. John 2.3.

38. Michael O'Carroll, Mary's Intercession, *Theotokos*, p. 188, note 21, DS 1821.

39. The first use of this title is attributed to Cynewulf in eighth-century England. See Eric Hester, England: The Dowry of Mary, in *Our Lady, A Catholic Life Special Publication*, ed. J. Kelly (Manchester: Gabriel Publications, 2001). I have not been able to confirm this but the title 'Lady' is found in Anglo-Saxon prayers and hymns of the eleventh century, see Bridgett, *Our Lady's Dowry*, p. 141, note 8 and p. 442, note 7.

The Angelus and *Memorare*

These prayers are important in their own right. They are included here because they reflect Catholic devotion to Mary and form part of the spiritual background to the rosary. The origins and history of the prayers were investigated by Herbert Thurston, who published his findings in *The Month* in 1901–2 and in the posthumous book *Familiar Prayers* (1953). What follows relies very much on Fr Thurston's work.

The Angelus

In his Apostolic Exhortation *Marialis cultus*, Pope Paul VI strove to enhance devotion to the Blessed Virgin Mary and selected two prayer forms for comment: the Angelus and the rosary. He described the Angelus as being in no need of revision,

> because of its simple structure, biblical character, its historical origin which links it to the prayer for peace and safety, and its quasi liturgical rhythm which sanctifies different moments of the day, and because it reminds us of the Paschal Mystery, in which recalling the Incarnation of the Son of God we pray that we may be led 'through his Passion and Cross to the glory of his Resurrection'. (n. 41).

One might add that both prayer forms include the Hail Mary, emphasize the Incarnation of Christ and evolved at about the same time.

The Angelus Prayer

The Angel of the Lord declared unto Mary.
And she conceived of the Holy Spirit.

> Hail Mary . . .

Behold the Handmaid of the Lord.
Let it be done unto me according to your word.

> Hail Mary . . .

The Word was made flesh.
And dwelt amongst us.

> Hail Mary . . .

Pray for us, O Holy Mother of God.
That we may be made worthy of the promises of Christ.

Let us pray.
Pour forth, we beseech Thee, O Lord, Thy grace into our hearts, that we, to whom the Incarnation of Christ, Thy Son, was made known by the message of an angel, may by His passion and cross, be brought to the glory of His resurrection. Through the same Christ our Lord. Amen.

This devotion is repeated three times a day: in the early morning, at noon and in the evening. It has long been the custom for a bell to be rung three times for each *Ave* and nine times for the final collect. The name comes from the first word of the opening versicle in the Latin. Fr Thurston, writing in *The Month*,[1] felt that there were reasonable grounds for connecting the origin of the Angelus with the ringing of the curfew bell. However, the curfew bell had a secular, not ecclesiastical, purpose. The erection of a belfry and the use of a bell were widespread in Europe for the purpose of calling the people to meetings, or as a warning. In England, the bell was more likely to be installed in the church tower. The use of the town bell seems to have been practically universal. The ringing of the curfew in England dates from about the time of the Norman Conquest. We know that a Synod held in Caen in 1061 ordered that a bell was to be rung each evening to call the people to prayer, after which hour they were to keep within their houses and to shut the doors. (The word 'curfew' comes from *couvre-feu,* meaning 'cover fire', the Latin equivalent being *ignitegium.* The use of the word in French dates from about 1263 where the curfew bell signalled the closing of the wine shops. In Italy they rang the *campana bibitorum.*)

A second possibility indicates an ecclesiastical purpose. There was a German custom belonging to the close of the tenth century which laid down that 'when Compline was finished, the children first of all say the three prayers, and after that the Abbot rings a bell and pours forth the three prayers together with his brethren'. The *trina oratio* were said in honour of the Trinity, morning and evening, as morning and evening prayers for the choir children, and it expressly mentions the ringing of the bell.

The origin of the Angelus has also been assigned to the Franciscan St Bonaventure (1217–74). The Acts of Canonization (1482) of this saint tell how he exhorted his brethren to greet Our Lady when the bell rang after Compline: 'when the bell rings after Compline, the people are devoutly to kneel and to say the *Ave Maria* thrice'.

Papal approval of a custom already established was given in 1318, when John XXII granted ten days indulgence to those 'who in the evening recite the Hail Mary three times on bended knee after hearing the sound of the bell'.

It seems likely that the triple bell and the triple Hail Mary of the fifteenth century were derived from the 'triple prayer' of the Saxon monks. The fact that this 'triple prayer' existed in the morning as well as in the evening would explain how the morning *Ave Marias*, recited after the Office of Prime, first came about.

Thurston believes it was not the Angelus which grew out of the curfew, but rather the curfew which developed out of the triple monastic peal. This, he suggests, is the true origin of the Angelus.

The origin of the midday Angelus is unclear. The practice of ringing the Angelus three times a day is a late development, and one not generally adopted till the seventeenth century. The practice of ringing a bell at noon occurred in medieval England on Saturdays and on the vigils of feasts, but was in no way connected to the Angelus.

In 1386 the Bishop of Prague gave an indulgence to the practice of ringing a bell and the recitation of five *Paternosters* in honour of the Passion on Fridays at None (or Noon). It is suggested that the midday Angelus may have grown out of this practice. In 1423 at Mainz, this new devotion to the Passion was formally brought into association with the Angelus bell as a method of honouring Our Lady's Sorrows.

A Bull of Callixtus III, issued in 1456, sought to unite all Christendom in a crusade of prayer to obtain the peace of the Church by the overthrow of the Turks. The Pontiff ordered that in every Christian church throughout the world, a bell should be rung 'between None and Vespers' (in practice this was interpreted as noon), in three peals, 'as is wont to be rung for the Angelic salutation in the evening', at which signal everyone should recite the Our Father and Hail Mary three times. This was to be done daily. It was primarily a prayer for peace.

The ringing of the midday bell was introduced into France

by Louis XI in 1472. He ordered that the great bell of Notre Dame should ring a peal at noon, at which signal all should kneel down and say a Hail Mary for the peace of the kingdom.

A little manual of devotions collected by an English Catholic (c. 1576) says:

> Of the ringing unto the salutation of the angel ... Thrice in the daytime is there usually a sign or ringing of the bell given unto prayer; in the morning, at noon and in the evening, that the Christian might be put in mind, that if oftener they cannot, yet at the least at these three several times of the day they ought to pray according to the Psalm, etc.
>
> In the morning and in the evening, say thou these three small verses with the Angel's salutation joined to every one of them.

> The Angel of our Lord showed forth unto Marie and she
> conceived of the Holy Ghost.
> *Ave Maria.*
> Behold the handmaid of the Lord, be it done unto me
> according to thy word.
> *Ave Maria*
> The word was made flesh and dwelled amongst us.
> *Ave Maria.*

> Some do also say these verses at the noon ring, which may be done very well, for although Christ perhaps was neither in the morning nor at noon Incarnate but in the evening (in the morning yet he rose from the dead, and he suffered at noon), not withstanding at these three several ringings of the bell, the Virgin is saluted for three mysteries sake, in which she is wont to be honoured by such as devoutly call on her.

The present form of the Angelus appears in several devotional works of the sixteenth century.

To the Reformers in England the *Ave* bell was thoroughly

obnoxious, and in 1536 Thomas Cromwell issued an ordinance, 'that the knolling of the *Aves* which has been brought in by the pretence of the Bishop of Rome's pardon, henceforth be omitted, lest the people do thereafter trust to have pardon'.

The rubric of kneeling to say the Angelus stems from the primitive but accurate concept that the Hail Mary is a salutation. This habit persisted in spite of contrary influences. It was widely practised in Italy and Spain even to the extreme of breaking off in the course of a theatrical production to recite the Angelus.

The Concluding Prayer, Gratiam tuam

Sister Benedicta Ward, in a lecture to the Ecumenical Society of the Blessed Virgin Mary at Oxford in August 2000, speaking of the double *kenosis* of Christ (that is, the emptying of himself as God in order to become man and the final emptying of himself as man on the cross for our redemption), pointed out that the two have been considered to be but one event and form a secure, non-sentimental foundation for the veneration of Mary. She continued:

> But that theme had been present in England much earlier. In 668 the Greek, Theodore of Tarsus, came from Rome to be the 7th Archbishop of Canterbury. He brought with him John, the Arch Chancellor of St Peter's, in order to teach the monks of the monastery the mode of chanting throughout the year as it was practised in St Peter's in Rome. It seems that among the many things he taught the Anglo-Saxons was· the collect *Gratiam tuam* which it is quite possible that he himself had composed, introducing just this link of Incarnation and Crucifixion. This admirable collect was later dropped from its place in the liturgy to a post communion prayer. But in the 16th century it was retrieved

by the Oxford scholar and theologian Archbishop Thomas Cranmer for the new book of Common Prayer, and translated in his incomparable English and restored to its proper place as the collect for the feast of the Annunciation, preserving the ancient insight in a new dimension in honour of Mary:

> We beseech Thee, O Lord, pour Thy grace into our hearts,
> that as we have known Christ Thy Son's incarnation by the
> message of an angel, so by his cross and passion we may be
> brought to the glory of his resurrection, through the same
> Christ our Lord. Amen.

The *Memorare*[2]

Remember, O most loving Virgin Mary, that never was it known
that any one who fled to thy protection, implored thy help,
and sought thy intercession, was left forsaken.
Filled, therefore, with confidence in thy goodness,
I fly to thee, O Mother, Virgin of Virgins;
to thee I come, before thee I stand a sorrowing sinner.
Despise not my words, O Mother of the Word,
but graciously hear and grant my prayer.

This popular Marian prayer has been attributed to St Bernard of Clairvaux, but that is uncertain. It was known to St Francis de Sales and it is to be found in print from the last quarter of the fifteenth century as part of a longer prayer to Our Lady, beginning *Ad sanctitatis tuae pedes, dulcissima Virgo Maria*. This was a long prayer with much repetition. It may be that in the sixteenth century it was abridged and from that we get the *Memorare*. It was indulgenced by Pius IX in 1846.

A French priest, Claude Bernard (1588–1641), known as the 'Poor Priest', was responsible for the popularity of the prayer in

France. The *Oraison du R. P. Bernard à la Vierge* was published and widely distributed. (It is possible that this particular title led to the belief that the prayer was composed by St Bernard of Clairvaux). Claude's devotion to the prayer stems from his own miraculous cure, an account of which he wrote for the queen of Louis XIII:

> I was dangerously ill and so overcome by the fear of death that to obtain my recovery I had recourse to Our Lady's intercession and for that end I recited the Memorare. Thereupon I instantaneously felt relief, but as I could not persuade myself that God had worked a miracle in my favour I attributed the cure to some natural cause. I was speaking in this sense to a friend who came to congratulate me on my recovery, when I heard a knock at the door. I opened it, and found outside the venerable Brother Fiacre, a discalced Augustinian, whom at that time I only knew by sight. Seeing that I was very much out of humour and that I turned away from him without speaking, 'Sir', he said, 'pray forgive me if I have come at an inopportune moment, but I only wished to inquire how you were, for the Blessed Virgin appeared to me last night, telling me of your illness, and that she had cured you, and bade me come in her name to assure you of the fact.' I was overwhelmed with confusion at the thought of my ingratitude in attributing to natural causes a cure which I owed entirely to the tender pity of the Mother of God. I at once besought her forgiveness, and at present I proclaim to all the world that since that moment I have never had another attack of the malady of which she has cured me and to which I was formerly very liable.

Notes

1. Thurston, The Angelus, *The Month*, 98 (1901): 483–99, 607–616; 99 (1902): 61–73, 518–32.
2. Thurston, *Familiar Prayers*, Chapter 9.

APPENDIX 3

The Liturgy of the Hours[1]

If indeed the recitation of 150 *Paternosters* was a substitute for the monastic Office of saying the 150 psalms, and this practice was influential in the development the Marian rosary, it is relevant that we should include a brief outline of the history of the Divine Office.

The monastic custom of reciting prayers and, in particular, the psalms at certain fixed hours of the day has its origins in Jewish practice. It was taken up by the early Christian Church in obedience to the command: 'Pray at all times in the Spirit, with all prayer and supplication' (Ephesians 6.18) and 'Rejoice always, pray constantly, give thanks in all circumstances; for this is the will of God in Christ Jesus for you' (1 Thessalonians 5.16–18).

In the psalms we find expressions such as:

But I, O Lord, cry to thee; in the morning my prayer comes before thee.

(Psalm 88.13)

At midnight I rise to praise thee.

(Psalm 119.62)

Evening and morning and at noon I utter my complaint and moan.

(Psalm 55.17)

Seven times a day I praise thee for thy righteous ordinances.

(Psalm 119.164)

The Apostles observed the Jewish custom of praying at midnight, the third, sixth and ninth hour:

Peter went up on the housetop to pray, about the sixth hour.

(Acts 10.9)

About the ninth hour of the day he saw clearly in a vision an angel of God coming in.

(Acts 10.3)

But about midnight Paul and Silas were praying and singing hymns to God.

(Acts 16.25)

The first Christians preserved the custom of going to the Temple or synagogue at the hour of prayer. In addition to this they also met in private houses for the celebration of the Eucharist. Such a meeting or synaxis adopted the prayer of the Synagogue with the recital or chanting of psalms, readings from the Old Testament, followed by a reading of an Epistle and the Gospel. A celebration of the Eucharist may or may not have followed. The combination of these two liturgies gives our present-day Mass. The meetings would have taken place in the evening and often continued until dawn. Separated from the Eucharist, such vigils became an independent liturgy and divided naturally into three parts: the evening prayer; the vigils properly so called; and the end of the vigils or the morning prayer. Thus we have the beginning of Vespers, Matins and Lauds.

During the day, prayer at the third, sixth and ninth hours became Terce, Sext and None. Compline appears as a repetition of Vespers, first in the fourth century. Prime was added at the end of the fourth century. So the Divine Office, or Liturgy of the Hours, was formed by the fifth century.

Custom varied according to time and place. The Irish monks were known to have recited the psalms as the 'Three Fifties'. While allowing a certain liberty as to the exterior form of the Office, the Church insisted from ancient times on its right to supervise the orthodoxy of the liturgical formulas. The Council of Milevis (416) forbade any liturgical formula not approved by a Council or by a competent authority. The Roman Liturgy tended gradually to replace the others, and this is additional proof of the right of the Church to control the Liturgy. The Council of Trent was unable to complete the reform of the Breviary, owing to a lack of time. Pius V promulgated the new Roman Breviary in 1568 to bring uniformity in this matter to the Latin Church. In 1911 Pius X issued a new Breviary restoring the tradition of the early Church of reciting the whole 150 psalms during the course of a week. Pius XII initiated further investigations which finally came to fruition after the Second Vatican Council with the promulgation of the new Liturgy of the Hours in November 1970 by Paul VI. The Apostolic Constitution stated: 'Since the Liturgy of the Hours should sanctify the different times of the day, in its revised form it can be fitted into the actual hours of people's daily lives.' The Office of Prime was abolished. The most important Hours are those of Lauds as Morning Prayer and Vespers as Evening Prayer: 'these become the two hinges, as it were, of the daily Office'. The Office of Readings, while retaining a nocturnal character, can be said at any time of the day. Prayer during the day is arranged for prayer before noon, at midday and in the afternoon. The day ends with Night Prayer. The Psalter is covered in a four-week cycle. Now that this form of prayer is more accessible we should strive to unite ourselves with the whole Church in daily and constant prayer.

Note

1. Fernand Canbrol, Divine Office, in *The Catholic Encyclopedia*, Vol. V.

Appendix 4

The Rosary and the Blessed Sacrament

There has in the recent past been some uncertainty as to the practice of reciting the rosary before the exposed Blessed Sacrament. The following extract was published in the *Southwark Liturgy Bulletin*.[1]

The following notes (annexed to Prot No 2287/96/L) were published in 1998 by the Congregation for Divine Worship and the Discipline of the Sacraments in 507–511 of its magazine *Notitiae*. The original notes appear in Spanish – this is an unofficial translation.

I *Origin*

1. The conciliar Constitution *Sacrosanctum Concilium*, number 13, says:

'Popular devotions of the Christian people are to be highly commended, provided that they accord with the laws and norms of the Church, above all when they are ordered by the Apostolic See ... But these devotions should be so drawn up that they harmonize with the liturgical seasons in such a way as to be in accord with the sacred liturgy, that they be in some fashion derived from it, since, in fact, the liturgy by its very nature far surpasses any of them.'

The Catechism of the Catholic Church adds to this citation from *Sacrosanctum Concilium*:

'These expressions are a prolongation of the liturgical life of the Church, but are not substitutes for it.'

- Eucharistic exposition is a celebration related to the liturgy as understood in the Instruction *Eucharisticum Mysterium*, n. 62, from the Roman Ritual: Holy Communion and Worship of the Eucharist outside Mass and from the Ceremonial of Bishops which dedicates chapter XXII to this same topic.

- The Holy Rosary is, without doubt, one of the pious exercises most recommended by ecclesiastical authority.

   (See also the *Catechism of the Catholic Church*, nn. 971, 1674, 2678, 2708.)

- A Catholic sensitivity never separates Christ from his mother or vice versa.

2. The Apostolic Letter *Vicesimus quintus annus*, n. 18, says:
'Finally, to safeguard the reform and ensure the promotion of the Liturgy it is necessary to take account of popular Christian devotion and its relation to liturgical life. This popular devotion should not be ignored or treated with indifference or contempt, since it is rich in values, and in itself it gives expression to the religious attitude towards God. But it needs to be continually evangelised, so that the faith which it expresses may become an ever more mature and authentic act. Both the pious exercises of the Christian people and also other forms of devotion are welcomed and encouraged, provided that they do not replace or intrude into liturgical celebrations. An authentic pastoral promotion of the Liturgy will build upon the riches of popular piety, purifying and directing them towards the Liturgy as the offering of the peoples.'

II Relationship between Eucharistic Exposition and the Holy Rosary

One quote from each of the three most important documents follows:

1. 'During the exposition everything should be so arranged that the faithful can devote themselves attentively in prayer to Christ the Lord . . .' (Instruction *Eucharisticum Mysterium*, n. 62).

2. 'To encourage a prayerful spirit there should be readings from Scripture with a homily or brief exhortations to develop a better understanding of the Eucharistic mystery' (*Rite for Holy Communion and Worship of the Eucharist outside Mass*, n. 95).

3. The Apostolic Exhortation *Marialis cultus* indicates that the Rosary 'as a prayer inspired by the Gospel and centred on the mystery of the Incarnation and the Redemption should be considered a prayer of deep Christological orientation' (n. 46).

III Observations

At this time it is important to note:

From the Second Vatican Council until the present, the following has been observed:

(a) In the first two decades after the Council, more or less, there arose within the Catholic Church a tendency to suppress adoration before the exposed Blessed Sacrament within a Christian community.

(b) In recent years, prayer before the exposed Blessed Sacrament has been increasingly appreciated once more. Two phenomena have been observed with adoration of the Blessed Sacrament, namely: adoration takes place according to the same style and mentality and with the same prayers as before the Council or it is celebrated in accordance with the guidelines provided by the Church's documents.

- Pastorally, this is an important time to encourage the prayer of adoration before the Blessed Sacrament according to the spirit of the Church's documents. An opportunity to re-orientate this popular practice should not be wasted.

- The restoration of the Rosary should be promoted in its authentic form, that is, with its Christological character. At times, the traditional manner of reciting the Rosary would seem to be limited to a recitation of the Our Father and the Hail Mary. Currently in some places, the stating of the mysteries is accompanied by a reading of a brief biblical text to assist meditation. This is very positive. *The Catechism of the Catholic Church* (cf. 2708) indicated that Christian prayer ought to go further. It should lead to a knowledge and love of the Lord Jesus, to union with him, finding great encouragement and support in liturgical prayer before the Eucharist.

- One should not expose the Eucharist only to recite the Rosary. However, among the prayers that are used during adoration, the recitation of the Rosary may certainly be included, emphasising the Christological aspects with biblical readings relating to the mysteries, and providing time for silent adoration and meditation on them.

- 'During the exposition, the prayers, songs and readings should be arranged so as to direct the attention of the faithful to the worship of Christ the Lord. To encourage a prayerful spirit, there should be readings from the scriptures with a homily or brief exhortations to develop a better understanding of the Eucharistic mystery' (*Rite for Holy Communion and Worship of the Eucharist outside Mass*, n. 95). In the area of popular piety there is still much to be done so that pious exercises will support liturgical life and vice versa. There is a need to educate the Christian community to deepen the understanding of this pious exercise in order to appreciate fully its true worth.

Note

1. Fr Stephen Boyle, *Southwark Liturgy Bulletin*, 111 (Summer 2000).

Rosaries in the Victoria and Albert Museum, London

The Langdale Rosary c. 1500
British Galleries 1500–1760; Gallery 58b, 'The Church', Exhibit 21 (M30-1934). This gold rosary (see Figure 8.3), consisting of fifty oval *Ave* beads, six lozenge-shaped *Paternoster* beads and a single pendant, was made in England. The hollow beads are engraved and enamelled in black on each side with a saint or a scene from the life of Christ, with an explanatory inscription around each rim. It is the only surviving gold rosary of the period. It is thought to have belonged to Lord William Howard (1563–1640), third son of Thomas Howard, 4th Duke of Norfolk (1536–72), and to have passed by later marriage to the Langdales, an old Yorkshire Catholic family.

Rosaries in the Jewellery Section
Case 12, Board G, Exhibit 11 (M517-1903): silver, wooden and amber beads with the instruments of the Passion and pendant of SS Catherine and Barbara. German, late fifteenth century.

Case 14, Board J, Exhibit 1 (M174-1866): glass and silver filigree, mounted with emblems of the Passion with pendant cross of St Walberga. Bohemian, third quarter seventeenth century.

Case 37, Board F, Exhibit 5 (M151-1872): coral and silver-gilt filigree, with pendant medallions commemorating the peace of Ryswick, dated 1697. South German, eighteenth century.

Case 37, Board F, Exhibit 7 (M155-1872): amber and silver filigree, with two pendants enclosing gilt medals of the Virgin of Allötting.

Case 40, Board B, Exhibit 9 (M741-1890): pink coral and filigree with Crucifix. Spanish, nineteenth century.

Bibliography

Articles

Breeze, Andrew, The Virgin's Rosary and St Michael's Scales, *Studia Celtica*, 24 (1991): 91–8.

Henry, H. T., Salve Regina, in *The Catholic Encyclopedia*, Vol. XIII (1912), online edition, © Kevin Knight.

Oakes, Catherine, The Scales: An Iconographic Motif of Justice, Redemption and Intercession, *MARIA: A Journal of Marian Studies*, 1 (August 2000): 11–31.

Rhodes, Jan, The Rosary in Sixteenth-Century England (I and II), *Mount Carmel*, 31/4 (1983): 180–91; 32/1 (1984): 4–17.

Thompson, Thomas A., The Rosary Encyclicals, *The Priest*, 12 (October 1998): 39–41.

Thurston, Herbert, series of articles, 'Our Popular Devotions', *The Month* 1900–2:

——, The Rosary, *The Month*, 96 (October 1900): 403–18.

——, The Rosary: The Rosary amongst the Carthusians, *The Month*, 96 (November 1900): 513–27.

——, The Rosary: The Fifteen Mysteries, *The Month*, 96 (December 1900): 620–37.

——, The Rosary: Was the Rosary Instituted by St Dominic?, *The Month*, 97 (January 1901): 67–79.

——, The Rosary: The Rebutting Evidence, *The Month*, 97 (February 1901): 172–88.

——, The Rosary: The Rise and Growth of the Dominican Tradition, *The Month*, 97 (March 1901): 286–304.

——, The Rosary: The Archaeology of the Beads, *The Month*, 97 (April 1901): 383–404.

——, The Dedication of the Month of May to Our Lady, *The Month*, 97 (May 1901): 470–83.

——, Benediction of the Blessed Sacrament, *The Month*, 98 (September 1901): 264–76.

——, The Angelus: The Hail Mary, *The Month*, 98 (November 1901): 483–99.

——, The Angelus: The Curfew Bell, *The Month*, 98 (December 1901): 607–16.

——, The Angelus: Compline or Curfew Bell – Which?, *The Month*, 99, (January 1902): 61–73.

——, The Angelus: The Mid-day Angelus, *The Month*, 99 (May 1902): 518–32.

——, The So-called Bridgettine Rosary, *The Month*, 100 (August 1902): 189–203.

Thurston, Herbert, The Name of the Rosary (I), *The Month*, 111 (May 1908): 518–29.

——, The Name of the Rosary (II), *The Month*, 111 (June 1908): 610–23.

Thurston, Herbert, series of articles, 'Notes on Familiar Prayers', *The Month*, 1913–16:

——, The Origins of the Hail Mary, *The Month*, 121 (February 1913): 162–76.

——, The Second Part of the Hail Mary, *The Month*, 121 (April 1913): 379–88.

——, Genuflections and *Aves* (I), *The Month*, 127 (May 1916): 441–51.

——, Genuflections and *Aves* (II), *The Month*, 127 (June 1916): 546–59.

——, The 'Salve Regina' (I), *The Month*, 128 (September 1916): 248–246.

——, The 'Salve Regina' (II), *The Month*, 128 (October 1916): 300–14.

Waterton, Edmund, Old English Devotions, *The Month*, 20 (April 1874): 515.

Winston, Anne, Tracing the Origins of the Rosary, *Speculum*, 68 (1993): 619–36.

Books

Balthasar, Hans Urs von, *The Threefold Garland* (San Francisco, CA: Ignatius Press, 1982).

Benson, Herbert, *The Relaxation Response* (London: Collins, 1976).

Boyce, James, *Praising God in Liturgy: Studies in Carmelite Liturgy* (Washington, DC: Carmelite Institute, 1999).

Bridgett, Thomas E., *Our Lady's Dowry: How England Gained that Title*, 3rd edn (London: Burns & Oates, 1903).

Brown, R. E., Donfried, K. P., Fitzmyer, J. A., Reumann, J. (eds), *Mary in the New Testament* (Philadelphia, PEN: Fortress Press, 1974).

Clayton, Mary, *The Cult of the Blessed Virgin Mary in Anglo-Saxon England* (Cambridge: Cambridge University Press, 1990).

de Montfort, Louis-Marie Grignion, *The Secret of the Rosary* (New York: Montfort Publications, 1965).

Drane, Augusta T., *A History of St Dominic* (London: Longmans Green, 1891).

du Manoir, Herbert (ed.), *Maria: Etudes sur la Sainte Virge* (Paris: Beauchesne, 1949–71).

Faber, Frederick W., *Growth in Holiness* (London: Thomas Richardson, 1855).

——, *Notes on Doctrinal Subjects* (London: Thomas Richardson, 1866) Vols I, XIII.

Fraternity of Our Lady de Salve Regina, *Revised Constitution and Daily Office* (London: Church of St Magnus the Martyr, 1985).

Gambero, Luigi, *Mary and the Fathers of the Church* (San Francisco, CA: Ignatius Press, 1991).

Graef, Hilda, *Mary: A History of Doctrine and Devotion*, 2 vols (combined edn; London: Sheed & Ward, 1985).

Gribble, Richard, *The History and Devotion of the Rosary* (Huntington, IN: Our Sunday Visitor, 1992).

Harding, John, The Place of Mary in the Writings of St Francis and St Clare, in *Mary and the Churches*, Ecumenical Society of the Blessed Virgin Mary, Chichester Congress Papers 1986, ed. Alberic Stacpoole (Dublin: Columba Press, 1987).

Harty, Gabriel, *Rediscovering the Rosary* (Dublin: Veritas, 1979).

Heimann, Mary, *Catholic Devotion in Victorian England* (Oxford: Clarendon Press, 1995).

Jaki, Stanley L., *Newman's Challenge* (Grand Rapids, MI: Eerdmans, 2000).

James, Fr, *The Story of Knock* (Knock: Knock Shrine Annual, 1950; issued as a pamphlet).

Johnston, Francis, *Fatima: The Great Sign* (Devon: Augustine Publishing, 1980).

——, *The Wonder of Guadalupe* (Chulmleigh, Devon: Augustine Publishing, 1981).

Kelly, John N. D., *Early Christian Creeds,* 3rd edn (Harlow: Longman, 1972).

King, Archdale A., *Liturgies of the Religious Orders* (London: Longmans Green, 1955).

Laffineur, M. and le Pelletier, M. T., *Star on the Mountain* (New York: Our Lady of Garabandal Inc., 1968).

Laurentin, René, *Bernadette of Lourdes* (London: Darton, Longman & Todd, 1979).

——, *Apparitions of the Blessed Virgin Mary Today*, 2nd edn (Dublin: Veritas, 1991).

Lokai, Louis J., *The White Monks: A History of the Cistercian Order* (Okauchee, WI: Cistercian Fathers, Our Lady of Spring Bank, 1953).

Maindron, Gabriel, *The Apparitions of Our Lady at Kibeho* (Godstone, Surrey: The Marian Spring Centre, 1996).

McGetrick, Matthew, *Meditation for Modern Men and Women* (Dublin: Dominican Publications, 1983).

McLoughlin, William M., Our Lady of Sorrows – A Devotion Within a Tradition, in *Mary and the Churches*, Ecumenical Society of the Blessed Virgin Mary, Chichester Congress Papers 1986, ed. Alberic Stacpoole (Dublin: Columba Press, 1987).

Miravalle, Mark I., *Mary, Coredemptrix Mediatrix Advocate* (Santa Barbara, CA: Queenship Publishing, 1993).

Moorman, John R. H., *St Francis of Assisi* (London: SPCK, 1976).

Mother Mary and Bishop Kallistos of Diokleia (trans.), *The Akathistos Hymn to the Most Holy Mother of God: With the Office of Small Compline* (Wallington, Surrey: The Ecumenical Society of the Blessed Virgin Mary, 1986).

Neuner, J. and Dupuis, J. (eds), *The Christian Faith in the Doctrinal Documents of the Catholic Church*, 6th edn (New York: Alba House, 1996).

Newman, John H., *Sayings of Cardinal Newman* (Dublin: Carraig Books, 1976; facsimile reprint).

O'Connor, Edward D., *Marian Apparitions Today – Why So Many?* (Santa

Barbara, CA: Queenship Publishing, 1996).

O'Donnell, Christopher, *At Worship with Mary, A Pastoral and Theological Study* (Wilmington, DE: Michael Glazier, 1988).

O'Dwyer, Peter, *Mary: A History of Devotion in Ireland* (Dublin: Four Courts Press, 1988).

——, *Towards a History of Irish Spirituality* (Dublin: Columba Press, 1995).

Rock, Daniel, *The Church of Our Fathers*, ed. G. W. Hart and W. H. Frere (new edition in 4 vols; (London: John Murray, 1903). Originally published 1849.

Thurston, Herbert, *Familiar Prayers: Their Origin and History*, arranged and selected by Paul Grosjean (London: Burns & Oates, 1953).

Vatican Council II, *The Basic Sixteen Documents*, ed. A. Flannery (Dublin: Dominican Publications, 1996).

Ward, Maisie, *The Splendour of the Rosary* (London: Sheed & Ward, 1946).

Waterton, Edmund, *Pietas Mariana Britannica: A History of Devotion to the Most Blessed Virgin Marye, Mother of God* (London: St Joseph's Catholic Library, 1879).

Wilkins, Eithne, *The Rose-Garden Game* (London: Victor Gollancz, 1969).

Willam, Franz M., *The Rosary: Its History and Meaning*, trans. E. Kaiser (New York: Benzinger Bros, 1953).

Winston-Allen, Anne, *Stories of the Rose* (Pennsylvania: Pennsylvania State University Press, 1997).

Papal Documents

Pius IX, Apostolic Constitution *Ineffabilis Deus* (1854), Acta of Pius IX, 1, 1, p. 616, D1641 (2803).

Pius XII, Apostolic Constitution *Munificentissimus Deus* (1950), *AAS* 42, pp. 753-71.

——, Encyclical Letter *Ingruentium malorum*, (1951), *AAS* 43, pp. 577-82.

——, Encyclical Letter *Ad caeli Reginam* (1954), *AAS* 46, pp. 625-40.

Paul VI, Apostolic Exhortation *Marialis cultus*, (1974), *AAS* 66, pp. 113-68.

John Paul II, Encyclical Letter *Redemptoris Mater*, (1987), *AAS* 79, pp. 361-4.

For English translations:

Callen, Claudia (ed.), *The Papal Encyclicals* (1740-1981), 5 vols, (Raleigh, NC: McGrath, 1981).

www.vatican va/holy_father/index/htm

Works of Reference

Catechism of the Catholic Church (English edition; London: Geoffrey Chapman, 1994).

Catechism of Christian Doctrine (London: Catholic Truth Society, 1937).

Catholic Encyclopedia, 15 vols (1907–12), online edition, © Kevin Knight.

Code of Canon Law, prepared by the Canon Law Society of Great Britain and Ireland (London: Collins, 1983).

Dictionary of the Bible, ed. J. L. McKenzie and L. John (London: Geoffrey Chapman, 1968).

Enchiridion indulgentiarum normae et concessiones, 4th edn (Vatican City, Rome: Libreria editrice vaticana, 1999).

Encyclopaedia Britannica CD 2000 (Chicago, IL: Encyclopaedia Britannica Inc.).

Encyclopaedia of Religion and Ethics, ed. James Hastings (Edinburgh: T. & T. Clark, 1918).

Le Dictionnaire d'archéologie chrétienne et de liturgie, Vol. 15, ed. H. Leclercq and F. Cabrol (Paris: Letouzey et Ané, 1956).

Oxford Dictionary of the Christian Church, 3rd edn, ed. F. L. Cross and E. A. Livingstone (Oxford: Oxford University Press, 1997).

The Revised Standard Version [of the Bible] (Logos Library System) (Oxford: Oxford University Press, 1973, 1977).

Theotokos: A Theological Encyclopedia of the Blessed Virgin Mary, ed. Michael O'Carroll (Wilmington, DE: Michael Glazier, 1982; reprint Collegeville, MN: Liturgical Press, 1990).

Websites

Anglican Beads *http://members.ols.net/~michael/PrayerBeads.html*

The Catholic Encyclopedia, The Fathers, The Summa Theologica *www.newadvent.org*

Papal Encyclicals *www.vatican.va/holy_father/index.htm*

Rosary Workshop *www.rosaryworkshop.com/HISTORYjournalingBead.htm*

University of Dayton Marian Library *www.udayton.edu/mary* [search on 'Resources']

Vatican II Documents *www.ourladyswarriors.org/teach/index.html*

Index

Note Page references in *italics* refer to illustrations and in **bold** to main treatment of topic within the given page range.

INDEX

Keating, Fr Geoffrey 137
Keble, John 129
Kerbala 85
Kibeho (Rwanda) 212
'The Knight and the World' 168
Knock apparition xiv, 158
knotted cord 92–3
knotting 77
Korean rosaries 82–3

Labouré, Catherine, vision of xiv,
    156, 163
Lady Godiva of Coventry 89, 95–6
Lamas 81, 82
Langdale rosary 106, 268–9
Le Bourgeois de Paris 168
Legion of Mary 143
Leo X xii, 28, 205
Leo XII 241
Leo XIII xiv, 177–80
Lepanto, Battle of xii, 28, 177
Lexikon der Marienerscheinungen
    (Ernest), 151–2
liberalism xiv
Life of Christ Meditations 13–15, 17
Limoges Exposition 205
Little Office of Our Lady (the Blessed
    Virgin) 41, 45, 66
Liturgy of the Hours (Divine Office)
    1, 149, 235, 261
Liturgy for the Queenship of Mary
    244
Living Rosary movement 180
Lollards 122
The Lord's Prayer 57–60
Loreto, Litany of 178
Loreto, Shrine of 243
Lourdes appariton 156
Lucas, Stephen (fishmonger) 238
Lumen Gentium 246, 247
Luther, Martin xii, 23, 240

McLoughlin, Fr William M. 209, 211
Magdalen, Mary 169
Margaret, Lady, Countess of
    Richmond 110
Marialis Cultus (Paul VI) xv, 148, 149,
    182, 193, 250
Marian apparitions 145, 151–65

Marian devotion 37–9, 45, 141
Marian guilds 118
Marian Movement 145–6
Marian psalters x, xi, 14–15, 18,
    47–50, 105–7
Marian rosary x, 1
Marien Rosenkrantz legend 13–14
Mary
    as Advocate 245–7
    as Chosen by God 5
    as Co-Redeemer 165
    Invocation to 50–3
    as Mother 161–2, 180, 242, 244–5
    as Queen 241–4
    role in the history of salvation 4–5
'Mary legends' 42
'Mastirs of the Salve' 239
Mater Misericordiae 244–5
materials used for rosaries 78, 79, 80
Mecca 85
meditation 196–203
meditation points see clausulae
meditation, rosary of 196–7
meditations 193, 196–203
Medjugorje apparition (Yugoslavia)
    xv, 159
Meissen brasses 97
The Memorare 256–7
metanies 92
A Method to Meditate on the Psalter or
    Great Rosary of our Blessed Lady 116
Miraculous Medal xiv, 156, 163, 164
More, Sir Thomas 108–10
Most Holy Rosary confraternity 232
Mother of Mercy 244–5
Much Marcle (Herefordshire) x
Mukangango, Marie-Claire 212
Munificentissimus Deus (Pius XII) 146
Muslim rosaries 84–5, 175
Mysteries 18, 24, 25, 27, 179, **190–1,
    224–7**
Mysteries of the Rosary xv
The Mystic Sweet Rosary of the Faithful
    Soul 115

Newman, Cardinal John Henry 4,
    127, 128–31
nineteenth-century England 126
nineteenth-century Ireland 140–1

279

Winston-Allen, Anne 2, 48–50, 169
Woman of the Apocalypse 166
woodcuts *20*, *101*, 116
World Trade Center xv

worry beads 85
Wycliffe, John 122

yoga mantra 202

CPSIA information can be obtained at www.ICGtesting.com
Printed in the USA
BVOW042201160112

280694BV00005B/27/P